CW00568373

JOHN THE BAPTIST

JOHN THE BAPTIST

HIS LIFE AND AFTERLIFE

JOSEPHINE WILKINSON

AMBERLEY

First published 2022

Amberley Publishing
The Hill, Stroud
Gloucestershire, GL5 4EP

www.amberley-books.com

Copyright © Josephine Wilkinson, 2022

The right of Josephine Wilkinson to be
identified as the Author of this work has been
asserted in accordance with the Copyright,
Designs and Patents Act 1988.

ISBN 978 1 4456 9896 0 (hardback)
ISBN 978 1 4456 9897 7 (ebook)

All rights reserved. No part of this book may
be reprinted or reproduced or utilised in any
form or by any electronic, mechanical or other
means, now known or hereafter invented,
including photocopying and recording, or in any
information storage or retrieval system, without
the permission in writing from the Publishers.

British Library Cataloguing in Publication Data.
A catalogue record for this book is available
from the British Library.

1 2 3 4 5 6 7 8 9 10

Typesetting by SJmagic DESIGN SERVICES, India.
Printed in the UK.

CONTENTS

INTRODUCTION

The appearance of John the Baptist in all four Gospels and reference to his baptism in the Acts of the Apostles suggests that John was regarded by early Christian communities as inextricably linked with the Jesus tradition from the earliest times. Jesus first comes to public notice in connection with John's baptism (Mk 1.9 and par.), or as a result of John's testimony (Jn 1.29-34). In all four Gospels, John is assigned the role of forerunner to Jesus. Were it not for the independent testimony of Josephus, John the Baptist would never have been seen as anything other than the prophet who proclaimed the Christ. Ironically, it was only when scholars began to research the life of Jesus that the true John began to emerge.

Life of Jesus research[1] arguably began in 1778 with Reimarus's *Fragments*. The German philosopher was the first writer of import to investigate the historical Jesus. This formative period ended when Schweitzer's *Van Reimarus zu Wrede* (1906) highlighted the largely subjective and liberal nature of what came to be termed the 'Old Quest'. The work of this period showed a lack of understanding of the traditions which led to the creation of the gospels, as well as the redactional methods used by the evangelists.

The second period, called the 'No Quest' or 'Bultmannian' period reversed Reimarus's anti-dogmatic stance and focused upon the theological nature of the gospels. Unlike the 'Old Quest', this period also took into account the development of the written and oral traditions concerning Jesus. The outcome was pessimistic. It concluded that the historical Jesus could not be freed from the dogma which surrounded the Christ of faith.

Such thinking prevailed until 1953 when a paper entitled *Das Problem des historischen Jesus* was presented by Käsemann. This heralded the 'New Quest', which took into account newly rediscovered sources such as the Nag Hammadi codices and the Dead Sea Scrolls, and used such critical tools as source, form and redaction criticism, and various criteria of authenticity. When applied to accounts of the actions and, especially, the sayings of Jesus, it was found that the critical tools could do much to assist scholars as they endeavoured to separate the historical Jesus from the Christ of faith. Unfortunately, the 'New Quest' was dominated by theological concerns, causing attempts to study the historical Jesus to decline.

The 1980s saw a renaissance in Life of Jesus studies, which saw the publication of such works as Sanders' *Jesus and Judaism* (1985). Five features characterise the Third Quest.[2]

1. it maintains individuals and groups within their social, cultural and political context.
2. it is primarily concerned with historical rather than theological questions.
3. it uses historical research methods, with the result that historical questions are answered on historical grounds.
4. it acknowledges that there is no such thing as mainstream, or normative, Judaism. Moreover, it relies less upon Rabbinic literature and more upon Second Temple Jewish literature. This is more appropriate, since it addresses events that occurred prior to 70 CE.

5. the Third Quest places growing emphasis upon Jesus'
   actions rather than his sayings. Each of these factors allows
   scholars to better understand Jesus' sayings in a life context.
   For example, it places Jesus' healings, exorcisms, and his
   eating with 'sinners' into their proper context, helping the
   researcher to discover what such events meant for those who
   witnessed them.

The conclusions so far drawn from the Third Quest show that the
pessimism of the 'No Quest' period was misplaced. Indeed, much
can be known about the person Jesus of Nazareth with a large
degree of certainty.[3] Jesus was baptised by John the Baptist. He
was a Galilaean preacher and healer. He called disciples, of whom
there was an inner core of twelve. He worked exclusively in Israel.
He was involved in a dispute concerning the Temple. Finally, he
was crucified outside the city walls of Jerusalem by the Roman
authorities.

The first fact, that Jesus was baptised by John the Baptist,
is particularly significant because it highlights the point made
earlier concerning the importance of John the Baptist in the life
of Jesus. John, it was noted, was important enough to be included
in all four canonical gospels, Acts, and several extra-canonical
texts. A man so prominent in the life of Jesus ought also to be
prominent in Life of Jesus research. Rather than simply accepting
that Jesus was baptised by John, it should also be asked why he
was baptised; what did it mean for Jesus? Several other questions
arise from this one. Did Jesus become John's disciple? Was Jesus'
ministry influenced by that of John? Did Jesus' ministry arise out
of a reinterpretation, or a rejection, of John's ministry? What was
the relationship between John the Baptist and Jesus?

Scholars have attempted to answer these questions. Indeed,
the Quests for the historical Jesus have been mirrored by similar
Quests for the historical John the Baptist.[4] The Quest for John
began at the same time as the 'Old Quest', with the publication

of Reimarus's work of 1778. Reimarus concluded that John and Jesus had collaborated in an attempt to inspire hope among the people of a deliverance from Roman rule by a messianic king. John's role was to preach and proclaim Jesus as the Messiah at his baptism. The earliest historical interpretation of John the Baptist, therefore, holds him to be a political revolutionary.

The 'New Quest' saw the publication of Kraeling's *John the Baptist* (1951), and Scobie's *John the Baptist* (1964), the latter being the first book in English to take into account evidence from the Dead Sea Scrolls. Meanwhile, the emergence of redaction criticism led to the study of the role given to John in the Gospels. Conzelmann's *The Theology of Luke* (1961) includes a section concerning Luke's interpretation of John. Wink's *John the Baptist in the Gospel Tradition* (1968) studies the redaction of traditions concerning John in all four canonical Gospels and Q source (*Quelle*).

Life of John research has now entered its 'Third Quest' period. Thanks to such works as Ernst's *Johannes der Tauter. Interpretation—Geschichte—Wirkungsgeschichte* (1989), Webb's *John the Baptizer and Prophet: A Socio-Historical Study* (1991), Kazmierski's *John the Baptist, Prophet and Evangelist* (1996), Taylor's *John the Baptist within Second Temple Judaism* (1997) and Murphy's *John the Baptist* (2003), John's actions and teachings can be fully understood within the context of Second Temple Judaism.

The results of Life of Jesus research and its parallel Life of John research make it appropriate to combine the two fields. Studies into the historical relationship between John and Jesus are included in many of the works mentioned above. Guyénot's *Jésus et Jean Baptiste. Enquête historique sur une rencontre légendaire* (1999) is the first major study in the field.

The aim of this book is to further the study of the historical relationship between John the Baptist and Jesus. However, it adds a new element to this research as it approaches the relationship from two perspectives. The first places John within his historical context, thus allowing the study of his relationship with Jesus, in which John's impact upon Jesus is evaluated, to be made against the authentic background of the Roman occupancy of Palestine. The second perspective looks at the traditions that arose shortly after the deaths of Jesus and John. It shows how various interpretations of Jesus influenced the redefinition and re-evaluation of John the Baptist, his message and his ministry.

A Note on Sources

This book accepts that the Gospel of Mark was the earliest of the four gospels to be written, and that it was used as a source by Matthew and Luke. Another source, the lost sayings source known as *Quelle* or Q, was also available to Matthew and Luke, who used it in their own gospels alongside material from Mark as well as text that was unique to them. The Gospel of John is of later date than the Synoptics and while its author may have been aware of the other gospels, or at least the events of which they speak, he has worked independently from them to produce a work that presents an entirely different interpretation of the Jesus traditions. To avoid confusion regarding which John is meant: John the Baptist or the Gospel of John, the gospel will be referred to in this book as the Fourth Gospel and its author as the Fourth Evangelist.

I

THE WILDERNESS

John the Baptist appeared in the wilderness, preaching a baptism of repentance for the forgiveness of sins (Mk 1.4).

The earliest mention of John the Baptist in the Christian Scriptures immediately associates him with the wilderness. The Fourth Gospel notes that John baptised 'in Bethany beyond the Jordan' (Jn 1.28), and at 'Aenon, near Salim' (3.23). These two places are generally accepted to be desert locations, relatively close to populated areas, but still somewhat remote. In his redaction of Mark, Matthew has maintained John's connection with the wilderness (3.1). The Lukan Infancy Narrative, while largely to be regarded as legendary, nevertheless ends by placing John in the wilderness (1.80), allowing Luke to discover John in the desert when he returns to him later (3.2). A strong historical tradition exists, therefore, which closely associates John the Baptist with the wilderness.

The most logical place to begin a search for the historical John the Baptist, then, is there. Several factors should be borne in mind, the first of which should be to establish what significance the wilderness held for John. The desert regions are also closely associated with the ancient prophets of Israel. As such, it would be revealing to see whether or not John's message reflected theirs. Moreover, since John felt that there were valid reasons to operate in the wilderness, it is possible that there were others who felt the same way. A study of their missions, which could then be compared and contrasted with that of John, would facilitate an understanding of John the Baptist's place in the desert tradition.

The Sources

The first task is to look at the sources supporting John the Baptist's association with the wilderness, beginning with the four Gospels. Mark describes John baptising in the Jordan River (1.5). Matthew places him in the deserts of Judaea (3.1), while Luke shows him to be working in the Jordan area (3.3). The Fourth Evangelist gives the scene of John's ministry as Bethany, beyond the Jordan (1.28). Later, he extends the range of John's environment to include Aenon, near Salim (3.23). Finally, he notes that Jesus withdrew beyond the Jordan 'to the place where John at first baptised' (10.40).

Because this study will make use of the Fourth Gospel as a historical source, some justification is necessary. Although a full discussion on the historicity of the Fourth Gospel cannot be entered into here, there are certain points to note. The primary argument against its use in historical study is its apparent late date. However, although the actual dating of the gospel is still disputed, even if it were relatively late, this need not be of concern. Some of the traditions and sources used by its author could have gone back as far as those of the Synoptic evangelists. It is possible some were known to one or more of them.

Next, the Fourth Gospel's dualistic references are unique to it, suggestive of a provenance far away in time and place from John and his immediate followers. In answer to this, the discovery of the Dead Sea Scrolls has revealed that a dualistic tradition did exist in Palestine during the period prior to and beyond that of both Jesus and John. The Gnostic/dualistic elements of the

Fourth Gospel are, therefore, compatible with first-century Jewish thought. Interestingly, the Gnostic Mandaeans claim John the Baptist as the founder of their movement. They revere him as a prophet, and their baptismal rite is based directly upon that of John. Nevertheless, that their manuscripts appeared relatively recently in their history does not invalidate their well-founded claim to be among the beneficiaries of John's earliest preaching.[1]

Another difficulty is that the Fourth Gospel makes no attempt to present a historically correct record of Jesus, his life and ministry, much less to show when and in what way the historical John the Baptist might have influenced it. This is entirely true. The Fourth Evangelist quite clearly states his reason for writing: 'that you may believe that Jesus is the Christ, the Son of God, and that believing you may have life in his name' (20.30). Clearly, then, the presentation of a biography of the historical Jesus was not the intent of the Fourth Evangelist. The purpose of the Fourth Gospel is to present to its readers and/or auditors the reality of Christ as its composer understood it. Consequently, anything said here about John the Baptist must be viewed within the context of the author's interpretation of Jesus. The approach to the Fourth Gospel, therefore, should be no different to that of the Synoptic Gospels. In any study in which the establishment of historical authenticity is the primary aim, all four gospels must be treated with caution, their evidence weighed against probably date, provenance and intent. This method will be followed in the present study as each factor of John's and Jesus' lives, and how they affected one another, is considered.

To return to the evidence for John's association with the wilderness, another source is Josephus. In contrast to the four Gospels, Josephus seems unaware of John's connection with the desert, or he ignores it. Only the Slavonic addition to *The Jewish War* shows John to be working by the Jordan. However, this work, as it now stands, cannot be accepted as authentic. The Slavonic additions show evidence of having been tampered with by an editor who wished to bring them more into harmony with Christian interpretation. Allied to this is their inconsistency with Jewish thought. They are at odds with Josephus's attitude towards the Romans. They contain errors that contradict Josephus's otherwise careful handling of historical facts. Finally, they betray an awareness of sources that did not exist or had limited distribution in Josephus's time, such as the New Testament, Hegesippus, early Christian writers and Christian apocrypha.

In his *Antiquities* (18.116-119), Josephus makes no mention of the setting of John's mission; he notes only that John was executed at Machaerus. Herod's fortress-palace, the ruins of which still stand, was situated in Peraea, less than fourteen kilometres south-east of the Jordan River and so comes within the general area suggested by the evangelists as the scene of John's ministry.

All three Synoptic Gospels show that John the Baptist appeared in the desert in fulfilment of the prophecy found in Isaiah 40.3: 'A voice cries; "In the wilderness prepare the way of the Lord, make straight in the desert a highway for our God."' The Fourth Evangelist assigns these words to John, thus making him declare himself to be the voice as he presents the purpose of his mission. This indicates that John's message and mission have been subject to interpretation, even at this early stage, but it does not mean that John's association with the wilderness should be dismissed. However it was presented, its inclusion in each of the gospels suggests that it was historically accurate. Had the evangelists chosen to alter or omit the association, John's followers and the general populace could easily have contradicted them. Moreover, their presentation of John's location indicates that there was some association with it that they felt they had to highlight.

John's desert association can be accepted as genuine and historical. It is multiply attested, since it appears in two or more independent documents, in this case, Mark and Josephus. It appears also in the Fourth Gospel, which might have used Mark as a source. On the other hand, it is more probable that the Fourth Evangelist, like Mark, had access to a pre-gospel tradition that placed John in the desert.[2] It can be concluded, therefore, that Mark, the Fourth Evangelist and Josephus appear to have drawn upon a sound historical tradition. It is acceptable to state that the desert wastes were indeed the authentic setting for the Baptist's mission of preaching and baptism. It is here that John the Baptist grew into manhood (Lk. 1.80) and where he first appeared to proclaim his message (Mk 1.4; Mt. 3.1). Jesus' comments about John indicate that crowds had gone into the wilderness in order to hear John's preaching (Q 7.24).

The Significance of the Wilderness

The term 'wilderness' meant many things to the first-century Jew. At its most fundamental, it simply referred to a region or a physical feature. Usually, water and vegetation are scarce. Shepherds are obliged to move their flocks from place to place in order to provide feed and water for them. The nomadic lifestyle of those who inhabit the wastelands was the main reason why the region was described as 'a land where there is no man' (Job 38.26). Conversely, Joshua notes six cities with their villages, Beth-arabah, Middin, Secacah, Nibshan, the City of Salt and Engedi, that are to be found in the desert (15.61). That Engedi, a city in Judaea east of the Dead Sea, was known to have produced henna (Song 1.14), and where palms grew (Sirach 24.14). Joel (2.22-3) indicates that green pastures, fruit-bearing trees, figs and vines could all be found in the desert, as could rain in abundance, all of which are provided by the Lord. For the unworthy, however, the gifts of the desert are short-lived, 'and the pastures of the wilderness are dried up' (Jer. 23.10).

The wilderness was also seen as a place where one could find refuge, as did David (1 Sam. 23-26). This is perhaps reflected in the words, 'O God, thou art my God, I seek thee, my soul thirsts for thee; my flesh faints for thee, as in a dry and weary land where no water is' (Ps. 63.1). Alternatively, one might, like Elijah, encounter

God in the wilderness (1 Kings 19.9). It was here that 'the word of the Lord' came to the prophet and spoke to him. Elijah was served by angels during his desert sojourn (1 Kings 19 4-8) These supernatural beings fed him with cakes and water, which sustained him for a period of forty days and forty nights.

Elijah's experience finds an echo in Mark's succinct account of Jesus' Temptation (1.13), wherein Jesus was tended by angels during the forty days he spent in the wilderness. Also in Mark's account, the twin dangers of demon and wild beast are brought together. This revives memories of Azazel, the demon to whom the scapegoat carrying the sins of the nation is sent (Lev. 16.8-10). The association of demons and deserts is also found in Mt. 12.43. Here, the evangelist notes that unclean spirits go to the wilderness when they have been exorcised. The demons look for rest in the desert but find none. On the other hand, Luke's story of the Gerasene Demoniac (8.29) suggests that the demon had led its victim into the desert.

The wilderness also has rich and powerful historical and religious connotations. The twin cities of Sodom and Gomorrah, situated at the southern shore of the Dead Sea, witnessed the power of God's wrath and paid the price of their defiance (Gen. 19). Conversely, it was in the wilderness that God intervened to bring about Israel's deliverance. The account of this, which appears in Exodus, begins with several miracles, the first of which are the plagues of Egypt (7-11) followed by the Passover (12.13). Next, the Israelites are protected from Pharaoh's men as they embark upon their epic journey (14). One miracle seems to have become especially significant to those who would return to the wilderness in the first century: the crossing of the sea. This event was facilitated by the direct intervention of the Lord (14.21-31), who held back the waters of the sea to allow the people to cross. Then, just as Pharaoh's soldiers were following on behind, the waters were released, thus drowning the enemy and allowing the people of Israel to proceed in safety.

God provides for the people as they cross the lonely wastes. In thanks, they sing songs of deliverance and praise (15.1-21). God supplies water for them when they are thirsty (15.22-27) and manna when they are hungry (16.4, 15). He gives them shelter (15.27), victory against the Amalekites, who dwelled in the Negeb between Sinai and Canaan (17.8.16), and human companionship (18).

The Exodus is linked to another event, which is perhaps the single most important feature of the sojourn in the wilderness, the institution of the Covenant. Once again, the account of this event is given in Exodus. Here, God reminds the Israelites of what he has already achieved on their behalf (19.4; 20.2), before presenting them with his demands (19.5a) and desires (19.5b, 6). God next gives the people a set of rules or laws according to which they are to live. Known as the Decalogue, or the Ten Commandments, the first four of these laws address humanity's relationship with God (20.3-11), while the remaining six apply to humanity's relationship with humanity (20.12-16). Each aspect of human life is catered for in the Decalogue, which reinforces the righteousness of God's people (21-23) and explains how they are to worship (24-40).

The Exodus ends when Joshua, Moses's successor, leads the Israelites into Canaan. This story, recounted in the book of Joshua, is the source of much of the imagery that will be exploited by those who would go again to the desert during the first century. One event of major significance is the crossing of the Jordan (Josh. 3.1-4.18). The crossing was accompanied by a miracle, in which God stopped the waters of the Jordan as the bearers of the Ark of the Covenant stood in the river. This miracle allowed the people to cross over dry ground as they entered the Promised Land.

Once across the Jordan, the people find themselves opposite the city of Jericho. At that time, the city is inhabited by a 'king and mighty men of valour' (Josh. 6.3) who, nevertheless, fear the

Israelites. Bearing the Ark of the Covenant before them, and led by priests carrying trumpets of ram's horns, Joshua and his men march round the city walls once daily for six days. On the seventh day, the priests sound their horns, causing the city walls to collapse and allowing the Israelites to enter (6.1-21). The significance of this account is that the Israelites, with God represented by the Ark of the Covenant, before them, could triumph over their enemies. In this case, the enemies are those who would prevent them from entering the land that God had promised them.

The historical and religious associations of the desert, so deeply embedded within the Jewish psyche, probably influenced the various eschatological, or end-times, end-of-the-world associations that came to be connected with the region. Just as God had led his people into the desert under Moses where he effected their salvation, so would he lead them back into the desert at the end of days. Here, he will speak to them and recover their love (Hos. 2.14-15), with the result that the desert shall 'rejoice and blossom; like the crocus it shall blossom abundantly and rejoice with joy and singing' (Isa. 35.1-2).

The wilderness is an area of immense significance. It is not merely a place of solitude for quiet and peaceful meditation but is the arena in which heavenly and infernal powers confront and engage one another. The desert wastes witnessed the severity of God's wrath, yet they also provided the scene of Israel's salvation by, and Covenant with, God. It came to be seen as the setting for eschatological determination and fulfilment.[3] God had acted in Israel's history to deliver the chosen people from oppression; he would do so again. Such thinking probably inspired many people to take refuge in the desert during the Maccabaean revolt,

> Then many who were seeking righteousness and justice went down to the wilderness to dwell there, they, their sons, their wives, and their cattle, because evils pressed heavily upon them (1 Macc. 2.29; cf. 2 Macc. 5.27, 6.11, 10.6; Pss. Sol. 17.19).

Whatever the case, the end-time was of prime concern to one particular section of society, the prophets.

Prophets and Prophecy

The prophets were believed to have possessed a profound understanding of the affairs and events of their day, the implications of which they could clearly envisage. Their main concern was that Israel had become disobedient towards God (Isa. 5, cf. Mt. 3.9; Lk. 3.8). Themes of idolatry and apostasy are recurrent in their writings. Because of their sin, God was justified in punishing his people (Ezek. 7). However, the prophets placed great emphasis upon God's willingness to forgive those who were truly repentant (Ezek. 18.21-23, 30-32; cf. Mk 1.4 and par.). They taught that a remnant would be saved (Isa. 28.5-6), who would enter into a new Covenant with God (Jer. 31.34). Such renewal is spoken of using wilderness imagery (Isa. 35.1-2). Great miracles are associated with it (Isa. 35.5-7), but only the redeemed will share in it (Isa. 35.9). The new Israel, therefore, will be born in the wilderness, where its relationship with a loving God will be re-established (Isa. 2.3; Hos. 2.14-23; Mic. 4.2).

It is little wonder, then, that the wilderness held such an important place in Jewish thought. The prophets looked forward to a time when Israel would once again be the nation of God. People would practice morality, be upright in dealings with their neighbours and offer right worship to God. Only those who were fit to live in this new Israel would do so. All others were condemned. The prophets, having transmitted God's intentions, would now be silent until the end of days, 'Thus there was great distress in Israel, such as had not been since the time that prophets ceased to appear among them' (1 Macc. 9.27; cf. Ps. 74.9; *t. Sota* 13.2).

The new age would be marked by a renaissance of prophecy. Many prophets, old and young, male and female, free as well as servants, would emerge, all filled with the spirit of God (Joel 2.28-29). This implies a new outpouring of prophecy on a grand scale. However, the intertestamental period saw this belief consolidate into the concept of a single prophet. Rather than many prophets, only one would arise as the new age dawned. Moreover, it came to be understood that the one prophet would return to accomplish an eschatological mission; he or she would preach of the end-time and the imminent judgement. This belief, as recorded by the Fourth Evangelist, finds expression in the Christian interpretation of John the Baptist as the forerunner of Jesus, '"Are you the Prophet?" And he answered, "No"' (1.21).

Notwithstanding the view that the spirit of prophecy had been withdrawn, prophets and prophecy appear to have continued throughout the intertestamental era and beyond. The Gospels allude to their existence, 'Why, then, did you go out? To see a prophet?' (Mt. 11.9 and par.). The evangelists warn the people against them, considering them to be false and/or dangerous. Such prophets, they say, 'show signs and wonders, to lead astray, if possible, the elect' (Mk 13.22 and par.). However, the greatest source for the study of such prophets is not the evangelists, but Josephus. As with those noted in the Gospels, the prophets mentioned by Josephus are judged to be false and dangerous. Josephus even shows a degree of hostility towards some of them. Those whom he does accept as genuine are really no more than fortune-tellers: Judas the Essene, who 'never happened to fall into error or mis-statement in his predictions', is one example (*War* 1.78-80). Josephus himself, who believed his gift of prophecy had come from God, is another (*War* 3.351-4).

Josephus's practice of reducing prophecy to fortune-telling is influenced by his adherence to Pharisaic belief that prophecy was currently suspended,

> It is true, our history hath been written since Artaxerxes very particularly, but hath not since been esteemed of the like authority with the former of our forefathers, because there hath not been an exact succession on prophets since that time. (*Apion* 1.41).

Josephus, however, does allow that God might use people in order to reveal the course of future events and to guide the people, but he does not consider them to be prophets in the true sense. Nevertheless, he does differentiate between those who genuinely interpret God's word and those who merely claim to have done so. Thus, he is able to give account of the activities of the latter group while qualifying those accounts by referring to them as false prophets (*War* 2.261). One example of this occurs in *War* 4.286-8. Here, Josephus tells of how some 6,000 people had been duped by a false prophet into going to the Temple to await signs of deliverance by God. Their gullibility prevented them from understanding warnings which were to be seen in and above the city. Josephus is careful to point out that the warnings were correctly interpreted by the sacred scribes as omens of the fall of Jerusalem.

It would appear, then, that the key to whether or not prophecy continued to exist lies in the question of authority. Clearly, prophets and prophesy did continue to be active during the period in question. However, the authority of these people, as well as the integrity of their utterances, were rejected by those in positions of power. Furthermore, for those who would condemn them as false, these prophets preserved certain qualities of the classical prophets, which they passed on to their successors (Zech. 13.3-6). While some in the first century continued to await the return of prophecy at the eschaton, prophecy itself, albeit unrecognised by the authorities, continued to flourish.

Prophets and Prophecy: Theudas

In a study of those who might be called 'unacknowledged prophets', there are several to choose from. In *Ant.* 20.97-99, Josephus gives an account of a prophet called Theudas:

> While Fadus was procurator of Judea, a certain magician named Theudas persuaded a great part of the people to take their effects with them, and to follow him to the river Jordan; for he told them

he was a prophet, and that he would, at his command, divide the river, and afford them an easy passage over it: and many were deluded by his words. However, Fadus did not permit them to make any advantaged of his wild attempt, but sent a troop of horseman against them, who, falling upon them unexpectedly, slew many of them, and took many of them alive. They also took Theudas alive, and cut off his head, and carried it to Jerusalem.

Beyond calling him a 'magician'[4] and so affirming his status as a 'false prophet', Josephus makes no attempt to evaluate Theudas or to understand his motives.

Theudas calling himself a 'prophet' is significant, as is his choice of locale. He led a large crowd to the Jordan, the waters of which he promised to part. Josephus notes that Theudas managed to persuade 'a great part of the people'. This might be an exaggeration, but there is no reason to suppose that Theudas would not have had wide appeal. His movement arose during the period when Judaea was once again under direct Roman administration.[5] There was every chance that payments of tribute to Rome would be reintroduced. As such, money that should have gone to the Temple, the house of the one true God, would instead go to a pagan ruler. Such a sensitive political climate ensured that many would have been interested enough to have at least listened to what Theudas had to say.

Theudas probably awakened profound nationalist sentiments in those who heard him. It is possible that he intended to lead pious Israelites into the wilderness where they might escape such a distasteful and offensive obligation to a pagan master. Moreover, he had promised to part the waters of the Jordan and lead the people through. He might have been attempting to re-enact a highly significant biblical event: the entry into the Promised Land, led by Joshua (Josh. 3-4).[6]

The Joshua story has many interesting parallels with the intentions of Theudas. Both Joshua and Theudas led a large group of people. Both wished to cross the Jordan. Joshua's followers by necessity had their belongings with them. Theudas urged his followers to do the same. Joshua entered the Promised Land by taking Jericho. Josephus's account suggests that Theudas' actions posed enough of a threat to Fadus that the procurator felt that he had to deal swiftly and decisively with him. In other words, Fadus, seeing the development of a potentially explosive political situation, interpreted it as a possible insurrection and took steps to suppress it.

While it is possible that Theudas was attempting to re-enact Joshua's entrance into the Promised Land, with all its connotations of salvation and deliverance, there is another possible explanation for his activity. Theudas might have been trying to re-enact the Exodus. His parting of the Jordan would, in this case, have symbolised the parting of the sea. However, since the Exodus and the entry into the Promised Land had become juxtaposed in the minds of the Jewish people (Isa. 51.9-11), it is possible that Theudas had both events in mind.

Whichever interpretation of Theudas' actions is the correct one, it is clear that he hoped God would act anew in the deliverance of his people. Moreover, since Theudas considered himself a prophet, he probably believed that he would act as God's agent in such an event. Perhaps he even saw himself and his followers as the 'remnant' who would become the new Israel. To take this scenario one step further, Theudas might have thought that acting out those events in which God had intervened in the history of Israel would 'prompt' God to act once again.[7] The belief that this could be done was not without precedent; it is found in the *Assumption of Moses* (9.1-7).

If this hypothesis is correct, then Theudas probably engaged in scriptural exegesis.[8] This does not mean that he was a scholar or a theologian. Rather, he could simply have heard Scripture being read out.[9] Instead of merely issuing predictions based upon what he had read or heard, he acted upon it, taking his followers to the

River Jordan, which held such significance for his countrymen (cf. Acts 7.44-45). Theudas did not intend to baptise, as John had done fifteen or so years before. Rather, he planned to act out a scene of political, spiritual and historical importance, and which would be recognised as such by his followers.

The timing of Theudas's mission, as well as his self-promotion as prophet and his choice of location, is significant. It coincides with the Roman occupation of his homeland. His people were no longer masters of the country they believed to be theirs by divine right. Theudas deliberately tried to re-create, as far as possible, the conditions under which God had once before delivered Israel. In so doing, he hoped to prompt God to act again. Aware of such a large gathering in the wilderness, and perhaps having some inkling of its intentions, Fadus immediately and violently quashed the movement. That Theudas and his followers could have been vanquished so swiftly suggests that they were unarmed. Rather than use force, their intention was to regain their lands by peaceful, divinely assisted means.

Before leaving Theudas, it is worth pointing out that Luke mentions a man of the same name in Acts 5.36. There are many similarities between this man and the Theudas mentioned by Josephus. Like Josephus's Theudas, the man spoken of by Luke attracted wide support. Luke states that he had some four hundred followers. Josephus describes Theudas as 'a magician'. For Luke, Theudas was 'giving himself out to be somebody'. In both accounts, Theudas was slain and his followers were dispersed.

On the other hand, if Luke is referring to the same Theudas mentioned by Josephus, his chronology is wrong. Luke's Theudas is succeeded by Judas the Galilaean (Acts 5.37). In fact, Judas the Galilaean, as we shall see, rebelled against the census ordered by Augustus in 6CE (*War* 2.118; *Ant*.17.4-6). Josephus's Theudas was active during the time of Fadus (*Ant*. 20.97), who was procurator of Judaea between 44-6CE. Clearly, Theudas should have come after Judas the Galilaean and not before.

A second mistake made by Luke is to make Gamaliel speak of Theudas. Gamaliel, a respected rabbi from Tarsus in Cilicia, was one of Paul's teachers (Acts 22.3). However, Theudas was not active until after the time Gamaliel is supposed to have made his speech.[10] Why Luke should place an anachronistic speech onto Gamaliel's lips could be inspired by his fondness for supporting his narrative with historical events (cf. Lk. 3.1-2). This might be one example of such a phenomenon.[11] His errors can be explained by the fact that Luke had not the means enjoyed by the modern historian of checking facts and dates. On the other hand, Luke might have attributed a speech to Gamaliel as a way of proving the validity of the early Christian church.[12] That is to say, Luke used Gamaliel, whose word carried authority, to show that those movements not blessed by God were doomed to failure. The Christian church, on the other hand, would succeed because 'it is of God' (Acts 5.39). As such, Luke is indulging in early church propaganda.

Prophets and Prophecy: The Unnamed Prophets

A decade after Theudas several more prophets emerged, about whom Josephus also speaks. Having mentioned a sect called the Sicarii, he notes that:

> There rose up another herd of villains, with purer hands indeed, but with views more impious, who not less than those assassins disturbed the happiness of the city. For these impostors and deceivers, under garb of inspiration aiming at innovation and change, persuaded the multitude to forgo their reason, and led them into the desert, assuring them, that God would there give them tokens of freedom. Against these, Felix, suspecting that this was but a prelude to insurrection, sent out a detachment of horse and foot, and put great numbers to the sword (*War* 2.259).

Josephus clearly regards these unnamed prophets as false. He compares them with the Sicarii, a splinter activist group who arose during Felix's time. Josephus considers the false prophets to be more dangerous than these people. As with Theudas, Josephus makes no further attempt to evaluate the nameless prophets except to say that they sought to bring about 'revolutionary changes'. As in the case of Theudas, their movements were decisively dealt with by the Roman authorities, who viewed them as insurrectionists. The swiftness with which Felix accomplished his action against them again suggests that this 'mob' was also unarmed.

Two features mark the movements led by the unnamed prophets. First, they are associated with the wilderness, which in turn is associated with the Exodus and the Conquest. Here, they awaited signs from God. However, the most important feature is once again their chosen locale, which in turn inspires the question of whether or not there was any cooperation between the prophetic movements of the first century. Against this, it must be remembered that had all the groups Josephus considered as revolutionary joined forces, he would certainly have noted it. That he did not must be taken into account.[13]

Of course, this conclusion does not mean that the unnamed prophets did not hold similar beliefs. Indeed, their missions featured at least one common aspect: eschatology. Moreover, while the Jewish authorities considered them charlatans, the people understood them to be prophets inspired by and acting as spokesmen for the Spirit of God.[14] It was expected that the revolutionary changes spoken of by Josephus would be brought about through the agency of this Spirit. The unnamed prophets anticipated a spiritual revolution wrought by God. As such, the preaching of these charismatic leaders induced the 'mob to act as if possessed'. The willingness of the people to leave everything behind and follow them into the wilderness was seen as foolishness by those who thought they knew better. Once in the wilderness, the believers would watch for signs of God's deliverance.

The faith shown by the followers of such prophets is not unlike that of the Covenanters at Qumran.[15] They all shared a belief that, in spite of the oppression of the times, God had not abandoned his people. Rather, they understood that God had an apocalyptic plan of salvation, the fulfilment of which was imminent. Just as the Covenanters went into the wilderness to await God's deliverance, so too did the followers of several unnamed prophets. Their plan was simply to watch for the signs that would show that God's deliverance was at hand. Their actions ended in disaster because the size of their movements led Felix to believe that they were planning a revolt. As a result, he dealt with them as decisively as his predecessor had done with Theudas and his followers.

Clearly, prophecy did continue into the first century. Unlike those of the classical period, the new prophets went unrecognised by the authorities. The main concern of the prophets of old, apostasy and idolatry, continued with the new generation of prophets. Now, however, it took a more subtle form. The failure of the Jewish authorities to protect their people from Roman oppression might have been seen by the masses as cooperation with Rome. The chance that they might once again be forced to pay tribute, and seeing no one fighting to prevent it, might have appeared to the people as though the authorities were accepting apostasy and idolatry as a means of preserving their status.

It is not impossible that the Jewish authorities were trying to attain peace for the people through negotiation with their Roman counterparts combined with acts of diplomacy.[16] The people, however, simply saw that God's laws were being transgressed. Feeling that they were unable to do anything to prevent it and thinking that the Jewish authorities were collaborating with Rome, they committed their cause to prophets such as Theudas and those who remain unnamed. In regarding the followers of the first century prophets as dupes, Josephus ignores the high probability that they had simply attached themselves to men whose cause they agreed with and who seemed to be the only people to have taken an active interest in their plight.

Prophets and Prophecy: Jeshua, son of Ananias

Given that Theudas and the unnamed prophets operated in the wilderness, it might be tempting to think that all prophets of the period used the desert regions as the scene of their ministries. This is not so. Josephus mentions a certain Jeshua, or Jesus, son of Ananias, who roamed the streets of Jerusalem and preached a message of doom against the Jewish aristocracy and the Temple:

> As he stood in the Temple he suddenly began to shout: 'A voice from the east, a voice from the west, a voice from the four winds, a voice against Jerusalem and the Sanctuary, a voice against bridegrooms and brides, a voice against the whole people (*War* 6.300-309).

The fact that Jeshua had no followers and did not seek to re-enact a biblical event also marks him out; in addition, he offered no means of deliverance, nor promise of salvation. The Jewish authorities attributed his behaviour to the agency of some supernatural force and handed him over to the Romans. Seen as a madman by the Roman authorities, he was simply beaten and then released.

Prophets and Prophecy: Judas the Galilaean

On the other hand, not all those who took to the desert did so with peaceful intentions. One person whose mission was far from peaceful was the aforementioned Judas the Galilaean,

> Archelaus's territory having been reduced to a province, Coponius, a Roman of the equestrian order, was sent thither as Procurator, invested by Caesar with authority to inflict capital punishment. During his administration, a certain Galilaean named Judas excited

the inhabitants to a revolt, denouncing them as dastards should they tolerate the payment of tribute to the Romans, and, after having God as their Lord, bow down to mortals as their masters. This man was the leader of a sect founded by himself, and totally different from the rest (*War* 2:118).

Josephus tells his readers that Judas and his followers were opposed to the census, which, according to 2 Sam. 24.1-17 and 1 Chron. 21, implied ownership. This was in direct opposition to Jewish belief that God alone owned the land, and that he had chosen to give it to his people for their own use. In carrying out a census Rome was seen to be supplanting God as owner of the land and reducing the people of Israel to slavery. Judas's belief that God alone should rule lay behind his revolt; but he also believed that, if the people acted, then God would intervene on their behalf. This, then, is another example of the understanding that God could be prompted to act.

Elsewhere, Josephus (*War* 4.264-6) speaks of 'scoundrels' who plundered villages and retreated into the wilderness, where they joined forces with others, forming companies and attacking sanctuaries and cities. Such people, it seems, were making use of the wilderness as a refuge and hideaway.

Josephus seeks to persuade his readers to believe that these bandits were wicked and mercenary. In fact, a clue to their intentions lies in the observation that their activity increased during times of difficulty. They became more prominent when the people faced famine, increased taxation and economic crisis. Rather than robbing the common people, their response to these crises was to target those in authority and the gentry who supported them at the expense of the people.[17]

Prophets and Prophecy: The Egyptian
Later, in 70 CE, when Jerusalem fell to Titus at the end of the Jewish War, the Jewish 'partisans and chiefs' met Titus and

begged to be allowed to leave the city and go into the desert with their wives and families (*War* 6.351-2). Titus, not surprisingly, refused this request. The Roman authorities had come to see the wilderness as a lure for those who would engage in revolutionary activity. The story of yet another revolutionary, known only as 'the Egyptian', serves to illustrate this point.

Like the unnamed prophets, the Egyptian made his presence felt during the time of Felix (52-59). According to Josephus (*War* 2.261-2; cf. Acts 21.38), the Egyptian was no more than a fraud posing as a prophet, who planned to lead his followers from the wilderness to the Mount of Olives with a view to forcing an entry into Jerusalem. Once there, he meant to overthrow the Roman garrison and seize power for himself. In the account of the same story given in *Antiquities* (20.169-70), Josephus adds that the Egyptian had wanted to show that, at his command, the walls of Jerusalem would fall down, through which he and his followers would gain entrance into the city. This shows the Egyptian to be in conformity with Theudas and the unnamed prophets, as far as his raison d'être, if not his method, is concerned. Like them, he seems to have been influenced by Joshua, who brought down the walls of Jericho (Josh. 6.1-21). Unlike them, however, he appeared to have posed a genuine threat because his movement was more openly militant.

The missions of Theudas, the unnamed prophets and the Egyptian were carried out in the desert, which was so closely associated with the salvation that God had already wrought there and was expected do so again. Their activity is based upon sound religious beliefs. Israel is God's chosen people. Only God, therefore, can rule over Israel. That it is ruled by pagan Romans and seemingly corrupt Jewish authorities is an affront to God. This belief lies behind the request by the Jews to be allowed to go to the desert rather than accept Titus's terms of surrender (*War* 6.351-2). It can also be seen in the activity of the bandits who joined forces with other rebels to successfully defeat Cestius Gallus and drive him away from Jerusalem in 66 CE (*War* 2.527-555).

Sustained, if not co-ordinated, attempts were made by certain sections of Jewish society to free the people of God. This is the climate, both political and religious, that existed prior to and following the time of John the Baptist. It remains now to assess John's place in it, as well as to enquire how far his ministry differed from or, indeed, reflected that of those with whom he unwittingly shared the desert wastes.

John the Baptist in the Desert Tradition

As with the prophets and the revolutionaries just discussed, John the Baptist emerged during a time of oppression and social difficulty. In fact, his appearance upon the world stage coincides with the oppressive rule of Pilate. However, in contrast with Judas the Galilaean before him and the Egyptian who followed, John was not a revolutionary in the militant sense. He was not the champion of a cause in the manner of Theudas and the unnamed prophets.

On the other hand, it would equally be incorrect to interpret John as a solitary prophet of doom like Jeshua, son of Ananias. As the evangelists make clear, John the Baptist had disciples. This can be accepted as historical fact because it is multiply attested. Mark compares the disciples of John with the Pharisees as well as Jesus' disciples (2.18). Luke also mentions them: 'Lord, teach us to pray, as John taught his disciples' (11.1). Indeed, these two passages give valuable insight into John and his ministry; they testify that he observed the laws of fasting and that he prayed. Acts speaks of their baptising activities (18.24-8; 19.1-7) The Fourth Evangelist also speaks of disciples of John. He asserts that John was 'standing with two of his disciples' (1.35), although they will leave him for Jesus. Here, they are used as a means of demonstrating the success of John's testimony in a gospel that treats him as little more than a witness. Elsewhere, the Fourth Gospel states that John did not have as many disciples as Jesus did, 'Now when the Lord knew that the Pharisees had heard that

Jesus was making and baptising more disciples than John...'(4.1). Again, this passage might serve the same purpose as the earlier one; however, the evangelist's gloss simply confirms that John did indeed have disciples. Moreover, while John might not have actively led a movement, he does seem to have inspired at least one (Acts 19.1-7).

The first century prophets and militants might have been informed by Scripture or were at least familiar with particular elements of Jewish tradition that are to be found in Scripture. As such, the movements of Theudas, the unnamed prophets and the Egyptian can be connected with one or more biblical acts of deliverance by God, each of which took place in the wilderness. Theudas led his followers to the river Jordan, the waters of which he promised to part in the manner of Moses, who parted the waters of the sea, or Joshua, who parted the waters of the Jordan. The unnamed prophets led their people into the desert to await signs of approaching freedom. The Egyptian was somewhat more war-like. He meant to overthrow the Roman garrison at Jerusalem after he had brought down that city's walls by the power of his command.

For those who would lead freedom movements, however they interpreted the word and however they sought to achieve their objective, the choice of location was paramount. The wilderness, a place of solitude where one could peacefully meditate and commune with God had been the scene of destruction wrought by God. It is also the setting of Israel's salvation by, and Covenant with, God. This last point led to its being understood as the setting for eschatological determination and fulfilment.

John the Baptist also chose the wilderness as the setting of his ministry. The locality in which John worked is variously given as the 'river Jordan' (Mk 1.5), 'the wilderness of Judaea' (Mt. 3.1) and 'all the region about the Jordan' (Lk. 3.3). The Fourth Evangelist places him 'in Bethany, beyond the Jordan' (1.28) and 'Aenon, near Salim' (3.23).[18] Those coming to John from Judaea and Jerusalem to be baptised were required to cross the desert and the Jordan to reach him. Similarly, they must re-cross the desert and the Jordan to return to their homes. It is tempting to think that John deliberately made use of the people's perception of the wilderness and the symbolism associated with it in the Jewish psyche.[19] First, he called upon them to leave their Judaean homes, where they were experiencing oppression not unlike that which had been experienced by their forefathers in Egypt. Second, he asked them to traverse the wilderness in response to his prophetic call as their ancestors had done in response to that of Moses. Their crossing of the Jordan would recall the parting of the sea during the Exodus and the crossing of the Jordan at the Conquest. Next, John baptised them. A full study of John's baptism will be made in the next chapter. For now, it should be noted that one of its possible functions was to create a 'remnant', or 'true Israel'. Those who submitted to baptism returned to their homes as changed people. They now saw themselves as the 'true Israel', comparable to those who were led into the Promised Land under Joshua's leadership.

Taking these various factors into account, it might be concluded that John had indeed drawn from Scripture as he devised the course and objective of his ministry. Certainly, he does appear to have had a profound knowledge of the Hebrew Bible. In his speech, given in Q 3.17, John speaks of the coming judgement using threshing floor imagery. This same imagery is used in the Hebrew Bible to signify the plenty and fertility due to those who would walk in the statutes and observe the commandments of God (Lev. 26.3-6; cf. Num. 15.18-20; 18.26-30). Thus, John could be using such imagery to refer to the future blessings of the people (cf. Joel 2.23-24). In addition, the release of God's chosen ones from exile is described as being threshed (Isa. 28.28-29; Hos. 9.2-3) or threshed and winnowed (Isa. 21.10). Here, exile might be used as a metaphor for the suffering and oppression that was afflicting the people at the time. That Israel is threshed out of the lands into which they have been dispersed and gathered back into their own land (Isa. 27.23-13) links very closely to John's prophecy as given in Q 3.17: '...to clear his threshing floor, and to gather the wheat into his granary...' More in keeping with John's eschatological perspective is the threshing floor imagery used in Dan. 2.35. This passage speaks of the destruction of worldly powers that will precede the institution of the kingdom of God at the end of days. Such powers shall 'become like the chaff of the summer threshing floors'. Conversely, Israel's vengeance against those who had oppressed them is also expressed using threshing floor imagery (Isa. 41.15-16; Mic. 4.10-13).

It is possible, therefore, that John took at least some of his inspiration from the Hebrew Bible. Unfortunately, such a conclusion cannot be demonstrated, but only deduced. To draw upon the historical and religious associations of the wilderness and the Jordan would have served John's purpose perfectly. He could have used such powerful connotations, representative of the greatest example of God's intervention on behalf of his chosen people, as an enticement to bring people to him. If an extensive knowledge of Scripture, which would have lent him even more authority, is added to the equation, it is not difficult to see why John's preaching would have been so successful.

Whatever the case, it must be remembered that John's preaching and baptism were the most important elements of his ministry. He was not concerned with revolution, whether spiritual (Theudas, the unnamed prophets) or militant (Judas the Galilaean, the various groups of bandits, the Egyptian). John differed in that he understood that the danger facing the people of Israel was greater than anything Rome could inflict upon them. It was nothing less than eschatological judgement. John did not seek to force God's hand, nor did he urge the people patiently and passively to await signs of freedom. His mission was to call upon them to repent in readiness for the judgement, 'John the baptiser appeared in the wilderness, preaching a baptism of repentance for the forgiveness of sins' (Mk 1.4; cf. Mt. 3.1-2, 11; Lk. 3.4). Moreover, he believed the judgement to be imminent, 'Even now the axe is laid to the root of the trees; every tree therefore that does not bear good fruit is cut down and thrown into the fire' (Q 3.9).

Considering the urgency and seriousness of John's mission, it is curious that he should confine himself to the desert wastes. The imperative nature of his message would surely have impelled him to take it to the people wherever they might be, in order to ensure that it reached as many as possible. While it is conceivable that John did come out onto the highways or into the towns and villages, even Jerusalem, to spread his message, he is mostly associated with the wilderness. More importantly, he is associated with those places where living, or running, water is to be found: the river Jordan and Aenon, near Salim. This choice of location provides John with the resources necessary for baptism: open spaces for many people to gather and living waters. This fact alone is indicative of the important place this rite held in his mission. In addition, to induce people to go into the wilderness brings them into the very area that is directly associated with salvation, the saving of the 'remnant' and the re-establishment of the Covenant spoken of by the ancient prophets: the wilderness.

Conclusion

A strong tradition associates John the Baptist with the wilderness. It is multiply attested, since it appears in Mark (1.4), Matthew (3.1) and Luke (3.3). The Fourth Evangelist is aware of traditions placing John in the desert (1.23, 28; 3.26). Josephus, while he does not explicitly speak of John conducting his ministry in the wilderness, does mention John's arrest and his being taken in chains to Machaerus. This palace-fortress belonging to Herod Antipas is situated in the desert of Peraea.

The significance of the wilderness for the Jewish people lies in its historical and religious associations. The most important of these are that it was the setting of Israel's deliverance from oppression by God and the establishment of the Covenant. The wilderness is also a place of refuge and a place where one might encounter both God and demons. Prophets had been drawn to it from antiquity. Here, they encountered these supernatural powers and relayed messages from God to his people. Such messages were usually exhortations to live righteously and return to God. There was a promise of restoration for those who did so, but God's wrath would ensure the destruction of those who refused. The wilderness, therefore, came to acquire powerful eschatological associations.

It was believed that once the prophets had spoken, prophecy would remain silent until the eschaton had come. It soon became obvious, however, that this was not the case. Men such as Judas the Galilaean, Theudas, several unnamed prophets, the Egyptian and John the Baptist each considered themselves to be the recipients of God's word, which they felt compelled to pass on to the people. Seen in this context, John the Baptist belonged to a tradition that reached back in time as far as the prophets of old.

Some first-century prophets, such as Jeshua, son of Ananias, took their message to the people in the city. Most, like John the Baptist, remained within or close to the desert wastes. With the exception of such men as Jeshua, most of the first-century prophets were leaders of movements, or, in the case of John, inspired later movements. The one thing they all shared in common was that their message was eschatological. This was not surprising, since Israel was once again living under the oppression of aggressive and seemingly intolerant rulers.

Nevertheless, there were differences in the way the first-century prophets approached their ministries. While the ancient prophets were content simply to preach their message, those of the first century chose to reinforce their message with action. Again, the exception is Jeshua, son of Ananias. Theudas, several unnamed prophets and even the militant Egyptian, appear to have attempted to re-enact certain significant biblical events.

The events they chose, specifically the Exodus and the Conquest, highlighted God's intervention in the salvation of his people and their release from oppression. Perhaps their actions were inspired by Scripture. More probable is that these events were so prominent in the minds of Jews anyway that there would be no need to scour the Hebrew Bible for them, or to explain them to their followers. It seems that the motive behind the staging of such acts was an attempt to 'provoke' God to act once again. Some of the first-century prophetic movements were peaceful. They undertook to hasten God's hand by passive means. The Egyptian and certain unspecified bandits sought to accelerate God's intervention by more violent means.

The Roman authorities considered each of these groups to be a threat to peace and stability and brutally quashed them. Jeshua, son of Ananias, whose ministry was seen as peaceful, was beaten by the Romans, who then released him. Clearly, his solitude, the obvious passiveness of his ministry, and probably the fact that he did not go into the wilderness, meant that he did not constitute a threat.

This, then, is the social, cultural and political context in which John the Baptist belongs. He is to be understood as a wilderness prophet, whose eschatological message reflected, and might have been informed by, that of the prophets of old. This hypothesis is supported by the content of some of his speeches as reported by the evangelists. However, his ministry differed from those of the classical prophets in that he supported his message with action. In this, he had more in common with his contemporaries.

There are strong reasons for believing that John the Baptist might have endeavoured to re-enact the Exodus by causing his audience to cross the desert and the Jordan. Certainly, the symbolism was there, should he have chosen to exploit it. However, the most important element of his message was not the exploitation of wilderness symbolism. Indeed, John did not look for freedom from oppression as his contemporaries did. Rather, he saw the oppression under which his countrymen were living as a sign of the approaching eschaton. He knew there was no escape from the judgement that was to come. There was, however, a means by which people could survive it. John offered a 'baptism of repentance for the forgiveness of sins' (Mk 1.4 and par.) that would in some way protect them from the coming judgement. The next step is to make a study of the baptism offered by John, and to evaluate it in its context as part of his eschatological mission.

2

BAPTISM

I baptise you with water for repentance... (Mt. 3.11).

John the Baptist preached a 'baptism of repentance for the forgiveness of sins'. Among those who came to hear him was Jesus of Nazareth, who listened to his preaching and submitted to the baptism. John's baptism was central to his ministry, and as such, is worthy of thorough investigation. Particular attention will be paid to what might have inspired John to offer baptism. It would be useful to make a comparison between it and other lustration rites known to Jews to see what differences there might be between them. What function did John's baptism serve, and what did it mean to John and to those who submitted to it?

The Sources

There is no doubt that John used a rite of baptism. It is multiply attested, appearing as it does in Q (3.16), Mark (1.4) and Josephus (*Ant.* 18.117). The Fourth Evangelist also mentions John's baptism (1.31), adding that the ritual took place at 'Bethany beyond the Jordan' (1.28) and at 'Aenon near Salim' (3.23). Because baptism is one among many forms of ritual ablutions used in contemporary Judaism, it is supported by the criterion of authentic context.

On the other hand, it is supported by the criterion of dissimilarity, because it shows important differences when compared with those practices. Moreover, a baptism designed for repentance and the forgiveness of sins contradicts the church's view that only Jesus could forgive sins (Mk 2.1-12 and par.; Mt. 26.28).[1] The fact that the sources include material that goes against Christian teaching strongly suggests that they preserve an authentic tradition concerning John's baptism.

The earliest Gospel designates John *Iōannēs ho Baptizōv* (Mk 1.4). Mark's use of the participle shows baptising to be a characteristic action of John. Indeed, he reiterates several times that John personally administered his rite: 'they were baptised by him...' (Mk 1.5) Jesus was 'baptised by John...' (Mk 1.9), 'I baptise you with water...' (Q 3.16). Matthew, in his redaction of Mark, replaces this participle with a noun: *Iōannēs ho Baptistiēs* (3.1). This slight alteration reflects the advanced view that the rite has become synonymous with John. 'The Baptist' now serves John almost as a surname in much the same way that 'Christ' came to be used for Jesus.

Jewish Lustration Rites

Clearly, John's baptism singled him out in the eyes of his contemporaries. Yet, his lustration rite is simply one of many such rites practised within Judaism. However, it must have been sufficiently different from existing lustrations known to Jews at the time, otherwise it would not have received the attention it did.

First-century Judaism consisted of several distinct strands, as the formation of various groups or sects clearly shows. Some of these groups had many members and were influential, such as the Pharisees. Others were small and often insignificant. What they all had in common was their use of ablutions.

Water rites have their origins in Torah. Leviticus 11-15 is especially significant. Here, the various ways of regaining purity are given, the form of the rite prescribed depending upon the type of contagion from which the person wished to be cleansed. However, all are concerned with ritual purification. It is important to note that ritual purification was distinct from personal hygiene. It had to do with being pure enough to serve God. Moreover, to be ritually impure did not mean that one was morally sinful. It simply meant that one had become contaminated by the impure things of the world: dead flesh, leprosy, semen, menstrual blood. Contact with such things was often unavoidable. The rituals given in Leviticus are designed to restore people to purity. Many of these rituals involve water, whether it is the washing of a garment (Lev. 13.55, 58), or sprinkling water onto a person (Lev. 14.7). Some call for total immersion (Lev. 14.8, 9; 15.5-18, 21). However, the most serious cases of contagion required cleansing in living water. Bathing in water was also part of the process by which a priest made himself ritually pure (Lev.16.4). Judaism used the symbolism of water as a purifying agent.[2]

Much later, several groups emerged who set themselves apart from their contemporaries by their attitude towards ritual cleanliness. For example, there are the 'morning bathers', who chose to bathe rather than merely wash their hands before prayer, thus ensuring ritual purity. Another group, the Hemerobaptists, took a daily bath as a normal part of their religious observances. Unfortunately, it cannot be said for certain whether these groups existed in John's time.[3] It is acceptable to assert, however, that baptising movements of some kind were extant prior to the fall of Jerusalem.

One group that certainly is contemporary with John the Baptist are the Essenes, whose lustration rites involved a ritual bath taken twice daily before meals (*War* 2.129, 132). At Qumran, an elaborate water system consisting of aqueducts, plaster-lined cisterns and pools with steps have been excavated. These are often taken as an indication that ritual bathing played an important role in the life of the Covenanters.[4] Another 'sect', if such a term is appropriate in this case, is that of Bannus. This wilderness ascetic, as described by Josephus, his former disciple, 'spent his life in the desert, wearing such clothing as might be had from trees, eating the food which the earth spontaneously supplied, and using frequent ablutions of cold water, by day and by night, for purposes of purity.' (Life 2.2).

Bannus bathed in cold water, indicating that it was running, or 'living' water. Thus he must have used springs, streams, or perhaps the most obvious choice for one living in the desert, the Jordan.

Quite why Bannus, who lived in conditions of extreme asceticism, should have felt the need to bathe so often is unclear. He might have sought to cleanse himself of some perceived moral contagion. More probable, and Josephus hints at this when he mentions purity, is that Bannus wanted to make himself ritually pure in readiness for taking meals. If this is the correct interpretation, Bannus's practice compares with that of the Essenes, who required new members to undergo a probationary period of one year before they were allowed to share the communal waters of purification.

It is evident that the ablutions required by Torah had already been adapted by those whose interpretation of Scripture took it to a higher level. Bathing, which often took the form of total immersion, formed a regular part of the religious observances of many devout Jews since before John's time. Whatever form they took, Jewish lustration practices had three important things in common. First, they were repeatable. Second, with the exception of Num. 19.19 and possibly the rite described in the Dead Sea Scroll 1QS 5.7-15, they were self-administered. Finally, they were concerned with ritual purity as opposed to physical cleanliness. John's baptism differed in several respects: it was to be taken only once, and John administered the baptism himself. Its raison d'être went much deeper than ritual purity.

John's Baptism

In order to gain a full picture of John baptism and how he understood it to work, a careful analysis of how it is presented in each of the sources is required. John's baptism is mentioned by the evangelists and by Josephus.

According to Mark (1.4) and Luke (3.3), John preached a 'baptism of repentance for the forgiveness of sins'. Matthew (3.11) omits 'for the forgiveness of sins', stating only that John's baptism is 'for repentance'. This discrepancy is easily explained by the fact that Matthew drew his material concerning John's baptism from two sources. One, 3.11, is Q material. The other, that in which Matthew found John's preaching of repentance, comes from Mark 1.4.

In 3.11, Matthew has added Mark's 'for repentance' to 'I baptise you with water...', which is preserved in Luke's redaction of the Q material (3.16). It can safely be assumed that 'for repentance' was absent from the original Q version since, had it been present, Luke would surely have included it. Luke is greatly interested in repentance motifs, which occur throughout his Gospel (3.3, 8; 5.32; 24.47) and Acts (5.31; 13.24; 19.4; 26.20). Matthew's reason for placing 'for repentance' where he did was to confirm that John's baptism was indeed one of repentance. He did not clarify this point in an earlier passage (3.2) because he wanted to show that John's preaching concerning the kingdom of heaven was consistent with that of Jesus. Moreover, Matthew understood that only Jesus' death had the power to forgive sins (26.28). As such, he omitted this aspect of John's baptism.[5] It is reasonable to state, then, that all three of the Synoptic evangelists agree that John's baptism was for repentance and the forgiveness of sins.

Mark is careful to note that John preached his baptism, going on to record the success of that preaching: 'There went out to him all the country of Judaea, and all the people of Jerusalem.' In showing that John baptised the people as they confessed their sins, Mark clearly shows that the baptism was an integral feature of John's ministry. Moreover, John required the people to participate by declaring themselves to be sinners, rather than passively accepting baptism. This was an ingenious measure implemented by John to force people to confront their past and to express a sincere desire to change.

In contrast to Mark, Matthew and Luke do not state outright that John preached his baptism. Instead, they give examples of John's preaching of repentance, which they then inextricably link to the baptism. This preaching is taken from Q 3.7-9. Here, John urges people to 'bear fruits worthy of repentance' (Q 3.8). In other words, John called upon people to change their ways, otherwise the baptism would not be efficacious. Furthermore, the theme is continued by Jesus (Q 6.43-45), whose parable of the blind man shifts into an interpretation of John's teaching of inner purity being linked to the fruits befitting repentance.

Josephus also mentions John's baptism:

> [John] had commanded the Jews to exercise virtue, both as to righteousness towards one another, and piety towards God, and so to come to baptism; for that the washing with water would be acceptable to him, if they made use of it, not in order to the putting away, or the remission of some sins only, but for the purification of the body; supposing that the soul was thoroughly purified beforehand by righteousness. (*Ant.* 18.116-117).

Josephus focuses entirely upon the fact that John's baptism, in order to be effectual, required a change of heart on the part of the person submitting to it. In other words, unlike Mark, Matthew and Luke, who directly mention repentance, Josephus represents repentance by describing what it entails. His explanation includes the observation that baptism must not be used for seeking forgiveness, but rather to purify the body once repentance has been expressed. Of prime importance is the prerequisite that the penitent must sincerely repent prior to submitting to baptism.

John's Baptism and Repentance

John the Baptist was aware of two types of repentance,[6] the first of which was marked by a sense of remorse for having sinned and required the sinner to atone for his or her actions through a ritual, such as fasting, bathing or sacrifice. This form of repentance, which can be referred to as 'penitential repentance', is illustrated in a passage taken from the Slavonic Life of Adam and Eve (35.1-34.4).

> Eve said to Adam, 'Rise up, my lord, let us pray to God in this cause that He set us free from that devil, for thou art in this strait on my account.'
>
> But Adam said: 'Eve, since thou repentest of thy misdeed, my heart will hearken to thee, for the Lord created thee out of my ribs. Let us fast forty days perchance the Lord will have pity on us and will leave us understanding and life.' I, for my part, said: 'Do thou, (my) lord, fast forty days, but I will fast forty-four.'
>
> And Adam said to me: 'Haste thee to the river, named Tigris, and take a great stone and place it under thy feet, and enter into the stream and clothe thyself with water, as with a cloak, up to the neck, and pray to God in thy heart and let no word proceed out of thy mouth.' And I said: 'O (my) lord, with my whole heart will I call upon God.' And Adam said to me: 'Take great care of thyself. Except thou seest me and all my tokens, depart not out of the water, nor trust in the words, which are said to thee, lest thou fall again into the snare.' And Adam came to Jordan and he entered into the water and he plunged himself altogether into the flood, even (to) the hairs of his head, while he made supplication to God and sent (up) prayers to Him.[7]

Here, Adam and Eve, recognising that they have sinned, seek to appease God by engaging in a ritual bathing. Their penitence reflects that which is prescribed in Torah. Adam prays as he stands in the water, and perhaps his prayers contain an acknowledgment of his sins. His bathing in water is the method used to express repentance for those sins. However, there is no indication that he or Eve seek to 'bear fruits that befit repentance'.

No matter how sincerely it might be expressed, 'penitential repentance' came to be viewed as inadequate by the prophets. They realised that it often constituted no more than an outward show of sorrow, making it an empty gesture of atonement. A person could sin, repent, atone and be forgiven, and then sin again, knowing that they would be forgiven once more. In order to ensure that those who atoned for their sins did so with sincerity, the prophets advocated a second type of repentance, one that involved a turning back, or a return.

This form of repentance comprised two elements, one negative, the other positive. The negative element calls for a rejection or a turning away from sin (Isa. 59.20; Ezek. 14.6), while the positive element involves a return to God (Isa. 10.20-1; Jer. 3.22-3; 18.8; 26.3-5; Zech. 1.3-4; Mal. 3.7).[8] Penitents were now required to undergo a readjustment in all the areas of their life so that they could enter into a new relationship with God. In other words, they had to convert, and this revised type of repentance was designated 'conversionary repentance'.

References to conversionary repentance are found throughout the prophetic books of the Hebrew Bible. All who answer the call to turn away from sin and return to God are rewarded with forgiveness, life and merciful judgement (Isa. 55.7; Jon. 3.9-10; Ezek. 33.13-16). Those in exile will be restored to Israel (Isa. 10.20-22; Jer. 12.15-16). On the other hand, those who refuse to repent will be punished (Ezek. 33.9-11; Hos. 11.5-6; Amos 4.6-8). The urge to repent sometimes comes from God himself (Jer. 31.15-20; Lam. 5.21), who usually speaks through the prophets (Zech. 1 3-6). God will then accept those who have returned to him and restore them (Jer. 24.7; 31.33-4; Ezek. 36.22-9). This would not necessarily happen at once (Isa. 6.10; Hos. 5.4), but it will certainly be affected at the eschaton (Deut. 4.30-1; Isa. 59.20; Hos.3.4; Mal. 4.5-6). A later text, the *Sibylline Oracles* 4.62-70, suggests that 'conversionary repentance' continued at least into the first century:

> O ill-starred mortals, let not these things be, and drive not the great God to divers deeds of wrath; but have done with swords and meanings and killing of men, and deeds of violence, and wash your whole bodies in ever-running rivers, and, stretching your hands to heaven, seek forgiveness for your former deeds, and with praises ask pardon for your bitter ungodliness. God will grant repentance and will not slay: He will stay his wrath once more if with one accord ye practise precious godliness in your hearts.[9]

Here, immersion in the perennial river is associated with a change in behaviour; the penitent is required to engage in certain actions: they must reject sin, pray for forgiveness and give praise to God. Once they have made the commitment to live according to the codes set out in the text, God's wrath will cease. Although the act of bathing can be seen as an expression of penitential repentance, the acts of piety are to be understood as conversionary repentance. In short, bathing alone will not work; it had to be accompanied by the required actions in order to be efficacious. Together, immersion and acts of piety form a rite that both expresses repentance and earns the penitent God's forgiveness. The *Sibylline Oracles* 4.62-70 reflects the interpretation of John's baptism that is given in the Synoptic Gospels and, even more explicitly, in Josephus's account. The rite worked because John understood and drew inspiration from the Jewish concept of the soul.

John's Baptism and the Concept of the Soul

Most Jews saw human beings as a whole entity rather than as a soul living within a corruptible body.[10] This was not an absolute concept, since the Pharisaic belief in a resurrection at the eschaton suggests the existence of some form of independent human spirit, which would be transferred into another body in the age to come.[11] However, this appears to be a very rare concept in Judaism.

There was a further distinction between the inner and the outer being of a person (Ps. 73.13, 26; 84.3; Lam. 3.41; Num. 15.39; I Sam. 16.7; Ezek. 3.10; Deut. 30.14). The inner being is לבב. This is described as the 'inner man, mind, will, heart.'[12] The outer being is רבש, meaning 'flesh' or the body.[13]

Both the inner and the outer being of a person are affected by impurity.[14] Physical impurity, as noted above, resulted from coming into contact with impure things. Although natural, certain things are seen as corrupting because they are considered unclean, and a rite designed to restore ritual purity would render the person physically clean again. However, physical impurity could not affect the heart, which could be rendered impure only by disobedience to Torah and unrighteous behaviour. Consequently, the only way a heart could be cleansed was by turning away from sin, embracing Torah and living righteously. Indeed, the Greek verb μετανοεω, although usually translated as 'repentance', could more accurately be described as 'a change of mind'.[15] The mind, of course, is part of the inner being of a person.

The distinction between the inner and outer being of a person was perfectly understood by John the Baptist. He also understood the effect impurity had upon each component of a person's being and how it could be remedied. John, therefore, shows himself to be in complete harmony with beliefs and teachings of the prophets of old. His views are particularly represented in Isa. 1.12-20 and 58.1-21. Such passages as these support Josephus's comment that John called for righteous behaviour, which alone entitled people to 'come to baptism' (*Ant.*18.117). Moreover, they reflect John's call to 'bear fruits that befit repentance' (Q 3.8). Clearly, people were not to submit to baptism until they had repented, changed their hearts and begun to live righteously.

Indeed, baptism would not be accepted by God unless the person concerned had repented. This is entirely consistent with Jewish belief that the heart could only be cleansed by righteous conduct. Repentance renders the person inwardly pure. The person is then baptised, emerging from the water physically pure. John's baptism served to purify the body once the heart had been purified.

The accounts of the Synoptic evangelists and Josephus regarding John's baptism are perfectly reconciled with each other. Mark describes it as a rite of 'repentance for the forgiveness of sins' (1.4). He observes that people were baptised while 'confessing their sins' (Mk 1.5). This suggests that penitents had admitted to their sins, were genuinely sorry and had undergone a change of heart, all of which made them eligible for baptism. Mark's account says nothing about the need to live righteously; such an imperative exists only in the Q tradition (Q 3.8) and special Lukan passages (3.10-14). In Q, it is stated but not explained.

Luke portrays John's teaching in a series of three formulaic questions and answers. Each question represents an area of special interest to the evangelist. First and foremost is his concern for the poor,[16] a major theme in his Gospel. Jesus proclaims the good news to the poor (4.16-20; 7.22), blesses them (6.20) and tells parables on their behalf (12.13-21; 16.19-31). Wealth and possessions are unimportant (12.15) or are distracting (12.34). Second is Luke's interest in tax collectors, such as Levi (5.27) and Zacchaeus (19.8), both of whom respond positively to Jesus' preaching. The passage concerning Zacchaeus, especially, strongly echoes Lk 3.12-13. Last is the suggestion that Luke is addressing readers living under Roman rule. In verse 14 John offers ethical advice to Roman soldiers who had not otherwise shown an interest in John's baptism.[17]

All this suggests that Lk 3.12-14 is a product of Hellenistic Christianity,[18] possibly invented by Luke and attributed to John. The specifically Lukan concerns support this theory. On the other hand, this discourse does reflect John's ethical imperative as found in Q.[19] The words spoken to the special groups would, therefore, belong to the same category as 'bear fruits that befit repentance' (Q 3,8) and John's exhortation to Jews to live righteously and piously (*Ant.* 18.117).

If Lk 3.12-14 is authentic to John, why Matthew should have omitted it is unclear. Matthew might have wanted to concentrate upon John's polemic against the ruling priestly classes. Conversely, Luke could have preserved this teaching precisely because it reflected his own special interest. More probable, however, is that Luke composed this passage using John's authentic ethical teaching as a base and applied it to those groups and situations that were of particular concern to him in a speech attributed to John. As such, Luke depicted John as a moral preacher.[20]

This leaves only Josephus to provide a full account of John's ethical imperative (*Ant.* 18.117). Josephus is correct to assert that baptism was not to be used to gain pardon for sin. Unless a person's heart was cleaned through right behaviour, they would not receive God's forgiveness. Baptism alone would not suffice because, without true repentance, it would be an empty ritual. However, if a person approached John with a clean heart and submitted to baptism, God would accept their baptism and restore them. Mark condenses the function of John's rite into a single sentence. Q, as used by Matthew and Luke, retains a memory of John's exhortation to live righteously and piously. However, Josephus presents this exhortation more fully.

John's baptism, therefore, worked in the following way. First, John called upon people to repent. This involved a rejection of sin and a turning back to God. Those who accepted John's call responded by changing their way of life; they bore 'fruits that befit repentance'. This made them worthy of God's forgiveness. They were then immersed in water by John. The baptism rendered the person ritually clean, as would any Jewish rite of penitence. More than this, though, the baptism was acceptable to God as a rite of penance because the former sinner had expressed a sincere change of heart. As such, John's baptism also served to mediate God's forgiveness upon them. Those submitting to it were cleansed in their inner and outer being. The inner being was cleansed by the power of God's forgiveness. The outer being was cleansed by the purifying water ritual. John's baptism and the ethical imperative that lay behind it was fully in concert with Jewish thought.

John's Baptism as a Protest against the Temple Establishment

John's baptism can accurately be described as a 'baptism of repentance for the forgiveness of sins'. However, it might have served purposes other than this. It is possible that John developed and used it as a protest against the Temple establishment,[21] and to replace the sacrifice. This hypothesis is based upon the previously drawn conclusion that the baptism mediated divine forgiveness and, as such, it took the place of the sacrifice in many of the rites described in Leviticus.

This view is supported by Josephus's observation that John's baptism had to be acceptable to God (*Ant.* 18.117). John, in common with his predecessors, believed that the Temple sacrifice had become empty and so was unacceptable to God. Josephus, in using language evocative of the Temple system, expresses his own interpretation of the nature of John's baptism.[22]

According to this system, the penitent confesses their sin (cf. Lev. 5.5). They bring a sacrifice to the priest who makes atonement for that sin (cf. Lev. 5.6-9). The penitent's sins are forgiven (cf. Lev. 5.10). However, John's baptism directly conveyed God's forgiveness to the penitent. Since this was so, John himself could be seen as acting the role of priest. That John performed the baptism himself further reinforces this view. If this conclusion is accepted, then a condemnation of the priesthood might be included as a motive for John's baptism. If John were indeed of priestly descent (Lk. 1.5), such a protest would take on a deeper significance. His turning his back upon his hereditary duty would constitute a rejection of the entire Temple establishment.

Why John should want to protest against the Temple establishment is more difficult to address, but the problem becomes clearer once it is understood what the Temple stood for. To begin with, the Temple was believed to be the dwelling place of God (Isa. 6.1) and that a divinely appointed hereditary priesthood was responsible for conducting rites of worship (Ex. 28.1, cf. 1 Chron. 6.48, 49). The Temple establishment therefore represented the centre of Israel's spiritual life, but in times of oppression, it also became the focus of Israel's hoped-for release through devotion to Torah (1 Macc. 11-2.2.68; 3.47; 51; 13.3-6) and even to the Temple itself (1 Macc. 3.43, 45, 49; 4.36, 60; 7.33-8).

However, under the Roman oppression of the first century, many members of the Temple aristocracy were seen to be collaborating with the enemy.[23] Moreover, high priests were often seen as corrupt and greedy, flaunting their wealth and even showing violence towards the people. It is possible that John viewed their presence in the Temple as defiling, or that it in some way invalidated Temple rites. As a result, John offered baptism as a replacement. In support of this hypothesis is the suggestion that John had altercations with the priestly classes (Mt. 3.7).

If John had preached against the Temple aristocracy and promoted his baptism as an alternative to the Temple rites, his activity might have prompted such confrontation. Certainly, his actions in this regard are not without precedent. The community at Qumran originally began as a protest movement. There, too, the Temple sacrifice was replaced by a system of prayers and ablutions. Seen in this context, John's baptism can be understood as part of a wider dissatisfaction with the Temple establishment. It must be emphasised, however, that this function of John's rite is only a possibility. It is not directly supported by the accounts of Josephus or the evangelists, although it can be inferred by what is already known about John, his beliefs and activities.

John's Baptism as an Initiation Rite

Another function of John's baptism might have been to initiate those who submitted to it into a sectarian movement.[24] This movement might be interpreted as the 'remnant' or the 'true Israel' who would dwell in the new age inaugurated by God at the eschaton. The concept of a remnant occurs several times in the Hebrew Bible (2 Kings 19.31; Jer. 23.3; Mic. 4.7; Isa. 10.21, 22; 11.11, 16).[25] As John's baptism was meant to be taken once only, it could be understood as an initiation rite. Moreover, that early Christian baptism was also used as an initiation rite suggests that John's baptism could be appealed to as a model for this.[26]

That John's baptism served as an initiation rite does not find universal scholarly support.[27] The main points of contention are that John did not gather about him an exclusive, or closed, community, which meant that there was no sect or movement to be initiated into. The fact that a Baptist group did emerge was a secondary development that did not reflect John's original intentions. Another objection is that John's message focused upon judgement rather than restoration. As such, his message could have been seen as no more than a warning to escape the coming wrath.

In answer to the first point, an initiation rite does not necessarily initiate a person into an exclusive community.[28] Several Jewish sectarian groups, such as the Pharisees and the early Christian movement, continued to live within the general community. However, the fact that the disciples of John were known for their praying, fasting and baptising activities (Mk 2.18; Lk. 1.1; Acts 18.24-8; 19.1-7) is significant. That they were noticed by their contemporaries suggests that they were set apart to some degree. As such, it might be concluded that John's baptism did indeed serve as an initiation rite into this group. This does not imply that every person who was baptised by John became a disciple. Most of them returned to their daily lives.[29] The important factor for them was the knowledge that they were purified in their inner and outer being. Thus, John's baptism had the effect of creating two groups of people: those who had been baptised and those who had not. The first group had rejected a life of sin and returned to God. They had changed their ways. Their sins had been forgiven them. They had been purified. The second group had not repented. They continued to live sinful lives. Their sins had been not forgiven. They were not purified.

In answer to the second objection, while it is true that judgement is the emphasis of John's message, a promise of restoration can also be discerned.[30] This occurs in John's announcement of a future baptism with the Holy Spirit as well as in the imagery of grain being gathered into the granary. Seen in the context of eschatological judgement, it can be deduced that the group who accepted baptism would find restoration. Those who rejected it would be condemned.

Josephus speaks of John asking people 'to come baptism' (*Ant.* 18.117). This should not be construed as being 'united in baptism', since John appears not to have advocated group baptism. Josephus's use of the dative, $\beta\alpha\pi\tau\iota\sigma\mu\omega$, is significant. While the dative is usually translated as 'in baptism', 'for baptism', or 'to baptism', it can also be used in the instrumental sense: 'through baptism'.[31] It is possible, therefore, that John was attempting to gather people into a group, and that he used his baptism as the means to achieve his objective. This conclusion is, of course, based upon Josephus's view of John's baptism as recorded in *Antiquities*, and so might not accurately reflect John's own intentions. However, Josephus has so far shown a remarkable understanding of John the Baptist and his ministry. There appears to be no reason to doubt him regarding this point, especially if Jewish self-understanding as the chosen, covenant people of God, and the hope of restoration on a national scale, is taken into account. The prophets had spoken about this in their writings. Now, at a time of oppression, Jews once again looked to a time when God would affect their salvation. John the Baptist's message intensified their hope that such an event was imminent. As such, although responding individually to his call, the people would have understood John's message collectively.

Another important point is that John rebuked those who felt that being 'sons of Abraham' (Q 3.8) would be protection enough against the coming wrath. He knew that simply being a member of ethnic Israel was not sufficient. Only those who had undergone baptism could claim to be members of the true Israel.[32] Considering the conclusions reached about John's baptism and its primary function, this makes perfect sense. John, like the prophets of old, viewed empty ritual with contempt. He knew that a person had to sincerely repent in their hearts in order to be worthy of God's forgiveness. Similarly, simply being one of God's chosen people was not enough to ensure salvation. People had to show their worthiness to be saved at the eschaton. They did this by responding positively to John's call and submitting to his baptism.

It is appropriate to interpret John's baptism as a rite by which people were initiated into the true Israel, or the 'remnant'. This conclusion is supported by four arguments. First, it separated people into two distinct groups. The first group consisted of those who had rejected sin and returned to God. Their repentance had been accepted by God, who then forgave them. These people were now purified in readiness for the imminent judgement, at which they would be restored. The second group consisted of those who were still sinful. They had not repented, their sins were not forgiven, nor were they accepted by God. They had not been purified, and so were not prepared to face the coming judgement. Rather than be restored, they would be condemned. Second, Jews believed that they were God's elect. This understanding was felt upon a communal, rather than an individual, basis. Since those who submitted to baptism were accepted by God, John's baptism formed a collective of God's elect: a true Israel or 'remnant'. Third, Josephus's interpretation of John's baptism supports the view that John gathered people into a group of some kind. Finally, simply being Jewish was not enough to save people from the coming wrath. People had to show themselves worthy of God's grace at the eschaton. Were it otherwise, John would have had no need to offer baptism to Jews.

John's Target Audience

John the Baptist's message of judgement, repentance and baptism was clearly in harmony with Jewish thought. Moreover, it was to Jews that he proclaimed his message. This is evident from Josephus, who explicitly states that John 'commanded the Jews to exercise virtue, both as to righteousness towards one another, and piety towards God.' (*Ant.* 18.117). However, simply to state 'the Jews' is vague; it is possible that John's message was aimed at a more specific section of society. The Gospels offer no further clarification of this interesting point: who was John's target audience?

The opening passage of Q 3.7-9 suggests that John directed his message at the ruling classes and other powerful social groups.[33] Certainly, while delivering his message, John spoke some harsh words. 'You brood of vipers', he says to the Pharisees and Sadducees (Mt. 3.7), throwing in accusations of hypocrisy and complacency for good measure. However, these words are directed at 'the multitudes' in Lk. 3.7. Here is another discrepancy that must be resolved.

It is highly probable that the introductions to this Q narrative reflect the interests of the respective evangelists.[34] For instance, Matthew often places Pharisees and Sadducees together, even where his source does not (Mt. 16.1; cf. Mk 8.11). Luke, on the other hand, displays a fondness for referring to 'the people' (3.21), or the 'crowds' (11.29; cf. Mt. 12.38). Clearly, then, the opening passages are original to the writer concerned, who then adds them to his redaction of the Q saying. On the other hand, it is possible that one or the other of the evangelists has faithfully represented the original Q account.

In support of Matthew's version as the most authentic representation of the original Q source is that fact that Matthew, in another passage (16.1-12), does not invent an association between Pharisees and Sadducees. Rather, he simply adds 'Sadducees' to the 'Pharisees' already present in his source. In support of this is the suggestion that much of Q appears to involve polemic against the Pharisees and/or lawyers (cf. 11.39-12.1).[35] The clue to the correct version lies in the observation that John's address as a whole, which includes the reproof, 'you brood of vipers' (Q 3.7) better fits those who actively oppose him.[36] Moreover, the appeal to Abrahamic descent (Q 3.8b) represents a theological argument which, in turn, makes it is easier to accept that it came from educated priests, such as Pharisees and Sadducees, rather than the common people.[37] However, it cannot be said for certain whether they came to John for baptism, or simply to hear him. It is possible that they wanted to be baptised without committing themselves to the ethical imperative, hence John's hostility towards them.

The proposal that Luke's version is the most faithful rendering of Q is supported by evidence found in Josephus (*Ant.* 13.16-17; *War* 2.165-6) and the rabbinic literature (*m. Yad.* 4.6; *b. Yom.* 19b). Here, the Pharisees and Sadducees are usually shown to oppose one another. It is questionable whether they would unite to challenge John. Moreover, Luke's version is supported by Josephus's account, wherein 'the crowds' came to John for baptism (*Ant* 18.118). John's message could not have been addressed exclusively to Pharisees and Sadducees, since all Israel would face God's wrath, not just the ruling classes. Luke singled out special groups (3.12-14) who were likewise in positions of authority, being tax collectors and soldiers. To these John also gave ethical teaching and a reminder of their obligations. As has been noted, however, the authenticity of Lk 3.12-14 is not assured.[38] The conclusion is that Luke's version, in which John addresses his fiery speech to the multitudes, should be considered the most faithful representation of the original Q tradition.

In support of this conclusion, the Gospels note that 'there went out to him all the country of Judaea, and all the people of Jerusalem' (Mk 1.5). Matthew (3.5) adds 'and all the region about the Jordan'. It might be something of an exaggeration to say that 'all the people' went to hear John the Baptist, but the evangelists nevertheless do convey a sense of how widespread his appeal was. Josephus simply observes that John 'commanded the Jews' (*Ant.* 18.117).

This is not to say that John kept to one location, forcing the crowds to come out to him as Lk. 3.7 might imply. The Fourth Gospel affirms that he baptised at 'Bethany beyond the Jordan' (1.28) and at 'Aenon near Salim' (3.23). John's travels took him across the Jordan into Peraea. The implication is that he spoke to the general populace. This deduction is supported by Q, which preserves a tradition that many people accepted John's teaching and were baptised (Lk. 7.29; cf. *Gospel of Thomas* 78). Moreover, John's success with the common people is reflected in Herod's desire to remove him.[39] As Josephus (*Ant.* 18.118; cf. Lk. 3.10) notes, the people John attracted were then joined by 'many others'. Had John not stirred up so much excitement among the people, he perhaps would not have faced such danger. On the other hand, his success would not have been so great had he addressed himself only to those who were likely to reject him. As a result, it can be accepted that John's message and baptism were preached to the general populace. It must be remembered that John's ministry was in response to his belief that the eschaton was imminent. He addressed his message to everyone, no matter to which section of society they belonged, because all Israel was facing judgement.

The Administration of John's Baptism

The importance of John's baptism is evident not only because of the message that accompanied it, but also because of the way in which it was administered. Josephus notes that John urged

Jews to consolidate their promise to lead righteous lives and their commitment to justice and piety by coming 'to baptism'. Further than this, he gives no information about how the baptism was administered. By contrast, the evangelists provide several clues. Mark (1.5), followed by Matthew (3.6), notes that the people were baptised by John in the river Jordan. This passive rendering is still more prominent in the original Greek, where Mark uses εβαπτίζοντο 'υπ αυτου. It is clear that John baptised the people, rather than that they baptised themselves. Luke (3.21) also uses the passive βαπτισθηναι for the people collectively, and the passive βαπτισθέντος for Jesus. His description, when read alongside those of Mark and Matthew, indicates that John himself administered the baptism.

Several methods were available to John as he administered his baptism, one of which is that he could have watched as penitents immersed themselves, perhaps by means of a total immersion or a quick ducking. Given the evidence presented above, however, it is doubtful that this would be the method used, since it reduces John's role to that of witness.

Another possibility is that John physically held the penitent, pushing him or her down into the water before raising them up again. However, a discussion found in the Mishnah,[40] indicates that there would have been some concern over the validity of an immersion if the water could not touch every part of person being immersed. Thus, if John had held the penitent as they went into the water, there would have been some part of them that the water could not touch: the part covered by John's hands. The Mishna suggests that, if the person holding the one being immersed had rinsed his or her hands in water prior to the immersion, this would remove the problem.

A third method would be for John to have held the penitent under the water before letting go of them at some point so that he or she could re-emerge on their own. This might have been the technique used in the baptism of Jesus (Mk 1.9; cf. Mt. 3.16), who, having been baptised, 'came up' out of the water. The Greek term used by Mark is αναβαινων, an active participle. This indicates that Jesus himself came out of the water, rather than waiting for John to raise him up.

It cannot be said for certain which of these possibilities most accurately represents John's baptism. However, another example, that of the baptism of the Ethiopian eunuch by Philip as it is described in Acts of the Apostles (8.36-9), might be illustrative of John's method. Here, Philip and the Ethiopian go down into the water together and re-emerge at the same time. There is no suggestion of physical contact. Instead, the impression is of a baptism in which both the baptiser and the one being baptised actively participate.

What makes Philip's baptism such a good example is that it does not reflect the rite as it was developing within the church. As in the case of the baptisms at Samaria, Philip would baptise people, not in the Holy Spirit, but rather, in the name of the Lord Jesus (Acts 8.16). It was only when Peter and John were sent to Samaria that the people there received the Holy Spirit through the laying on of hands (Acts 8.17).[41] If Philip's baptising method was closer to John's rather than that of the apostles, it is quite conceivable that John accompanied the penitent into the water, immersing himself at the same time.

Connected to the method of baptism is the question of whether or not the penitent was naked when he or she took part in the rite. Certainly, Christian art frequently depicts Jesus naked at his baptism, but other images show him fully clothed. It must be remembered that John's baptism, despite its raison d'être, was still a Jewish rite and should be evaluated within that context. Historically, Judaism has viewed nakedness negatively. It was a source of shame (cf. Gen. 2.25; 3.7) and was used as punishment for women found guilty of adultery (Isa. 3.17; 47.3; Hos. 2.3, 9-10; Jer. 13.26; Ezek. 23.26). Jews, anxious to preserve their traditions in the wake of the Hellenisation of their country, rejected the nakedness of the gymnasium (1 Macc. 1.14-15; 2 Macc. 4.12-15; cf. Ant. 12.241). The Qumran Community also had strict rules governing the circumstances in which nakedness would be acceptable (1QS 8.12, 13-14). The weight of evidence against nakedness suggests that John did not expect it of penitents coming to him for baptism. Moreover, to be clothed does not invalidate baptism as a purification rite, since John himself wore garments of camel's hair. It is possible that certain types of cloth or clothing were deemed capable of allowing water to freely circulate and reach every part of the penitent's body.[42]

Conclusion

Baptism was of course a predominant feature of John's ministry. Immersion in water was not unknown to Jews, and Torah prescribed water rituals in several forms for various types of physical impurity. Once undergone, the person would be rendered ritually pure and worthy to serve God again. John's baptism differed from these forms of ablutions in three ways. First, while the ablutions prescribed in Torah were designed to be taken whenever the need arose, John's baptism was meant to be taken once. Second, with rare exceptions, Jewish lustration rites were self-administered. John's baptism was performed by John himself. Third, the rites mentioned in Torah were concerned with physical purity. John's baptism was also concerned with this. However, John knew that physical purity alone would not prepare people for the coming judgement. Rather, they had to meet this event with a pure heart. Like the prophets of old, John knew that rituals designed to restore the body to ritual purity could do nothing to cleanse a heart rendered impure by immoral behaviour. As a consequence, he called upon people to change their hearts, to reject sin and return to God. In a word, he asked them to repent. This they did by expressing sincere sorrow for their sins, by acting justly towards their neighbours and showing piety towards God. Having done that, they were allowed to submit to baptism. This water rite, serving fundamentally as a penitential ritual, was accepted by God because the heart of the penitent was truly changed. As a result, God forgave them their sins. Baptism mediated God's forgiveness upon the penitent, who was then purified in their inner and outer being. This prepared them for the imminent judgement.

John's baptism, therefore, was entirely in concert with Jewish tradition. It was acceptable as a purification ritual in accordance with Torah and would have been understood as such by those who agreed to submit to it. It also reflected prophetic teaching of the necessity to come to God in sincere repentance. However, it differed from tradition in that John took ritual away from the Temple. He did not ask people to sacrifice. Instead, he made them come into the wilderness, which he would have considered to be more holy because it was the natural dwelling place of God and the scene of the Covenant. Here, John baptised in living water; that is, he used water that had not been collected by people but had been given to humanity by God in the form of rivers and springs. Finally, John's baptism was preached and administered in anticipation of the eschaton. In its function, to prepare the people for imminent judgement, its method – it was administered by John – and its location, the wilderness, John's baptism was unique among Jewish rituals. Its uniqueness meant that John had to preach his baptism; he had to explain what it meant and how it worked. John the Baptist's rite singled him out from the prophets of old, as well as from those who were his contemporaries.

John's baptism served a similar function to the sacrifice that would normally be offered by a penitent at the Temple. Once offered, the priest would communicate God's forgiveness to the penitent, who would then be restored. In a similar way, baptism mediated God's forgiveness. John, who performed the baptism himself, can be seen as acting the role of a priest. As such, another function of John's baptism might have been as a means of protest against the Temple establishment. John, like many of his contemporaries, could have seen the priestly aristocracy as unworthy of fulfilling their roles as mediators of God's forgiveness because of their perceived collaboration with the enemy of Israel: the Romans. Were this the case, John might have thought that rites conducted by them in the Temple would be ineffective. He offered the people his rite of baptism as a more efficacious alternative.

Another function of John's baptism could have been to initiate people into a sect. This does not mean that those who had been baptised then formed a closed or exclusive sect, like the community at Qumran. Rather, they became a people set apart by the fact that they had responded positively to John's call for repentance and been baptised. John, therefore, was attempting to restore as many people as possible to God in preparation for the eschaton. John's actions in this regard would have created a group akin to the 'remnant' or the 'true Israel' spoken of in the Hebrew Bible, especially the prophetic literature. John the Baptist certainly appears to have been familiar with such literature.

Finally, the hypothesis that John's target audience was the ruling priestly classes and other powerful social groups is rejected because it does not take into account the many references to 'crowds', 'multitudes' or 'the people' that are to be found throughout Josephus's account of John's baptism, as well as those of the evangelists. In addition, John's success brought him to the attention of Herod Antipas. Had John preached merely to those who were likely to oppose him, he would have been less successful and would not have drawn crowds large enough to be noticed. Moreover, John was working in anticipation of the imminent eschaton. All Israel faced judgement, not just the ruling classes. This is reflected in the wide-ranging area in which John chose to work. It can be concluded, then, that John directed his message at everyone.

3

THE COMING ONE

After me comes he who is mightier than I... (Mk 1.7).

John the Baptist expected an imminent eschatological judgement of humankind. In preparation for this event, he embarked upon a ministry of baptism. However, baptism, vital though it was, was not the only element of John's ministry. The Gospels unanimously state that he spoke of another who was to come after him (Mk 1.7 and par; Jn 1.1.26-7; cf. Acts 13.25). Indeed, the announcement of an expected figure was the most significant element of John the Baptist's proclamation, making it essential to explore this figure and what John had to say about him.

It is possible that the evangelists invented John's proclamation of a coming figure in order to show that such an important and influential prophet as John had announced the coming of Jesus. For this reason, it is imperative that the authenticity or otherwise of John's announcement should be established. This chapter, therefore, will seek to verify whether or not John really did proclaim another to follow after him.[1] Other factors to be considered are the identity of this figure, as well as what function John expected this figure to perform.

The Sources

Mark (1.7) says of John the Baptist, 'and he preached, saying, "After me comes he who is mightier than I, the thong of whose sandals I am not worthy to stoop down and untie. I have baptised you with water; but he will baptise you with the Holy Spirit."' Matthew (3.11) emphasises the point that John's baptism was for repentance before going on to describe the baptism of the Coming One as being with 'the Holy Spirit and with fire'. Luke (3.16) omits Matthew's reference to repentance but retains 'the Holy Spirit and fire'. The Fourth Evangelist (1.26-27) reports a slightly different speech, 'I baptise with water; but among you stands one whom you do not know, even he who comes after me, the thong of whose sandal I am not worthy to untie.' In the Fourth Gospel, then, John indicates that this important figure is already present. It is a question of timing. In the Synoptics, the coming of this figure will arrive at some point in the future. For the Fourth Evangelist, he has already arrived.

John's Announcement of the Coming One

Each of these sayings denote that John was aware of someone who was yet to come (the Synoptics) or who was already present in the midst of the people but who was as yet unknown (the Fourth Gospel) and that it was his duty to announce this person. They also show that John thought himself to be subordinate to him. The context in which John made this announcement, as he baptised, indicates that the ministries of John and this figure were closely linked, and that John was in some way preparing the ground for this person. Since John's ministry was carried out under an atmosphere of increased eschatological expectation, complete with its associations of judgement and restoration, it can be assumed that the Coming One was expected to be a judgement and restoration figure.

The Christian tradition has interpreted the Coming One as Jesus. For this reason, it might be supposed that, of all the sayings of John the Baptist as they are reported in the Gospels, the pronouncement of the Coming One should be the least authentic. The reasons are not hard to find; Jesus could only benefit from being seen as the fulfilment of the proclamation of such a prophet as John. Furthermore, it is easy to see how the evangelists could have approached the task of making up a proclamation and placing it onto the lips of the Baptist. To begin with, since the evangelists knew that Jesus' ministry continued after that of John, the latter could be made to say that Jesus was coming after him. Second, Jesus' disciples saw him as mightier than John, hence John's assertion that the Coming One would be mightier than he. This would also explain John's declaration that he was unworthy to untie or carry this person's sandals. Third, Christians believed that the resurrected Jesus baptised them with the Holy Spirit, beginning with the 'tongues like fire' at Pentecost. Thus, John 'announced' that the Coming One would baptise 'with the Holy Spirit and with fire'. Finally, Jesus was expected to return to judge the unrighteous. As such, John is made to speak of the Coming One as having a winnowing fork in his hand, while his mission is described using the image of the threshing floor as a metaphor for the division of the repentant from the unrepentant.

These points, while feasible upon a cursory reading, do not withstand closer scrutiny. They cannot support the hypothesis that John's proclamation of the Coming One was created by the early church for several reasons. First, references to the Coming One are vague and could apply to almost anyone; many people came after John, not just Jesus. Second, if those who followed after John were religious leaders or were involved in politics, they could be seen as mightier or more worthy than John. Third, the Coming One's baptism in Holy Spirit and fire has nothing to do with Jesus' earthly life. Rather, it belongs to his post-resurrection ministry. As such, it would do little to convert non-Christians, since they could easily question or reject this aspect of Christian belief. In order to be convincing, a prophecy about Jesus should reflect events that took place during his own lifetime. Conversely, prophecies invented by the church and attributed to John the Baptist in order to win converts could just as easily be denied by John's own disciples. On the other hand, Christians would need no convincing because they were believers anyway. Finally, Christians did not need to invent prophecies and attribute them to John because their belief was based upon their interpretation of the Hebrew Bible and Jesus' own teaching. Therefore, they did not require John to prophesy Jesus' future role as judge.

John's proclamation of the Coming One can confidently be accepted as authentic.[2] To begin with, it is multiply attested, since it appears in Q (3.16b) and Mark (1.7). That the Fourth Evangelist makes John proclaim Jesus as Christ (1.26-7) does not invalidate the historicity of his proclamation. Rather, the fact that this evangelist had to reinterpret the message to fit his own view of Jesus serves to enhance it. In addition, if the version given in Acts (13.26) came from a different source to that presented in Luke, then a fourth source can be added. Second, the proclamation is not presented in especially Christian terms. In fact, as will be demonstrated, each component of John's proclamation harmonises with Jewish belief in the Second Temple period. Thus, it is doubtful that it originated within the early church. Third, such a proclamation coheres with John's wilderness baptising and preaching ministry. Fourth, the fact that it does not appear in Josephus is no cause for concern. Josephus shows an aversion to the messianic expectation held by many of his people. Such expectation led to unrest and, subsequently, to the disastrous Romano-Jewish war. On the other hand, Josephus's account does seem to imply that John's preaching had eschatological, perhaps even messianic, elements. This is reflected in Herod Antipas's perception of John as a political threat and it corresponds with the Gospel accounts of the excitement engendered by raised eschatological expectation stimulated by John's announcement. Consequently, Josephus can be viewed as a silent witness to John's proclamation of the Coming One.

There is, therefore, every reason to accept that John the Baptist proclaimed a Coming One. It is supported by the criterion of dissimilarity or distinctiveness, since the fact that John made such a proclamation showed him to be unique among prophets. Its appearance in Q, Mark and, perhaps, Acts, means that it is multiply attested. The Fourth Evangelist has also acknowledged it, although he has altered the proclamation radically in order to fit it into his Christology. It is also supported by the criterion of cohesion or consistency, since it harmonises with what is already known of John: that he is a prophet and baptiser associated with the wilderness tradition of eschatological expectation. Another area of support for John's announcement of a Coming One is the fact that, as noted above, had the church invented it, his disciples would probably have risen up to deny it. On the other hand, had John done so, it is easy to see why the church seized upon it. Similarities between John's preaching of the Coming One and their own understanding of Jesus inspired in them the belief that John had proclaimed their master.

The Identity of the Coming One

John's proclamation of someone who would come after him was of great importance. In addition to his baptism, it formed the central theme of his preaching. It also defined John's relationship with Jesus in the eyes of the early church.

Christianity is in no doubt that the Coming One spoken of by John was Jesus. This is in spite of the fact that John, as far as the sources allow such a conclusion to be drawn, appears not to have identified this person. In fact, John could have been speaking about one of several figures, each of whom could be said to be 'expected' by people living in the Second Temple period. The list includes human beings, such as the Davidic messiah, the Aaronic messiah and an eschatological prophet, often interpreted as Elijah *redivivus*. Some supernatural figures are often referred to in eschatological writings. These include the archangel Michael, who is sometimes equated with Melchizedek, the 'One like a Son of Man' and God.[3]

Josephus, even if the speculation entered into above were accepted, makes no direct mention of the proclamation of a Coming One in his account of John the Baptist and his mission (*Ant.* 18.116-119). Therefore, any attempt to determine who John was speaking about must be based upon the Synoptic and the Fourth Gospel accounts.

The Identity of the Coming One in the Synoptic Gospels

According to the Synoptic accounts, the Coming One would baptise with the Holy Spirit (Mk 1.8), or with the Holy Spirit and with fire (Q 3.16). John the Baptist places this activity within a framework of eschatological judgement (Q 3.17). There are images of unfruitful trees being felled and burned. The Coming One stands ready, his winnowing fork[4] in his hand, to clear the threshing floor. The wheat is gathered into his granary. The chaff is burned with an unquenchable fire. The evangelists allow certain things to be known about the Coming One: he[5] will judge and restore, he is coming, he is mightier than John, he will baptise with Holy Spirit and fire and he will perform a task that can be described using the metaphor of the threshing floor.[6] These clues are useful indicators of what John expected the Coming One to do. They hint at his power. They can also reveal who John thought the Coming One would be.

The first clue is that the Coming One will judge and restore. This process in fact began with John's own baptism. People effectively judged themselves when they accepted or rejected John's message and rite of baptism. The process would be completed by the Coming One by means of his baptism with Holy Spirit or Holy Spirit and fire.

At this point, it should be clarified whether or not John could have spoken about both Holy Spirit and fire as reported in Q.

John's baptism with water is one of reconciliation with God. The Coming One's fire baptism appears to be one of divine wrath poured out upon those who are not reconciled with God. One objection to the presence of the Holy Spirit in the Coming One's baptism is that it appears to destroy the balance of opposition created by water and fire.[7] Another is that John twice mentions fire on its own: trees are 'cut down and thrown into the fire' (Q 3.9), while the Coming One burns chaff 'with unquenchable fire' (Q 3.17). Each time, fire is seen in a negative sense. A third objection is that John belongs to an apocalyptic tradition in which an association between destructive fire and Holy Spirit is not found. The Holy Spirit, therefore, would surely have no place in this context. Yet another objection to the presence of the Holy Spirit is that the small Ephesian church mentioned in Acts 19.1-7 knew only of John's baptism. Had teaching of the Holy Spirit been part of John's original proclamation, they would surely have known about it.[8] Finally, if, in his original proclamation, John spoke about both Holy Spirit and fire, Mark's omission of this element (1.8) must be explained.

In answer to the first of these objections, it should be pointed out that John did not appear to be interested in creating or maintaining a balance of any sort. It was his mission to save as many souls as he could, which he achieved by trying to turn as many people as possible back to God. The second objection, that John spoke of fire in a negative sense, can be upheld if fire can be seen exclusively as a punishing and destructive force. Certainly it could be interpreted this way,[9] and a correlation between fire, judgement and punishment is shown throughout the Hebrew Bible as well as in texts belonging to the intertestamental period (Amos 7.4; Ezek. 38.22; Mal. 4.1; *Enoch* 90.24-27; 1QS 2.8). Moreover, Sodom and Gomorrah are destroyed by fire and brimstone (Gen. 19.24). The seventh plague of Egypt was hail 'and fire flashing continually in the midst of the hail' (Ex. 9.24; cf. Rev. 8.7).

It is imperative that any assessment of John's proclamation should be kept within its historical context. John spoke of fire within the context of judgement and punishment, so this is where it belongs. The two baptisms spoken of by John are combined into a single baptism by the use of the υμας and the solitary εν.[10] This suggests that the penitents, who had already undergone John's water baptism, will undergo the second baptism. Since one of the reasons they submitted to water baptism was to be physically cleansed after having been absolved of their sins, fire ought to serve a different function for them. Indeed it does, for fire can also be a means of refining or purification.[11] For example, Q 3.17 speaks of a figure removing the useless chaff and burning it. This provides a powerful analogy with purification. The description of the Coming One's role comes immediately after the verse in which he is announced. As such, John must have expected an eschatological cleansing of the penitents. Fire as a means of purification and renewal would not be a new concept to Jews. It is encountered in this context in Isa. 1.25; Zech. 13.9; Mal. 3.2.

In addressing the second objection, the third objection has also, in a sense, been addressed. This was that John belonged to an apocalyptic tradition wherein no correlation is found between destructive fire and Holy Spirit. However, as has been seen, fire does not have to be perceived solely as a destructive force. Fire is one of the means by which God appears in physical form (Ex 3.2f; 24.17; Judg. 6.21f). It is also a sign of divine grace. In this context which, admittedly, is rarer than its use as a force for destruction, fire is usually found in relation to God's acceptance of sacrifices (Gen. 15.17-18; Lev. 9.23-24; Judg. 6.21-24; 1 Kings 18.38-39; 1 Chron. 21.26-27; 2 Chron. 7.1). This is particularly significant if it is accepted that John's baptism served as a substitute for sacrifice.[12] A subsequent baptism in fire could underline God's acceptance of the baptism/sacrifice of the penitent, thus reiterating his or her forgiveness by God. Indeed, Isa. 6.6-7 shows fire in connection with the forgiveness of sins.

Finally, fire is sometimes used as a term for God (Deut. 4.24; 9.3; Isa. 33.14).[13] Thus, God will judge and condemn the unworthy, while accepting those who are fitted into salvation (Isa. 10.16-29).

Fire, then, functions as an instrument of refining or purification. John did speak of destructive fire. It was part of his general message. Everyone who came to him heard this aspect of it, not just the penitents. It can be assumed that John expected fire to form some part of the apocalyptic event that was about to unfold. However, it was only to the repentant that John spoke of fire in conjunction with the Holy Spirit. Therefore, the effect of the fire, when it came, would be dictated by the state of the soul upon which it was unleashed. Those who had been baptised in water and had become reconciled with God would feel only its benefits and would be refined and purified. The unrepentant, who were not reconciled with God, would be destroyed. Seen this way, it is possible to see how fire would work in conjunction with Holy Spirit.

Another objection to a correlation between Holy Spirit and fire in John's speech is that the small Ephesian church mentioned in Acts 19.17 knew only of John's baptism. Had teaching of the Holy Spirit been part of John's original proclamation, they would have been aware of it. In answer to this, it should be noted that the lack of any knowledge of the Holy Spirit on the part of the Ephesians shows them to have been unfamiliar with Jewish thought in general or John's message in particular.[14] This scenario would be improbable for two reasons. First, were the Ephesians Jews, even a basic knowledge of the Hebrew Bible would make them aware of the Holy Spirit. Second, were they Gentiles, the fact that they were disciples of John would indicate that they must have been aware of his teaching of the Holy Spirit.

The problem surrounding the Ephesian church's awareness of the Holy Spirit lies in the fact that *Αλλ' ουδ' ει πνευμα αγιον εστιν ηκουσαμεν* is usually taken to mean that the Ephesians had not even heard of such a thing as a Holy Spirit. That is to say, they were not aware that the Holy Spirit existed. However, it is doubtful that this would be the case. To translate ειμι as 'to be' or 'exist' is not appropriate in this context.[15] Rather, this passage should be taken to mean that the Ephesians had not heard that the Holy Spirit had arrived or that they had not heard that people were now receiving the Holy Spirit. In this instance, ειμι should be used in the same sense as it is in Jn 7.39, wherein it states 'for as yet the Spirit had not been given, because Jesus was not yet glorified.' Interpreted this way, Acts 19.2 would indicate that the Ephesians had not heard of anyone yet receiving the Holy Spirit. In either case, Acts 19.2 supports John's proclamation that the Coming One's baptism would include Holy Spirit; the Ephesians show an awareness of John's teaching, but are unaware of the Christian belief that it had been fulfilled.

There is one more discrepancy to address: if, in his original proclamation, John spoke about both Holy Spirit and fire, why did Mark (1.8) fail to mention it? The answer probably lies in the provenance of Mark. The Gospel is largely believed to have been written in Rome.[16] Since Christians had been persecuted by Nero, who blamed them for the fire of Rome, Mark might have felt it prudent to leave any references to fire out of his Gospel.

The Fourth Gospel also omits fire, as does Acts. It is especially curious that Acts should do so since the author, Luke, includes it in his Gospel. However, it should be borne in mind that by the time Luke came to write Acts, he was writing a history of the early church. There was no longer any need to mention fire because Jesus did not bring the fiery judgement John had spoken about. Instead, fire finds a place in the tongues of flame in which the Holy Spirit descended at Pentecost. It has therefore taken on a new meaning.

With regard to the Fourth Gospel, it could be that the evangelist had access to the Markan version which omits 'fire',[17] although it seems more probable that Jesus' failure to bring fiery judgement led to John's reference to fire being dropped from the accounts of his proclamation. Greater emphasis was placed on the Holy

Spirit instead because this came to be interpreted as a prophecy of the dispensation of the Holy Spirit at Pentecost and by means of baptism. By the time the Fourth Gospel came to be written, Jesus' earthly history had been superseded by the Christian interpretation of it. John's proclamation was altered to show that he had testified to the Saviour. The judgement he had expected the Coming One to perform was transformed into an act of salvation.

There are many reasons to accept that John the Baptist expected the Coming One to baptise in both Holy Spirit and fire. However, what inspired John to speak of these two elements working in conjunction with each other? Certainly, they are found together in Isa. 4.4: 'when the Lord shall have washed away the filth of the daughters of Zion and cleansed the bloodstains of Jerusalem from its midst by a spirit of judgement and by a spirit of burning,' but this only suggests where John might have found his idea. It can be conjectured that John largely invented the concept of a baptism in Holy Spirit and fire. Using metaphors taken from the Hebrew Bible relating to judgement and purification, he combined them to form a vision of the Coming One's expected activity. This does not explain, however, why John saw a need for Holy Spirit and fire if both performed the same function for penitents, unless, of course, the Holy Spirit was expected to do more than cleanse and purify. Little is known of the rewards the repentant could expect. It might have had something to do with the kingdom of God, which John preaches in Mt. 3.2. John might have seen some connection between the kingdom of God and the Holy Spirit.[18]

John the Baptist could legitimately have spoken of Holy Spirit and fire in his proclamation. Of the two versions, that of Mark and the Fourth Gospel without fire and Q with fire, the latter appears to be more acceptable as authentic. Fire is not out of place in the context of John's general prediction of apocalyptic judgement, and it would have been understood by those listening to John. It is more difficult to connect fire with Holy Spirit, but it is conceivable that John saw the two elements working in conjunction. The

Coming One would use fire to destroy the unrepentant, but the repentant would be purified by that same fire and receive the Holy Spirit at the same time. The wheat being gathered into the granary could signify restoration.[19] Perhaps, then, the granary serves as a metaphor for the kingdom of God. The purified souls are restored by God and allowed to live in his kingdom. The unrepentant sinners are the chaff, which is removed and destroyed. Thus, the Coming One performs a dual function of judging and restoring.

The Hebrew Bible and intertestamental literature mentions several expected figures, each of whom might be the one spoken of by John. As we have seen, the list includes human figures: the Davidic messiah, the Aaronic messiah and an eschatological prophet, usually interpreted as Elijah *redivivus*. There are also some supernatural figures: the archangel Michael/Melchizedek, the Son of Man, God. There are five essential elements in John's prophecy of the Coming One: he will judge and restore, he is coming, he is mightier than John, he will baptise with Holy Spirit and fire, and he will perform a task that can be described using threshing floor imagery.

Elijah

Elijah can instantly be dismissed because John's description of the Coming One's task rules him out. Mal. 4.1 clearly shows that the returning Elijah would restore familial harmony: 'he will turn the hearts of fathers to their children and the hearts of children to their fathers.' A later text upholds this prophecy, while adding a social element: 'to turn the heart of the father to the son, and to restore the tribes of Jacob' (Sir. 48.10). This plainly does not accord with John's proclamation of the Coming One, since Elijah fulfils only one of the factors John outlined: he is coming. While initiating a return to filial harmony and the restoration of the tribes of Jacob do come under the heading of restoration, there is no judgement involved. There is no mention of Elijah being mightier that John, nor are there any references to Holy Spirit and fire. Finally, his mission is not described in terms of the threshing floor. As such, Elijah must be rejected as a candidate for the Coming One.

The Davidic Messiah

Perhaps John was alluding to the Davidic messiah as he spoke of the Coming One? Several factors support his candidature. He is described as 'mighty' or 'powerful' in the Hebrew Bible, the apocrypha and pseudepigrapha, as well as the Dead Sea Scrolls (Isa. 9.6; 11.2; Pss. Sol. 17.22, 37-40; *Jub.* 31.18; 1QSb 5.24-5; 1QH 3.10; cf. Mk 1.7; Q 3.16). He is said to be 'coming' (Zech. 9.9) or will 'come forth' (Isa. 11.1; Jer. 30.21; Mic. 5.2). 2 Esdras 12.32 adds that the messiah will 'arise from the posterity of David'.

John's expected figure would judge and restore. Certain Hebrew Bible texts (Isa. 9.7; 16.4-5; Jer. 23.3-4, 5-6) indicate that the Davidic messiah was also expected to restore and judge (Isa. 9.7; 11.4; Jer. 23.5-6; 33.15-16). However, his role as judge of Israel (Pss. Sol. 17.26-7, 36; 18.7; CD 7.20-8; 14.19; 19.10-3) and punisher of sinners (Pss. Sol. 17.2-5, 29; *Jub.* 31.20; 1QSb 5.24, 27) did not come until later.

There are three areas of agreement between John's expected figure and the Davidic messiah: both are mighty or powerful, both are coming, and both are acceptable as judgement and restoration figures. However, the Davidic messiah would be required to impart the Holy Spirit (Mk 1.8; Q 3.16). While he is himself endowed with the Holy Spirit (Isa. 11.2; Jer. 3.15; 23.5; Pss. Sol. 18.7; 1QSb 5.25), there is no explicit indication that he will communicate it. Moreover, no texts contain fire or threshing-floor imagery in connection with the Davidic messiah's ministry. As such, it is unlikely that John's Coming One was this figure.

The Aaronic Messiah

References to an expected high priest can be found in the Hebrew Bible, where he is often represented in association with the Davidic messiah (Jer. 33.14-26; Zech. 6.12-14). However, by far the best evidence for such a figure is found in the Qumran literature. Nevertheless, even here, the concept of dual messianism, although often considered to be standard, is in fact the exception rather than the rule.[20] In fact, there is only one reference to the 'messiahs of Aaron and Israel', which occurs in 1QS.9.11, and there are only two closely related expressions: 'the messiah of Aaron and Israel' (CD 12.23; 14.19; 19.10) and 'a messiah from Aaron and from Israel' (CD 20.1).

In spite of such limited evidence, the Covenanters at Qumran did appear to expect two messiahs: one royal, the other priestly.[21] The important factor is not how many texts speak of two messiahs, but how many of them refer to another figure of equal or greater authority than that of the Davidic messiah. Looked at this way, there is much to support the concept of an expected priestly messiah. 1QSa seems to refer to such a figure, whose importance is such that no one is allowed to touch the bread until he has 'extended his hand' over it. Other texts indicate that the Davidic messiah must defer to the authority of the priest (4Q161.20; 4Q285, fr.5), or at least to share his own authority with him (*Florilegium* 1.11; CD 7.18). Furthermore, the blessing of the High Priest takes precedence over that of the Prince of the Congregation (1QSb).

Evidence does exist, therefore, that a priestly figure was expected to take a prominent place in the messianic era. In fact, the concept can be traced beyond Zech. 6.12-14, which speaks of both a kingly and a priestly messiah, to Moses and Aaron. As such, the Aaronic messiah could be the figure about whom John spoke as the Coming One. Clearly, the Aaronic messiah is expected, and so he fulfils the 'coming' aspect of John's message. Since he will preside over the liturgical blessings of those going to battle (1QM 15.4), returning (1QM 16.13) and at the end of the day (1QM 18.5), his role could be seen as judgemental.[22] He can also be regarded as a restoration figure, since he and the

Davidic messiah would 'pardon the iniquity' of those who broke the community's laws (CD 14.19). If the quotation from Deut. 33.8-11 in 4QTest 14-20 refers to the Aaronic messiah, then might is one of his qualities: 'Bless his power, O Lord ...' On the other hand, there is no reliable evidence that he will baptise in the Holy Spirit. Missing also is the all-important threshing-floor imagery.

The Aaronic messiah fulfils perhaps three of the criteria stipulated by John in connection with the Coming One. He is coming, he can be interpreted as a judgement and restoration figure and, if an ambiguous text does indeed allude to him, he is described as mighty. However, the essential element of communicating the Holy Spirit is missing, as are references to fire and the threshing-floor. He must be ruled out.

Michael/Melchizedek

If the human figures do not satisfy the criteria required of John's Coming One, perhaps the identity of this figure will be found in the supernatural realm. One such figure is the archangel Michael. In the Dead Sea Scrolls, Michael is identified as the heavenly prince Melchizedek, a mysterious figure who is equated with the Prince of Light of the Qumran scrolls.[23] Michael/Melchizedek fits the role of one who judges. This is implied in Dan. 12.1-2, wherein a description of Michael as having 'great charge of your people' introduces a judgement scene. A more concrete example is 11QMelch 9, 11, 13, wherein Melchizedek is seen to be an agent of both judgement and restoration.

In favour of Michael/Melchizedek is that he fulfils the judgement and restoration element of John's proclamation. Second, he is coming: he 'shall arise' (Dan. 12.1). Third, he is 'mighty': 'and he will, by his strength ...' (11QMelch 9), 'He will send eternal succour to the company of His redeemed by the might of the princely Angel of the kingdom of Michael' (1QM17.6). Michael/Melchizedek could also be seen to fulfil the fire element of John's message: 'Belial will be consumed with fire'

(11QMelch 3.7). Since Melchizedek judged Belial in 11QMelch
2.12-13, this fiery judgement could be associated with him.
However, Michael/Melchizedek must be rejected for two reasons.
There is no suggestion that he will baptise in the Holy Spirit.
Secondly, the threshing-floor imagery is lacking.

The One like a Son of Man

The 'one like a son of man' at first had no active part to play
in judgement and restoration. Rather, he was served by all the
peoples and nations, and his 'dominion is an everlasting dominion
... and his kingdom one that shall not be destroyed' (Dan. 7.14).
Although the one like a son of man could act as an agent of the
Ancient of Days, the one who judges and restores is God himself.

Nevertheless, the traditions surrounding the one like a son
of man later underwent a transformation. In *Enoch*, he is seen
enthroned and passing judgement (1 *Enoch* 69.27-8). Similarly,
he has become a restoration figure (1 *Enoch* 48.4; 49.2), whose
blessings even extend to those who died before his reign began
(1 *Enoch* 51.1-2; 61.5). Clearly, the transformation of the one
like a son of man gave him a new quality, and this allows him to
be seen to satisfy the judgement element of John's proclamation.
Moreover, he is coming (1 *Enoch* 69.29; cf. Dan. 7.13) and came
to be seen as mighty (*Enoch* 1 49.2-3; 52.4; 69.29). While there is
no mention of the Holy Spirit in connection with this figure, the
blessings bestowed by him are described using ablution imagery
(1 *Enoch* 48.1; 49.1; 53.7). Also, although there is no direct
use of fire and threshing-floor imagery in connection with the
ministry of the one like a son of man, he will hand over those to
be punished, who will be 'as stubble in the fire', after judgement
(1 *Enoch* 48.9). Therefore, there is an indirect association with
fire and threshing-floor imagery, albeit in connection with the
agents of the one like a son of man rather than with that figure
himself. Nevertheless, the 'one like a son of man' does not fulfil all
the criteria of John's proclamation, and so he cannot be accepted.

God

As it is, there is one figure whose judgement and restoration activity is described using threshing-floor imagery: God (Isa. 27.12-13; Jer. 13.24; 15.7; Mal. 4.1; Wis. 5.23). Elsewhere (Isa. 10.33-34), an account of God judging the Assyrians is given in terms of trees being cut down with an axe (cf. Q 3.9). God fulfils the judgement and restoration elements of John's proclamation.

God also fulfils the Holy Spirit and fire elements. While the Messiah (Isa. 11.2; Pss. Sol. 17.37) and the one like a son of man (1 *Enoch* 62.2) receive the Holy Spirit, God alone imparts it (Ezek. 36.26-27; Joel 2.28). This is sometimes portrayed in terms of water or ablution imagery. As such, it can be seen as a baptism (1QS 4.21). Fire is used to portray God's judgement in the *Sibylline Oracles* (2.196-7; 203-5; 252-4; 315) and in the Qumran literature (1QH 3.28-31). Finally, God is shown to be 'coming' (Isa. 62.11; 63.1; 66.15; Mic. 1.3; Zech. 14.3-4; 1 *Enoch* 1.3-4, 7-9; 1QS 3.18; 4.19; CD 8.2-3).

John did not refer to God explicitly. Instead, he referred to him as 'the one who comes'. His approach allowed him to proclaim the coming of God while complying with the Pharisaic influenced interdiction against anyone mentioning the name of God.[24] It also allowed him to avoid giving offence when he made the comparison between himself and God.

The fact that John spoke of the Coming One wearing sandals does not imply that he thought that this figure would be a man.[25] John's reference to the Coming One wearing sandals is supported by Pss. 60.8 and 108.9, wherein it states: 'upon Edom I cast my shoe.' Here, God's shoes are used as a metaphor for his seizure of Edom.

That John used the term 'mighty' to describe the Coming One, as opposed to the 'almighty' one might expect in reference to God also has support in the Hebrew Bible and the apocalyptic literature. Isaiah. 9.6 speaks of 'Mighty God'. However, this is given as one of the names of the messiah, and probably means that he would be endowed with divine powers. A less ambiguous example is found in Ps 24.8: 'The Lord, strong and mighty, the Lord, mighty in battle!' In 1 Chron. 29.12, David pays tribute to God's 'power and might'.

The figure with a winnowing fork will clear the threshing floor. He will gather the wheat into his granary and burn the chaff with unquenchable fire. The repentant, represented by the wheat, will be saved. The unrepentant, represented by the chaff, will perish. The Coming One does not separate the wheat from the chaff. This has been done already by John's baptism. Instead, he will carry the repentant and the unrepentant to their appropriate destinies. As noted above, the literal translation of πτουν is winnowing shovel. This implement was used by the farmers of Palestine to heap up the grain before winnowing, to gather the wheat and the straw into two piles after winnowing, and to clear the threshing floor of the two piles.[26] The wheat, of course, would be moved into the granary. The actual separation of the wheat from the chaff was done using a θρινας or winnowing fork. John's words suggest that the winnowing process had already taken place. It is the threshing floor which is cleaned out, not the grain. The owner of the winnowing shovel is also the owner of the threshing floor (Q 3.17). Matthew (3.12) also shows that the wheat belongs to this figure. Luke (3.17) shows that the granary belongs to him. This indicates that it is God himself who will accomplish the task of judgement and restoration over his own people. He will gather the true Israel who have returned to him through John's baptism and take them into his kingdom. Thus, God is the Coming One proclaimed by John the Baptist.

There is, therefore, much support for the hypothesis that John the Baptist proclaimed the coming of God, who would carry out a baptism in Holy Spirit and fire. However, there is one difficulty that must be addressed before the question can finally be settled: the imprisoned John would hardly have sent a delegation to ask Jesus if he were 'he who is to come' (Mt. 3.11; Lk.7.19) had he expected God and not a human figure.

To solve this ambiguity, it is necessary to look at how God had previously used human agents in order to accomplish his judgement and restoration. Often the agent was a Davidic messiah (Isa. 9.2-7; Jer. 23.5-6; Ezek. 34.22-23; 37.21-24). In the same way, God used Moses to rescue his people from Egypt. John the Baptist concentrated upon the divine, or heavenly, aspect of restoration and judgement. He made little reference to the earthly aspect of it, although he was anxious to stop any speculation that he himself might be the Messiah (Lk. 3.15). John might have considered himself to be an agent of God but saw that as the limit of his importance: he was the one through whom God achieved the separation of the wheat from the chaff.

It was not inconceivable to John that another human person might be chosen to realise the next stage of God's plan. This person would act solely as God's agent. God would be working through that person as he had done with Moses, the Davidic Messiah and John himself. John could have seen in Jesus that earthly agent chosen by God to fulfil a specific task. However, this was of little concern to John. What was important to him was what God would do, rather than whom he might choose to do it.

Having studied John's proclamation of the Coming One as reported in the Synoptic Gospels, it can only be concluded that John thought that this figure would be God. Only God fulfils all the elements of John's description of the Coming One and his ministry: that he will judge and restore, that he is coming, that he is mightier than John, that he will baptise with the Holy Spirit and with fire, and that his ministry can be described using threshing floor imagery.

The Lamb of God Motif in the Fourth Gospel

The Fourth Gospel differs markedly from the Synoptics in that it portrays John the Baptist specifically identifying Jesus as the Coming One. Here, John points to Jesus and says to one or more unidentified persons, 'Behold the Lamb of God, who takes away the sin of the world' (1.29). If this passage is to be accepted as authentic, it is necessary to show that the lamb motif would have been known to John the Baptist. That is to say, that the lamb motif was an element of Jewish belief and that its use as a title would be appropriate within the context of John the Baptist's eschatological ministry. In other words, it must apply to someone who would fulfil the criteria stipulated by John: that he would judge and restore.

The Lamb of God motif might have originated in a Jewish-Hellenistic belief that equates Jesus with the ἀμνός of the Suffering Servant story (Isa. 52.13-53.12) taken from the LXX. Another possibility is the purely Jewish concept relating to the Paschal Lamb, or to the sin-offering. Alternatively, it could be a reference to the lamb of the apocalypse. The term 'lamb' also has a place in Jewish tradition as a messianic title.

The first of these hypotheses is that the 'Lamb of God' could be used to compare Jesus to the Suffering Servant of Isa. 52.13-53.13. In favour of it is that the phrase 'the Lamb of God, who takes away the sins of the world' harmonises with the account of the Suffering Servant, with Isaiah describing the Servant as 'an offering for sin' (53.10c) who 'he bore the sins of many' (53.12e). Another favourable element is that there is a correlation between the voluntary nature of the respective deaths of the Servant and Jesus. Thus, the Servant 'makes himself an offering for sin' (Isa. 53.10c). Jesus does not seek to evade his captors (Jn 18.6-8), nor does he make any attempt to avoid his fate: 'Jesus commanded Peter, "Put your sword away! Shall I not drink the cup the Father has given me?"' (Jn 18.11). Similarly, the silence of the Servant in his suffering (Isa. 53.7) is paralleled with that of Jesus before Pilate (Jn 19.9). However, the association between Jesus and the Suffering Servant is incomplete because of Jesus' lively defence before Pilate (Jn 18.34-7; 19.11), and the High Priest Annas and his officer (Jn 18.20-3).

It is clear that the association between the Lamb of God and the Suffering Servant relies upon the interpretation of Jesus as

Christ, and the belief that his death was redemptive. As such, it comes from within the early Church and not the context in which John the Baptist was working. Specifically, it could have been an invention of the Fourth Evangelist, or perhaps it had already developed as a concept within the community in which he lived and for whom he was writing. Indeed, the Fourth Evangelist makes a direct reference to the Suffering Servant story elsewhere (12.38; cf. Isa. 53.1). Either way, the christology that would allow an association to be made between Jesus and the lamb/messiah motif is too advanced to go back to John.

The second hypothesis associates Jesus with the Paschal Lamb or the sin offering. This link is a common feature throughout the New Testament (Acts 8.32; 1 Cor. 5.3; 5.7; Heb. 7.26-8; 1 Pet. 1.19). It is particularly emphasised in the Gospels by the timing of Jesus' crucifixion, which takes place at the Passover. However, there are several problems that must be overcome if this hypothesis is to be acceptable as support for the authenticity of the 'Lamb of God' speech attributed to John the Baptist. To begin with, the traditional sin offering is not a lamb, but a young bull (Lev. 4.3, 14) or a goat (Lev. 4.23, 28; 16.5, 7-10). If a lamb were to be offered, it should be female (Lev. 4.32; 5.6). As such, John could not have equated Jesus or anyone else with a lamb offered up in expiation of sins.

As to the Paschal Lamb, such a correlation could have come from Ex. 12.46 and Num. 9.12, each of which refers to the sin-offering. However, another source could have been Ps. 34.21, which does not. In the Johannine literature itself, Jn 19.24 reflects Ps. 22.18, Jn 19.28 reflects Ps. 69.21 and Jn 19.36 reflects Ps. 34.21. There is a consistency in which each of the passages cited from the Psalms refer to the 'afflictions of the righteous' (34.19) and their deliverance. It appears, then, that the Fourth Evangelist might have formulated, or drawn from, a link between the Paschal Lamb in the deliverance of Israel from Egypt and the death of Jesus. The sacrificial death of the Paschal Lamb was the means by which Israel was saved. Jesus' death was seen by the Fourth Evangelist as a sacrificial act (6.51; 10.15; 11.50; 17.19), through which the sins of the people of Israel, as well as Gentiles (10.16; 11.52; 17.21), were expiated. Taking this into consideration, the hypothesis that John the Baptist equated Jesus with the Paschal Lamb or the sin offering cannot be upheld.

In the hypothesis, the 'Lamb of God' refers to the lamb of the apocalypse. This is especially interesting, since it reflects imagery that appears in several apocalyptic texts, including Revelation. Here, αρνιον (the diminutive of 'lamb') is found throughout as a title for Christ. Two interpretations are given. In the first, the lamb is sacrificed (5.6, 12; 7.14) for the redemption of humanity (5.9). In the second, the lamb is the leader or shepherd of the people of God (7.17; cf. Jn 10.11). He stands upon Mount Sion surrounded by many saints (14.1-5). He wages war against the enemies of God and defeats them (17.14). His wrath causes fear among the kings and great men of the earth (6.16). The lamb shares the throne of God (22.1, 3). This paradox, in which a lamb is associated with power, wrath and violence, has its roots in Jewish apocalyptic tradition. For instance, *Enoch* 84.46 represents David as a lamb who then becomes a ruler and leader of the people of God. *Enoch* (90.6-19) also contains an archetype of the seven-horned lamb of Rev. 5.6.

The lamb motif, therefore, appears in connection with the removal of evil from the world as well as a general restoration (cf. The Syriac Apocalypse of Baruch 73.1-4). The Testament of Levi 18.9 notes that 'in his priesthood shall sin come to an end, and the lawless shall cease to do evil.'[27] Ps Sol. 17.29 assert that 'he shall not suffer unrighteousness to lodge any more in their midst, nor shall there dwell with them any man that knoweth wickedness.'[28] This brings it within John's context of judgement and restoration. Moreover, the Lamb motif exists within Jewish tradition in conjunction with a messianic figure. Indeed, the term 'Lamb of God' could be used as a messianic title, a view supported by the fact that Andrew is later made to say 'we have found the Messiah' (Jn 1.41). Although the lamb/messiah motif could have been known to John the Baptist, the application of the concept in the Fourth Gospel reflects that evangelist's theology regarding Jesus as Christ, rather than the view of the Baptist himself.

As provocative as they are, there are problems with each of these suggestions. While some of the concepts addressed were known in John's time, the application of those concepts to the person and ministry of Jesus could not possibly have gone back to John the Baptist himself. They conflict too radically with the Synoptic reports of John's Coming One. There is no mention of fire. Gone, too, is the threshing-floor imagery. The 'Lamb of God' is the one who 'takes away the sins of the world', which reflects an authentic Jewish concept. However, that the lamb is equated with Jesus represents too closely the concerns of the Fourth Evangelist to be accepted as the authentic belief of John the Baptist.[29]

By the time the Fourth Gospel came to be written, Jesus had already become identified with John's Coming One. The Fourth Evangelist has merely incorporated John's proclamation into his own theological concept of Jesus. John the Baptist no longer announces a figure who has to do with the terrible day of judgement; instead, he bears witness to the Saviour. For the writer of the Fourth Gospel, Jesus' death on the cross is the means by which the sins of the world are taken away. As such, Jesus is equated with the Paschal Lamb. This correlation is further enhanced by the Fourth Evangelist's use of imagery from Ex. 12.46 and Num. 9.12, wherein no bones of the sin-offering are to be broken. 'But when they came to Jesus and saw that he was already dead, they did not break his legs. Instead, one of the soldiers pierced his side with a spear, and at once blood and water came out' (Jn 19.33); and 'For these things were done, that the scripture should be fulfilled, A bone of him shall not be broken' (Jn 19.36).

The Fourth Gospel, therefore, shows a christology that is far too developed for it to be useful in the quest to establish the identity of John's Coming One. It appears to acknowledge John's authentic proclamation. However, it is too far removed from the context in which John was working to represent its original meaning. Even if the 'Lamb of God' passage could be supported by the criteria of dissimilarity (because it is not found in the Synoptics) and authentic context (because it relates to traditional Jewish concepts), the highly developed christology it so clearly betrays would still have to be explained.

Conclusion

The early church could have invented John's proclamation of a Coming One in order to make it appear as though he had announced Jesus. However, whatever proof might be brought to support this hypothesis is too vague to be credible.

On the other hand, there is reason to accept that John did indeed proclaim a Coming One. It is supported by three criteria of authenticity. It is multiply attested, since it appears in Mark, Q and, perhaps, Acts, as well as in a redacted form in the Fourth Gospel. It fulfils the criterion of dissimilarity, since such a declaration singles John out among the prophets of old, as well as those of the first century. It is supported by the criterion of cohesion because it harmonises with what is already known about John: that he is a prophet and baptiser associated with the wilderness tradition of eschatological expectation.

Still, John had made no attempt to identify the Coming One. The passage in the Fourth Gospel in which he appears to do so betrayed a too evolved christology for it to be accepted as authentic to John.

In order to establish the identity of the Coming One, it is necessary first to look at what John thought this figure, who was mightier than he, was expected to do. John expected him to baptise with Holy Spirit and fire. Because the repentant had responded positively to John's call, the fire when it came would purify or refine, rather than destroy them. This, combined with the reception of the Holy Spirit, is at least one consequence of their reconciliation with God.

John thought that the Coming One would complete the process that he himself had begun: that of judgement and restoration. Those souls who had responded positively to John's baptism were prepared for the divine wrath that would be unleashed. They would be saved. Those who responded negatively to John's message would face damnation.

The question of who John thought the Coming One would be is best approached by taking into consideration John's expectation that the Coming One's baptism would comprise Holy Spirit and fire. Several things are noted about the Coming One: he was mighty, he was expected to come and he would judge and restore. In addition, his activity could be described using threshing floor imagery. These elements provided clues to the identity of the expected figure. A list drawn up of judgement/ restoration figures most commonly associated with the eschaton includes such human figures as the Davidic messiah, the Aaronic messiah or Elijah. There were also supernatural figures: Michael/ Melchizedek, the one like a son of man and God. When the expected activity of each of these candidates is compared with that of the Coming One, it is found that all of them fulfilled some of the elements of John's proclamation. Only one fulfilled them all: God. The Coming One proclaimed by John the Baptist was, therefore, God.

4

JESUS THE BAPTISER

...Jesus was making and baptising more disciples than John (Jn 4.1).

John the Baptist proclaimed the imminent arrival of a Coming One who was, in all probability, God. Christian tradition takes the view that John in fact proclaimed the coming of Jesus, and that Jesus' mission began with his baptism by John. This is in spite of the fact that Jesus' ministry differed considerably from the task of the Coming One as described by John. Such contradictory views make it appropriate to study the relationship between John the Baptist and Jesus. Several factors should be considered, including an analysis of Jesus' response to John's eschatological message. Did he agree with what John had to say? If so, how did he express that agreement? Was he really baptised by John? If so, what did he do afterwards? Did he help John to spread his message? Perhaps there was rivalry between John the Baptist and Jesus?

An investigation into whatever relationship might have existed between John the Baptist and Jesus is too long and complex a subject to be carried out in one chapter. It will, therefore, be divided between two, each of which will focus upon one of two points of contact between the two men. The present chapter will consider the only recorded direct encounter between John and Jesus: Jesus' baptism by John. The next chapter will focus upon an indirect point of contact: John's question to Jesus, via his disciples, while in prison.

The Sources

These questions set out in the introduction are suggested by a discrepancy that exists between the Synoptic accounts of the timing of Jesus' public ministry and that found in the Fourth Gospel. According to the Synoptic Gospels, Jesus approached John and was then baptised by him. The evangelists then begin an account of Jesus' Galilaean ministry. Jesus is variously described as a healer (Mk 1.29-31 and par.), an exorcist (Mk 1.23-26 and par.), a man who mixes with sinners (Mt. 11.19 and par.), a miracle worker (Mk 6.30-44), the Messiah (Mk 8.27-33 and par.) and one who sacrifices his life 'for many' (Mk 14.24) or 'for the forgiveness of sins' (Mt. 26.28).

According to Mark (1.14) and Matthew (4.12), Jesus' ministry takes place after the arrest of John the Baptist. Luke's account (3.21) implies that Jesus was baptised after John's arrest (3.19-20), although he does not disclose who might have baptised him if not John. The reader is left to assume that, following his baptism, Jesus had no further direct contact with John. This is where the discrepancy lies. It is not certain whether or not Jesus remained in Judaea until after John's arrest. The Synoptics affirm that he did, and they describe Jesus going into the wilderness where he was tempted by Satan (Mk 1.12-13 and par.). However, this event could have happened days, weeks or even months after his baptism. The temptation story does not adequately answer the question. The Fourth Gospel appears to confirm that Jesus did not begin his Galilaean ministry until after John's death (Jn 6.1).[1] Prior to this, however, it notes that 'Jesus and his disciples went into the land of Judaea; there he remained with them and baptised' (Jn 3.22). The following verse notes that 'John was also baptising.' Although this verse shows Jesus going into Judaea (i.e., from elsewhere), the reader has already been told that Jesus had attended a wedding at Cana, which is in Galilee (Jn 2.1-12). There are difficulties with this text, not the least of which involves explaining how the Fourth Evangelist could speak of Jesus going into Judaea from Jerusalem (Jn 2.13-3.21). Perhaps it is not really 'blatant harmonization'[2] to suggest that Jesus moved from Jerusalem into the Judaean countryside, but the fact that the Fourth Evangelist openly states that Jesus and his disciples were baptising in Judaea cannot be overlooked. Could the Synoptic Gospels have ignored a Judaean baptising ministry of Jesus', which the Fourth Gospel alone has preserved? This question holds important implications for the relationship between John the Baptist and Jesus.

Establishing the Existence of a Relationship between John the Baptist and Jesus

Before any relationship that might have existed between John the Baptist and Jesus can be appraised, it must first be established whether or not there was one. Of the primary sources that are available to us, Josephus makes no mention whatsoever of an association between John and Jesus. This leaves the Gospels, where a direct encounter between John and Jesus is described: Jesus' baptism by John (Mk 1.9-11 and par.).

Unless the birth narratives are accepted as historically accurate, Jesus' coming to hear John and to be baptised by him marks his debut onto the world stage. This event is narrated in the Synoptic Gospels, while reference to it is made in the Fourth Gospel. When those references that are found in the independent extra-canonical Gospels are taken into consideration, it can be agreed that the historical authenticity of Jesus' baptism by John is supported by the criterion of multiple attestation.

Even a cursory reading of the Gospel accounts reveals an increasing sense of disquiet among the evangelists surrounding

Jesus' baptism. The reasons are not difficult to find. John's baptism was for 'repentance and the forgiveness of sins' (Mk 1.4 and par.) The *Gospel of the Nazoraeans* brings the problem into sharp relief: 'Wherein have I sinned that I should go and be baptised by him?'

The implications of Jesus' submission to John's baptism could have been spotted as early as Mark. The evangelist, as he presents his account of the event, betrays his theological concerns surrounding Jesus' baptism by balancing it with the voice from heaven and the descent of the Holy Spirit (1.9-11). This implies that the theophany is an invention of the evangelist. It could be that Mark used the presence of the Holy Spirit at Jesus' baptism, which signifies his calling by God, to show that God has broken his silence and that prophecy had come alive once more.[3] However, as we have seen, prophecy had not come to an end.[4] Mark 1.9-11, therefore, possibly reflects early church teaching rather than the true experience of Jesus.

On the other hand, Mark openly shows that Jesus came to John and not the other way round. He also indicates that Jesus is simply one penitent among many. Perhaps, then, the theophany is indeed an invention of the early church designed to qualify Jesus' submission to baptism. Thus, John is depicted merely as the unwitting agent of God's inauguration of Jesus. Alternatively, it is just possible that the story of the dove (i.e. the Holy Spirit), the opening of the heavens, and the voice could reflect a genuine experience of Jesus', who then passed it on to his disciples. Such imagery is in keeping with the experiences of other prophets and men of God who experience the Holy Spirit (cf. Gen. 28.17; Isa 61.1; Ezek. 1.1; 3.22, 24; 11.5; Rev.1.10, 4.1).

Matthew (3.13-15) solves the dilemma by adding a short dialogue, the ending of which is Jesus' assertion that John should perform the rite in order to 'fulfil all righteousness'. Thus, Matthew shows that Jesus simply wanted to set a standard of righteousness. Indeed, Matthew appears to dislike the idea that

Jesus may have sinned. For example, a saying attributed to Jesus by Mark: 'Why do you call me good? No one is good but God alone' (10.18), becomes the slightly more ambiguous: 'Why do you ask me about what is good? One there is who is good' (19.16) in Matthew's hands. Teaching of the removal of sins is transferred to the Last Supper, 'Drink of it, all of you; for this is my blood of the covenant, which is poured out for many for the forgiveness of sins' (Mt. 26.28). Thus, Matthew reveals that Jesus' death and not John's baptism is the means by which forgiveness is bestowed.

Nevertheless, Matthew does not entirely deny that John's baptism is for the forgiveness of sins, since he places it in the context of John's speech about the Coming One (3.11). Matthew's presentation of Jesus' baptism takes whatever awkwardness there might be out of it by showing that Jesus chose to submit to the rite because he saw it as the proper thing to do (3.15). Moreover, Matthew, unlike Mark, makes it clear that John knows who Jesus is from the beginning (3.14); he is no longer an unwitting agent.

Luke's solution to the problem is to set Jesus' baptism after John's arrest (3.19-22). The effect of this is that, if Luke were the only Gospel available, readers would think that Jesus was baptised only after John had been removed from the scene.[5] As it is, the question whether or not Luke wanted to show that Jesus was in fact baptised by John is an open one. It appears that Luke preferred to place greater emphasis upon the theophany, an event for which Jesus' baptism merely served as a stage.

Luke's handling of Jesus' baptism is difficult to explain. He might have seen it as having little or no significance, and that he included it in his account simply because he had found it in Mark and Q. Alternatively, it is possible that he found the fact of Jesus' baptism by John too disconcerting and sought to suppress John's role in it. In this case, he was unable to ignore the event because it was too well known. Of course, he could have invented a suitable dialogue as Matthew did.

Several factors should be taken into consideration when trying to understand Luke's treatment of Jesus' baptism. First, Luke thought that Mark's account implied that John, like his proclaimed Coming One, baptised in Holy Spirit. As Mark clearly states, the Holy Spirit came upon Jesus in the form of a dove as Jesus emerged from the water. In order to avoid the difficulties such an interpretation would cause, Luke removes John from the scene as soon as possible. Secondly, Luke is fully aware that John did not announce Jesus as the Coming One.[6] For example, in Acts 19.4, Paul is made to qualify a statement by adding, 'that is, Jesus'. This reflects Luke's own belief rather than that of Paul. Furthermore, a speech attributed to Paul (Acts 13.25) fails to name Jesus as the Coming One. Had Luke believed that John did bear such testimony, he missed a perfect opportunity to express it. The conclusions reached in the previous chapter, that it is highly probable that John referred to God and not Jesus when he spoke of the Coming One, support this view. Therefore, Luke, who was as aware as the community he represented that John had not proclaimed Jesus, saw no reason to link Jesus' baptism with his ordination by God. Thus, he removed John, whom he probably viewed as quite superfluous at this stage, from the scene. A third area of consideration, and one that is not unrelated to the previous one, is Luke's division of salvation history into periods.[7] For Luke, salvation history takes place as a three-stage event. John the Baptist belongs to the first period, or the 'period of Israel'; his ministry marks the end of the epoch of the 'law and the prophets' (Lk. 16.16). Jesus, on the other hand, belongs to the second period, or the 'period of Jesus', which encompasses his Galilaean ministry as far as Jerusalem. The third period of salvation history, that of the church, begins with the descent of the Holy Spirit at Pentecost and ends with the *parousia*, the Second Coming. By placing Jesus' baptism after John's arrest, Luke is effectively denying John any further significant role in the period of Jesus.

Luke's actions, if not his reasons, are in concert with a growing trend in which John's role as the baptiser of Jesus is undermined or diminished. By the time the Fourth Gospel was written, John's baptismal mission had no other aim than to reveal Jesus to Israel (Jn 1.31). This is entirely in keeping with Johannine theology, which holds that Jesus was the Logos. It was through Jesus, who was with God from the beginning and who was God, that the universe was created (Jn 1.1-3). What need did God have to reveal himself before such a one as John? In effect, he would be revealing himself to himself. The Fourth Evangelist, therefore, altered the significance of John's baptism. No longer was it the occasion upon which the Holy Spirit entered Jesus, and at which God revealed himself to Jesus. Instead, it was the means by which Jesus was revealed to John, who then announced him to Israel.

The trend of diminishing John's role becomes even more apparent when the accounts of Jesus' baptism as they appear in the extra-canonical Gospels are considered. The *Gospel of the Hebrews* does not appear to depend upon the canonical sources and so can be viewed as an independent account of Jesus' baptism. Note, however, that while this Gospel gives an account of Jesus' baptism, it fails to mention John's role in the rite. The *Gospel of the Nazoraeans* acknowledges John as a baptiser but denies that Jesus was baptised by him or indeed by anyone else. The *Gospel of the Ebionites* shows too much reliance upon the Matthaean and Lukan accounts to be considered an independent witness. The *Gospel of Thomas* mentions John (46) but says nothing of his baptism.

The purpose of denying John his part in Jesus' baptism, or indeed, of denying Jesus' baptism *per se* is probably to reduce the significance of the event, or possibly even to influence the reader into believing that it had never occurred at all. Its effect, however, inclines him or her to the opposite conclusion, that one is more disposed to believing that Jesus was indeed baptised, and that he was baptised by John. All this suggests that the event bore a greater significance than the early church was willing to allow. The discomfort felt by the church concerning Jesus' baptism is plain to see. It could not be omitted from the Gospel accounts because it was too well known historically. However, submission to such a rite also implied submission, even if it were only for a short while, to the one who performed it. Jesus' baptism by John, with all that it implies, goes against early church teaching. Thus, the historical authenticity of the event is supported by two criteria of authenticity: multiple attestation and dissimilarity.

It can be accepted without question that Jesus of Nazareth was baptised by John the Baptist, but what did this mean for Jesus? John used baptism as the means by which he expressed his ideological outlook. It was integral to his mission. However, John's baptism was unique. While Jews had long been used to ablutions for cleansing and purification, John's rite differed, both in its method and in its function. For this reason, John had to preach it, or explain it, to those who came to hear him. Those gathered about John, having listened to his message, were faced with a simple choice. Do they accept his preaching, or reject it? Accepting John's message also meant submitting to baptism. The two went hand in hand. Those who submitted to it showed that they agreed not only with John's message, but also with his ideological outlook. Since Jesus allowed himself to be baptised by John, he must have done so because he agreed with John's message and shared his viewpoint.

The Disciples of John the Baptist

John the Baptist had impressed upon his hearers the need to live righteously and piously as they awaited the eschaton. It is natural to assume that those who submitted to baptism took this message to heart and went on to live their lives according to John's teaching. Following their baptism, most of them would have returned to their everyday lives, which were now enhanced by the promise of the salvation to come.

Others, however, gave up their normal existence and became followers of John. The Gospels provide evidence that John had attracted disciples (Mk 6.29 and par.; Jn 1.35; 3.25-26) who fasted with him (Mk 2.18 and par.), served him (Mt. 11.2 and par.) and whom he taught to pray (Lk. 11.1). A hint of their existence can even be gleaned from the otherwise reticent Josephus, who refers to people who were 'greatly moved or pleased by hearing his words' (*Ant.* XVIII.118). Further on, he states: 'For they seemed to do anything he should advise.' Josephus could simply be referring to those who heard John and submitted to his baptism. However, this view is contradicted by the words 'when many others came in crowds about him'. Clearly, these 'others' are not simply penitents. Nor can they be those who constitute the 'brood of vipers' of Q 3.7, who rejected John's preaching and baptism, and so could not have been 'greatly moved or pleased' by it. Of course, one can be moved to anger, but the context in which the 'others' are mentioned excludes this interpretation. It might also be added that they would not have been sufficiently inspired by John to be guided by him. It is possible that Josephus might have been referring to 'special groups', such as those who appear in Lk. 3.10-14. If so they, like all who agreed with John's message, would have confirmed their commitment to it by being baptised. Thus, they would not have stood out from other penitents.

There is nothing to suggest that Josephus was referring to disciples of John when he spoke of the 'others.' On the other hand, he did separate this group from the penitents. As such, he leads his readers to think that they differed from the 'average' penitent in their attitude towards John. It would be reckless to say that Josephus, in a roundabout way, was insinuating that John had disciples. It would be better to acknowledge that Josephus mentioned people who had attached themselves to John, and who appeared to be more than repentant sinners. Even without

Josephus's witness, one might, nevertheless, appeal to the criterion of multiple attestation to show that John the Baptist did in fact have disciples; that they are independently referred to in the Gospels is sufficient.

Jesus, Disciple of John

There is, therefore, little doubt that John the Baptist had disciples. However, and perhaps controversially, the question of whether or not Jesus was one of them must be addressed. Certainly, Jesus was baptised. Thus, it is undeniable that he agreed with John's message and his perspective. Moreover, Jesus submitted to a baptism designed to mediate divine forgiveness for sins and to initiate the repentant sinner into the 'remnant', or the true Israel. The key question is: did Jesus then return home as did the majority of penitents, or did he become a follower of John?

A linguistic study of how Jesus is referred to in relation to John the Baptist in the Gospels reveals that the word used to denote 'after' is οπισω (Mk 1.7; Mt. 3.11; Jn 1.15, 27, 30).[8] Here, οπισω is used temporally to show that Jesus came after John in time. On the other hand, the term can also be used to indicate location. That is to say, it can be applied to one who comes after another in place rather than in time. Of the thirty-five occurrences of οπισω in the New Testament, only those found in the speech attributed to John the Baptist are interpreted temporally. It is plausible, therefore, that the temporal interpretation of οπισω is redactional. It was probably done in order to conform to the belief that Jesus was the Coming One proclaimed by John. It must be reiterated, however, that this belief is that of the early church and does not reflect the contemporary view of Jesus. The fact that οπισω is the stock phrase for affiliating oneself with the cause of a person, more usually applied to the disciples of Jesus, should not be overlooked. The evangelists' redactional use of the word could have served the purpose of disguising the fact that Jesus was a follower, or a disciple of John. This hypothesis will stand or fall according to what the Gospel accounts have to say about the early days of Jesus' mission.

Jesus' Public Ministry

According to the Synoptics, Jesus began his public ministry after the arrest of John the Baptist. The reader is allowed to assume that this event occurred soon after his baptism (Mk 1.14; Mt. 4.12; cf. Lk. 3.19; 4.14). However, no further information regarding why Jesus stayed in Judaea following his baptism is given.

Only in the Fourth Gospel is it made clear that Jesus' public ministry was divided into three distinct phases, the first of which speaks of Jesus working as a baptiser in Judaea (Jn 3.22-23).[9] The ministry recorded in the Synoptics, wherein Jesus is depicted as an eschatological prophet working in Galilee becomes the second phase in the Fourth Gospel, while the third begins on the road to Caesaraea Philippi (Mk 8.27 and par.).

The Fourth Evangelist's assertion that Jesus began his public ministry as a baptiser is supported by the criterion of dissimilarity, since the idea of 'Jesus the Baptiser' is so far removed from early church teaching. In addition, Jn 4.2 merely confirms that which it is intended to deny: 'although in fact it was not Jesus who baptised, but his disciples.' The fact that it is a parenthesis is a clue to its redactional origin. The use of καιτοι γε and the absence of the definite article in connection with Ιησους, found only here, confirm this conclusion. Since Jn 4.2 is inauthentic, it can be accepted that Jesus began his public career as a baptiser. If any doubts remain, they can be assuaged by noting that the use of the imperfect εβαπτιζεν emphasises the time factor.[10] The εκει διετριβεν μετ' αυτων (Jn 3.22) suggests that this was an established activity. Therefore, baptising must have formed the basis of Jesus' regular ministry as conducted in Judaea in the period following his own baptism. Indeed, this appears to be the only conclusion that can be drawn. In the first phase of his early public ministry, Jesus of Nazareth worked as a baptiser.

That Jesus began his ministry as a baptiser implies one or more of the following. First, that Jesus was running a baptising ministry aided by his own disciples. This was independent of that of John, although it was of a similar type and was continued within the same general area. Secondly, Jesus' ministry was run in conjunction with John's. The third alternative combines the first two and proposes that Jesus began baptising in conjunction with John but that their ministries eventually divided into two distinct movements.

The correct interpretation of Jesus' baptising ministry is of paramount importance because it holds the clue to the nature of the historical relationship that existed between John the Baptist and Jesus. We must therefore distinguish the historical data upon which Jn 3.22-24 is based from the Fourth Evangelist's redaction of it and the narrative framework in which it is placed. In doing so, it must be borne in mind that whatever conclusions are drawn concerning the nature of the relationship between John and Jesus must be consistent with what can be concluded from other sources.

The first interpretation of Jesus' baptising ministry asserts that it was separate from John's. Nevertheless, it was parallel to, and performed in similar locales to that of the Baptist. This might suggest that John and Jesus were in competition with each other, and certain passages in the Fourth Gospel could be used to support this conclusion. For instance, that two of John's disciples defect to Jesus (1.37) might indicate a sense of rivalry. Later, the Fourth Evangelist states that 'people came and were baptised' by John (3.23), while Jesus was 'making and baptising more disciples than John' (4.1). Still later, Jesus announces that 'the testimony which I have is greater than that of John' (5.36).

The acceptance or rejection of this hypothesis appears to turn upon the question of Jesus' disciples. It could be argued that Jesus' having disciples strengthens such a theory because it suggests a group working under a master and pursuing a systematic course of activity. Alternatively, to depict Jesus surrounded by disciples might simply be an extension of the Fourth Evangelist's theme of John bearing witness to Jesus.[11] Since Jesus' first disciples were originally attached to John, the reader is further convinced of the success of John's testimony.

In addition, the methodical approach taken by the Fourth Evangelist as he recounts the manner in which some of John's disciples transfer their allegiance to Jesus (Jn 1.29-51) is cause for concern.[12] The phrase τη επαυριον, 'the day after tomorrow', is used three times in this account. It probably serves the same purpose as the Markan και ευθυς, which is to condense into a short space of time events that, in reality, occurred within a larger timescale. The first τη επαυριον introduces the passage containing John's 'Lamb of God' saying (1.29-34). The second and third times the phrase appears, it is in conjunction with passages that show John's disciples defecting to Jesus (1.35-37) and Jesus' calling of Philip (1.43-44). The effect is that some of John's disciples appear to have defected to Jesus within the space of three days. This literary device probably disguises a more realistic timescale, allowing the possibility that Jesus stayed with John the Baptist as his disciple and carrying on his work for a longer period than the Fourth Evangelist felt comfortable with. On the other hand, the author might simply have wanted to hurry the story along.

The narrative content also gives cause for concern. Following John's proclamation of Jesus as the Lamb of God, two disciples leave him for Jesus. The reader learns a short while later that one of the two was Andrew, who 'first found his brother Simon, and said to him, "We have found the Messiah"' (Jn 1.41). It is significant that this passage uses πρωτος 'first', without the expected δευτερος 'second'. The reader might infer that Andrew must have gone to at least one other person after he had spoken to Simon.[13] This other person might have been Philip, the account of whose calling was redacted to look as though it had come from Jesus. This approach brings the Fourth Evangelist more in harmony with the Synoptic accounts, wherein Jesus simply asks Philip to follow him (Mk 1.16-20 and par.). John's pointing to Jesus as the Lamb of God might be the work of a redactor seeking to demonstrate that John directed some of his disciples to Jesus. As such, it does not reflect the relationship between the historical John and Jesus, but rather a later interpretation of it.

Nevertheless, there is no reason why Jesus should not have attracted disciples, since having them would not necessarily preclude his activities from being part of the movement that was beginning to form around John.[14] Indeed, to have disciples is part of an ancient Oriental tradition concerning men of God.[15] For Jesus to have disciples would, in fact, serve a practical purpose. The sense of urgency that enshrouded John's mission (Mt. 3.10 and par.) would make it prudent for him to take on an assistant.[16] Under such circumstances, it would be useful if Jesus himself could have assistance as he worked to accomplish his master's task. As such, John encouraged some of his own followers to go to Jesus for that purpose. There is nothing to suggest that any rivalry existed between John the Baptist and Jesus at this point. The first interpretation of Jesus' baptising ministry can be dismissed.

The second interpretation maintains that Jesus' baptising ministry was performed in conjunction with that of John the Baptist. This hypothesis has been found, so far, to be acceptable. Given the limited time in which he believed he had to accomplish his mission, it made sense for John to appoint an auxiliary. Moreover, if Jesus were a blood relative (cf. Lk. 1.36), this would predispose John to favour him for the task.[17] The two men shared the mission of baptising as many people as possible before the final days. What, then, was their *modus operandi*?

Jesus' baptising career probably followed the same lines as that of John. They both preached repentance (cf. Mt. 4.17) and offered a baptism against the coming judgement. In addition to recognising one's own sins and sinfulness, John's baptism also required a return to right behaviour towards one's neighbour. That is to say, John demanded the observation of the statute given in Lev. 19.18, and this is most clearly expressed in the words addressed to the 'special groups' of Lk. 3.10-14. That the same commandment is later mentioned by Jesus (Mk 12.31 and par.) suggests that Jesus maintained continuity with John's teaching.

It is interesting to note that Luke places Jesus' commandment within the context of his parable of the Good Samaritan (Lk. 10.25-37). Luke is the only evangelist to present this parable, which serves as an illustration to the commandment. It is no coincidence that Jesus should choose a Samaritan for the hero of his story, since there was hostility between Samaritans and Jews, which adds poignancy to the tale (cf. 2 Kings 17.29ff; Mt. 10.5; Jn 4.9). Jesus was himself turned away from one Samaritan village (Lk. 9.52-53).

However, there are hints that at least some Samaritans were receptive to Jesus' preaching and work. In Lk. 17.16-17, the Samaritan is the only one to thank Jesus for his cure. Of course, this passage might be early church 'propaganda', designed to show Jesus' success with Gentiles as opposed to his own people. It would, therefore, serve the purpose of justifying the taking of Jesus' word to the Gentiles. Another incident of Jesus' success with Samaritans would appear to confirm this. The Fourth Gospel relates an account of Jesus meeting a Samaritan woman at a well as he was travelling from Judaea to Galilee. The Fourth Evangelist notes that Jesus had to pass through Samaria on the way (Jn 4.3ff), although this is not necessarily the case. Jesus could have taken a route through the Jordan valley and on via the Bethshan gap.[18] After conversing with the woman, she comes to believe that Jesus is the Messiah her people were expecting (4.25).

She goes to her village, where her testimony is enough to convince many that Jesus is the Christ (4.39). They come out to see him for themselves (4.40), so that many more, having seen Jesus, believed in him (4.41-42). This story, then, could be another instance of the early church showing how appropriate it was to take Jesus' word to the Gentiles. On the other hand, there is a connection between the Samaritans and Jesus that would support an alternative view, that such passages as these are based in historical fact.

Jesus began his public ministry as a disciple of John. At some point, he served as a baptiser, working in conjunction with his master. Anyone searching for a link between Jesus and the Samaritans would do well to scour the ministry of John to see if anything could be found that might lead to Samaria. The Fourth Gospel proves most fruitful. Here, it is stated three times that John baptised in 'Bethany beyond the Jordan' (1.28; cf. 3.26; 10.40). Since Bethany is situated in Judaea, it cannot be used as evidence of a baptising ministry in Samaria. However, elsewhere it is noted that 'John was also baptising at Aenon, near Salim' (3.23). The lack of the phraseology peculiar to the Fourth Evangelist in this passage indicates that he found this information in traditional material.[19] In other words, he accepted a tradition in which John the Baptist worked at Aenon, near Salim.

Five springs follow a one-kilometre line on the eastern side of Mt Gerizim close to Aenon, near the town of Salim. The reason Aenon is not given to be near Shechem, as would be more appropriate, is because that town no longer existed in the first century; John Hyrcanus had sacked it in 107 BCE. Salim was the nearest inhabited site, hence the association of the two place names in the Fourth Gospel.[20] This leads to one simple conclusion: John the Baptist took his message and his baptism into the heart of Samaria. The enigmatic character of Jesus' saying about 'others' (Jn 4.38) is explained if it is accepted that 'others' refers to John and his disciples, among whom would probably be Jesus.[21] The Samaritans would more readily accept Jesus if he were already known to them in association with John, or if Jesus could speak to them about John's message.

Jesus' conversation with the Samaritan woman took place by Jacob's Well (Jn 4.12) and involved drinking the living waters. This is a subtle baptismal motif. It correlates with the image of the hart, a metaphor for the soul, quenching its thirst, or its longing for God, in living waters (Ps 42). Similarly, 1 Cor. 12.13 speaks of baptism in terms of drinking the Spirit, while the image of the Samaritan at the well is used as a baptismal motif in early catacomb art.[22] Jacob's Well is close to the eastern slope of Mt Gerizim. This was not untried territory; its links with baptism, and therefore, John, are especially significant. Later, when the followers of Jesus took their message into the world, the Samaritans responded well (Acts 8.5-25), even abandoning Simon, who had practised magic (Acts 8.9-13). Interestingly, the evangelist on this occasion was named Philip, which was also the name of one of the disciples who might have been sent to Jesus by John. If this is the same man, then here is another link in the chain connecting Jesus with the Samaritans.

It might be argued that the Samaritan connection is restricted to Luke and that the Fourth Evangelist has simply found it and made use of it. However, there is a strong tradition that John was buried at Sabaste. Another clue lies in the origins of the Mandaeans, a Gnostic sect whose rise approximately coincides with that of Christianity and whose baptism might have been influenced by that of Syrian Christianity.[23] The Mandaean language is one of the eastern Aramaic dialects.[24] It contains western Syriac elements that are used specifically as religious terms: *yardna*, 'Jordan' or 'running water' and *manda*, 'knowledge'.[25] A historical link between John the Baptist and Syria cannot be ruled out. It appears that at least some Samaritans did accept John and embraced his teaching. This would have made it easier for Jesus to be accepted when he returned to that region with his own disciples.

John and Jesus ran a co-ordinated campaign that took John's message and baptism to both Jews and Samaritans. Since time was of the essence (Q 3.9), John felt pressed to carry his message to as many people as he could in the shortest time possible and appointed Jesus as his assistant. Jesus continued his master's work among the Jews, where John had already made headway and the people had shown themselves to be receptive to it (Mk 1.5). Meanwhile, John took on the more difficult task of convincing the Samaritans. The Fourth Evangelist highlights Jesus' success as a baptiser (4.1), which is not surprising. Quite simply, Jesus had the easier task. Those passages in which the reader is assured that Jesus was a more proficient baptiser than John are not intended to confirm Jesus' superiority to John. Rather, they merely reflect the facts.

The conclusion to be drawn from this study of the second alternative is a simple one. Because time was short, John took the step of augmenting his ministry by taking on an assistant, and he appointed Jesus for this purpose. Why he chose Jesus is open to speculation. Perhaps Jesus was one of his most enthusiastic disciples. Indeed, dynamism would be a useful character trait for such a person to possess. Perhaps John found a charismatic quality in Jesus. If John and Jesus were indeed blood relatives, this would increase Jesus' chances of being chosen. Whatever the reasons for his appointment, Jesus began his public ministry as a baptiser in conjunction with John.

The third interpretation of Jesus' baptising ministry is that Jesus began his work in conjunction with John, but that the two of them later went their separate ways. The operative word here is 'later'. At first, as has been demonstrated, there was agreement and cooperation between the two men that allowed Jesus to work as John's assistant. The strongest suggestion of a break between John and Jesus is found in Jn 3.25. Here, it is stated that 'a discussion arose between John's disciples and a Jew over purifying.' This verse might refer to a disagreement between John's disciples and Jesus or one of his disciples.[26] If so, the dispute might have centred upon Jesus' and so his disciples', lax attitude towards purification. In support of this interpretation is a comment by Mark (7.1-23), which implies that Jesus was not observing the laws of purity as strictly as he ought.

There is no doubt that the dispute between 'John's disciples and a Jew' arose over purification. The Greek text uses the term καθαρισμος, meaning 'cleansing' or 'purification'. This term is used elsewhere in the Fourth Gospel (2.6), as well as in the Synoptics (Mk 1.44 and par.), to denote traditional Jewish cleansing rites. However, it is never used in connection with John's baptism. As such, the dispute more probably concerned the contrast between Jewish purification rites and John's baptism.[27] For this reason, it is doubtful that the Jew involved was Jesus or one of his disciples. Rather, he was probably someone who did not accept John's message, and who was taking his disciples to task over the rite of baptism.

The dispute over purification is not the only event in the Fourth Gospel that could be used to demonstrate opposition between John and Jesus. Two of Jesus' miracles can also be cited as evidence.[28] In the first of these, the Wedding at Cana, Jesus turns water into wine (Jn 2.1-11). For the Fourth Evangelist, Christians are baptised by the blood of Christ, as well as the Spirit. The account of the Wedding at Cana, therefore, is used to illustrate that Jesus' baptism in blood is more effective that John's water baptism. This intriguing interpretation is fully in keeping with Christian thought. Jesus turns the water into wine. Wine is consecrated at the Eucharist as Jesus' blood. Jesus is crucified: he sheds his blood. This act is understood in terms of salvation. However, it remains to be proven that the Fourth Evangelist meant the passage to be interpreted in this way. It is, after all, a particularly theological pericope. The good wine is the knowledge of God, which has been kept back until the time of the incarnation of the Logos.[29]

The Wedding at Cana story reflects traditional material concerning Jesus that can be found throughout the Gospels. Jesus is a good man for a party (Mt. 1.19 and par). There is some evidence of family tension (Mk 3.32-5; Lk. 2. 48-50; Jn 7.1-5). The New Age inaugurated by Christ is sometimes expressed in terms of wine (Mk 2.22; Lk. 5.39). Although the Wedding at Cana story is unique to the Fourth Gospel, weddings do feature in three Synoptic parables (Mt. 22.1-14; Mt. 25. 1-13; Lk. 12. 35-6), while Mk 2.19 and Jn 3.29 involve sayings about the bridegroom and his friend. To suggest that this story simply serves as anti-Baptist polemic is to ignore its basis in Jesus traditions that have no bearing upon his historical relationship with John the Baptist. Whatever the origins of the narrative, the finished redaction serves Johannine theology well. It belongs to a time much later than that under consideration. In addition, it is set in Galilee and not Judaea. The Wedding at Cana pericope cannot be used to establish rivalry between John and Jesus during Jesus' Judaean ministry.

The second of Jesus' miracles that might be used to demonstrate rivalry between John the Baptist and Jesus is the Healing at Bethzatha (Jn 5.1-9). Here, Jesus cures a man who had been ill for thirty-eight years. Throughout that time the man had been anxious to dip himself into the waters of the pool in the belief that this would cure him. Unable to do so, his suffering continued until Jesus cures him without requiring him to go into the water. This account, therefore, might contain a veiled reference to the inefficacy of John's water baptism as opposed to Jesus' powerfully effective Spirit baptism. As such, it is an example of anti-Baptist polemic.[30]

The fact that this story is set in Judaea, where both men had baptised, is a point in favour of this theory. However, it must still be rejected as evidence of rivalry between John and Jesus. The objections raised concerning the miracle at the Wedding at Cana apply equally to this one, which should become obvious when it is compared with other healing stories that occur in the Gospels: the Crippled Woman (Lk. 13.10-17), the Widow's Son of Nain (Lk. 7.11-17), the Man with the Withered Hand (Mk 3.1-6) and the Man with Dropsy (Lk. 14.1-6).[31] Each of these healing stories follows a similar pattern: the scene is set, the condition of the patient is described, Jesus intervenes, the patient recovers, leading to a sequel. The Bethzatha Healing story is probably based upon traditional material known to the Fourth Evangelist. The material was redacted so that it would better serve his purpose, which is related to its status as σημειον.[32] Thus, the Healing at Bethzatha story reflects a theology that has nothing to do with the historical relationship between John and Jesus. As such, no supportable evidence has yet been found that would sustain the hypothesis that opposition or competition existed between John the Baptist and Jesus during the time of Jesus' Judaean ministry.

Conclusion

Jesus of Nazareth came to John the Baptist, heard his message, and was baptised by him. The fact that an account of the baptism appears in all four canonical Gospels and several extra-canonical Gospels, notwithstanding the discomfort felt by the evangelists pertaining to such an event, attests to the authenticity of it. In addition, that Jesus should submit to a rite designed to purify sinners and reconcile them to God confirms its authenticity under the criterion of dissimilarity. Quite simply, the church would not have invented it. From this it can be concluded that Jesus agreed with John's message and that he showed his agreement in the same manner as everyone else who responded positively to it: he presented himself to John for baptism.

Most penitents returned to their homes after baptism to live their lives under a new commitment to right behaviour and piety. They probably thought themselves somehow changed by the experience of receiving baptism. Jesus, however, did not return to his home and his everyday work. The Synoptic Gospels suggest that he went into the wilderness where he, like many who went there, encountered the supernatural beings believed to inhabit the desert wastes. After this sojourn, and upon hearing of the arrest of John the Baptist, he embarked upon his own preaching ministry. However, the Fourth Evangelist clearly had access to a tradition wherein Jesus baptised (4.1). The fact that a later redactor tried, unsuccessfully, to assure readers that Jesus did not baptise (4.2) merely reinforces the belief that he did. This suggests that, rather than returning to his normal life or embarking immediately upon his prophetic career, Jesus stayed with John, learned from him and became his disciple. Certainly, John had disciples with whom he observed such rituals as fasting and praying. These disciples would have assisted him in his ministry. It is probable that Jesus was among this group. At some stage, he was nominated by John as a co-baptiser, a task at which he was particularly successful.

The relationship between John the Baptist was one of master/disciple. Jesus' appointment as a baptiser resulted from John's need to spread his message as far as possible in the short time that remained. Therefore, Jesus' baptising ministry included the teaching of John's message. Interestingly, this means that Jesus would also have proclaimed the Coming One. He would have warned of the imminent eschaton and the judgement that it would bring. He would have exhorted, as strongly as did John, the people to repent while there was still time for them to do so.

To help him in his important task, Jesus took with him some disciples of his own. It is possible that they were assigned to him by John to help him with his work. It is equally possible that Jesus called his own disciples. More probably, he set out on his baptising career with helpers assigned to him by John, but then appointed others where and when he found suitable candidates.

The fact that Jesus began his ministry as a baptiser implied that he ran it in conjunction with that of John. Certain passages in the

Fourth Gospel do seem to suggest that a rift occurred between John and Jesus. Upon analysis, it was discovered that they had originated at a later stage in the Christian tradition, although there is no reason why they should not have a historical basis. However, being of late origin, whatever evidence they offer has nothing to do with John or Jesus. At the time in question, Jesus remained firmly a disciple of John the Baptist. His mission ran in conjunction with that of John. Although it cannot be known how long John and Jesus worked together, it must have been a significant length of time. The time factor given in Jn 1.29-51 is a literary device and cannot be regarded as historical.

5

THE KINGDOM OF GOD

But if it is by the finger of God that I cast out demons, then the kingdom of God has come upon you (Lk. 11.20).

At some point in his career, Jesus of Nazareth went to Galilee instead of remaining in Judaea where John the Baptist had sent him. Here, he embarked upon an independent mission and became the leader of a movement. Several changes mark this stage of Jesus' career. His disciples are no longer encouraged to follow a system of fasting and prayer. More importantly, Jesus appears to have stopped baptising. Instead, he embarked upon a road which he knew would eventually lead to his death.

The aim of this chapter is to try to understand what factors were involved in this transformation. Was Jesus influenced by something he learned under John the Baptist? Did he outgrow John's teaching? He might have discovered something about himself that compelled him to move on; if so, what was it? Perhaps John's arrest and execution influenced Jesus' decision?

The Sources

Josephus makes no mention of any contact, either direct or indirect, between John the Baptist and Jesus. Thus, the four Gospels provide the source material for this investigation. All four evangelists agree that Jesus left Judaea and went to Galilee. The first step is to try to establish why he did so.

From Judaea to Galilee

The Fourth Gospel asserts that Jesus left Judaea because his success as a baptiser had brought him to the attention of the Jewish authorities (4.1-3). A few verses further on it adds a saying of Jesus' in which he 'testified that a prophet has no honour in his own country' (4.43-4; cf. Mk 6.4 and par.). Later, Jesus avoids Judaea because 'the Jews sought to kill him' (7.1). A pattern of persecution appears to be forming. The reader is invited to think that Jesus must have regarded Galilee as a safe haven. By going to Galilee, he would have placed himself beyond the reach of the Jerusalem authorities. However, such a move would then have made him vulnerable to Herod.[1] Indeed, Jesus seems to have been in danger wherever he went; Mk 3.22 shows him being attacked by 'the scribes who came down from Jerusalem'. So a sense of threat and the need for safe refuge cannot adequately explain Jesus' change of location.

According to Luke, Jesus left for Galilee because he was 'in the power of the Spirit' (4.14). His quality as a prophet is well recognised (Mk 6.4 and par.; Mk 6.15 and par.; Mk 8.28 and par.; Mk 14.65 and par.; Mt. 21.11, 46; Lk. 7.16, 39; 24.19). Moreover, it is not unusual for prophets to give their disciples an account of their vocation (Isa. 6; Jer. 1; Ezek. 1). Thus, the account of Jesus' experience of the Spirit in the form of a dove at his baptism might have come from his telling his disciples about his calling.[2] Jesus' being filled with the Spirit might be the reason why he left Judaea. His move might have been in response to a divine call.

Mark (1.14) and Matthew (4.12), attribute Jesus' departure from Judaea to the arrest of John the Baptist. It is important to note, however, that the Synoptic Gospels give the reader no reason to think that, following his baptism, Jesus remained in contact with John the Baptist. There is certainly no mention of their working together. Why Jesus would have been so affected by John's fate is not explained by either Mark or Matthew. Indeed, the one Gospel that does acknowledge a close association between John and Jesus, the Fourth Gospel, gives persecution as Jesus' motive for leaving Judaea. It does not mention John's fate in this, or any other, context.

As diverse as they might appear on the surface, the accounts of Mark, Matthew and the Fourth Evangelist are, in fact, mutually supportive. The Fourth Gospel indicates that Jesus was very much aware that he was under threat from the authorities, whether Jewish or Roman. Mark and Matthew show that he knew of John's arrest. The second of these two circumstances arises as a consequence of the first. If John had been arrested and was now in the custody of the Roman authorities, then the same fate probably awaited Jesus not too far hence. This supports the Fourth Evangelist's assertion that Jesus had aroused the interest of the authorities, and that this had placed him in danger.

John the Baptist was arrested in Peraea, a province under Herod Antipas's administration in whose power it was to arrest John. When Jesus heard of his master's fate, he realised that he had to continue John's mission to the Galilaeans. Indeed, he might have thought that he would be concluding John's ministry altogether. After all, once the Galilaeans had been preached to and baptised, there would be no province outstanding. John's message would have reached all Israel. Thus, it was Jesus' duty to go to Galilee, no matter what the cost to himself.

Jesus' Galilaean ministry, then, must have begun as a continuation of his Judaean ministry, which in turn was part of John's baptising mission. He did not go into Galilee as an autonomous and independent preacher. Rather, he went as a baptiser and a preacher of the word of John the Baptist.

This hypothesis, if correct, explains how Herod could think of Jesus as John the Baptist *redivivus* (Mk 6.16 and par.). There is no reason to doubt the authenticity of a passage in which Jesus is mistaken for John the Baptist. The criterion of dissimilarity alone would support it. Even allowing for the legendary character of the pericope of John's death, it must be acknowledged that the early church could never have invented a saying wherein it is suggested that Jesus and John are indistinguishable from each other.

The pericope of John's death comes soon after an account of Jesus' miracles, healings and exorcisms. Jesus has appointed his disciples to continue his work, and his activity has come to the attention of Herod. Nevertheless, Herod confuses Jesus for John the Baptist. The Fourth Evangelist (10.41) assures his readers that John performed no miracles. Of course, this passage might be a polemic against an otherwise unknown tradition in which John was indeed a miracle worker.[3] However, with no direct evidence to support such a claim, the statement has to be accepted at face value. If 'John did no sign', then something else must have connected the two of them in Herod's mind. Jesus' Galilaean mission must have been seen as very similar to that of John the Baptist. One shared aspect is the preaching of repentance, as suggested by such parables as that of the 'Lost Sheep' (Lk. 15.4-7 and par.), the authenticity of which is not in dispute.[4] Elsewhere, Jesus continues to uphold the importance of preaching repentance. In Mk 6.12, he sends his disciples out to help him in his mission in precisely the same way that Jesus helped John with his.

The problem with Jesus' preaching of repentance is that it is subtle. It is not certain that Herod would have known about it. The factor that led him to confuse the two men must have been more obvious, something highly visible. It must have been something that singled the two men out from all the other prophets, miracle workers and healers that were to be encountered at that time. It could only be that Jesus had continued to baptise, even during his Galilaean ministry. Indeed, he must have because baptism went hand in hand with John's preaching of repentance. One could not repent yet refuse baptism; that was not acceptable to John or to God.

The rite of baptism, which was so important to John, continued to be important to later Christians.[5] One of the functions of John's baptism was as an initiation rite. It was the means by which the penitent became part of the remnant, the True Israel, who would be saved when God came to usher in the new age. This, however, was re-interpreted by the early church, which saw baptism as the means of identifying those who had chosen to join its community.[6] Acts 1.21-2 implies that baptism was the only recognised means of entry into the Christian community. Only someone who had been part of the movement, beginning with John's baptism, could be considered an acceptable witness to 'his resurrection'.

Against this, however, is that it cannot be inferred from Luke's Gospel that Jesus' chosen apostles were present at Jesus' baptism, or that they were at all involved with John. As such, they could not really be understood as having 'accompanied us during all the time that the Lord Jesus went in and out among us, beginning from the baptism of John until the day when he was taken up from us...' According to Luke, Jesus does not begin to go 'in and out among us' until after his wilderness experience, which came after John's arrest. Moreover, Simon, James and John do not become disciples of Jesus until Lk. 5.1-11. This dilemma is solved if it is accepted that Simon, James and John, as well as Jesus' other disciples, were baptised by Jesus with John's baptism. In this case, Acts 1.21-2 does not speak of Jesus' own baptism by John, but rather the baptism that Jesus himself performed, and that he learned from John.

It seems almost inconceivable that Jesus would suddenly stop performing such an important rite. A cornerstone of John's preaching was the idea that inner purity had to precede outer purity. It follows that Jesus would also have required penitents to submit to baptism in order to be completely pure. Evidence that baptism remained an essential part of Jesus' ministry is found in Acts (2.38; 8.12-17; 9.17-18; 10.44-48; 11.15-17; 19.5-6), where water baptism and baptism in Spirit are found together. These passages demonstrate that a person must undergo both water baptism and Spirit baptism in order to be a full member of the church. Among the members of the early church were those who had been baptised by John. Acts 1.21-2 confirms that the legitimacy of their membership would not be in doubt. However, there must have been many who joined the church after John's arrest, not to mention those who became members at Pentecost (Acts 1.41) and afterwards. Such people would not have been baptised by John. This does not mean, however, that their membership was in doubt. Rather, it would be validated by Jesus' continuation of John's baptising ministry even after the death of John. Those who were baptised by Jesus or his disciples were accorded full membership of the early church, just as those who had been baptised by John were.

John's Question from Prison

If the hypothesis that Jesus did continue to baptise and preach repentance during his Galilaean ministry, is correct, it must be reconcilable with Q 7.19. Here, John sends his disciples to ask Jesus, 'Are you he who is to come, or shall we look for another?'

This is a crucial passage because it represents the second of only two points of contact between John the Baptist and Jesus that are to be found in the Synoptic Gospels. As explored in the previous chapter, the first contact occurred at Jesus' baptism, an important moment for Jesus because it marked the beginning of his eschatological mission. He was taught by John, whom he must have impressed to the point that he saw in Jesus a trustworthy partner who could help him in his work.

The second time contact was made, it was achieved indirectly, by means of a communication between John's disciples and Jesus. John, in fact, asks what could be seen as a rather awkward question of the one he had appointed as his co-baptiser. The implications are that Jesus was no longer performing the task allocated to him by John. As can be seen, this is an important passage. Even more important, therefore, is to establish its authenticity.

The first thing to note is that Q 7.19 does not press John into his traditional role of forerunner, or witness. Rather, he actively expresses doubts about Jesus. This goes against church tradition concerning John's role in relation to Jesus. Any saying in which John is seen to doubt Jesus ought to be taken seriously as potentially authentic. However, this entire Q passage is predicated upon the assumption that John the Baptist did in fact proclaim Jesus as the Coming One. It is almost certain that he did not. Rather, he anticipated the coming of God. It is, of course, possible that John might have expected God to make use of a human agent through whom he would act. If so, John might have come to accept Jesus as that agent. There is much to be said about this subject, and it can be condensed into five hypotheses.[7]

In the first hypothesis, John's doubts concerning Jesus' status as the Coming One were not genuine. Instead, John pretended to be uncertain in order to strengthen his own disciples' understanding of, and belief in, Jesus.[8] This hypothesis cannot stand because it is clearly inspired by theological, rather than historical, concerns. It assumes that John did in fact proclaim Jesus as the Coming One when it most probable that John's expected Coming One was God.

In a second hypothesis, John's question reveals that he had, until that point, been unaware of Jesus' true identity.[9] This hypothesis could be accepted on the grounds that John had come to see Jesus as a human agent sent by God. That it conflicts with John's recognition of Jesus in Mt. 3.13-14 is of no concern, since this Matthean passage is pure redaction. It originates with the evangelist, or his community, who invented it in order to justify Jesus' submission to John's baptism. Nevertheless, this hypothesis must be rejected because it assumes that John realised his mistake when he saw that Jesus was indeed the eschatological agent of God. What did Jesus do to inspire John to finally see him as such? There is no correlation between the activities of Jesus – baptising, healing, exorcising and the performance of miracles – and those expected of the Coming One or his agent, judgement and restoration. In short, Jesus was not acting as this eschatological agent should. This hypothesis cannot be accepted.

A third alternative is that John's question simply reflects the conflict that arose between John's disciples and the early Christian community.[10] This hypothesis is valid in so far as it acknowledges that there were differences between those who followed John and members of the movement that formed itself upon Jesus' teaching. However, this hypothesis is concerned with these differences as they had developed later, rather than with any personal relationship John might have shared with Jesus, and so must be rejected.

In a fourth hypothesis, John expresses a genuine doubt, which is inspired by the fact that Jesus is not acting in the way John expected him, as the Messiah, to act. In other words, John was experiencing a crisis of faith.[11] Clearly, this interpretation assumes that John proclaimed Jesus as the Coming One. It also implies that John thought that the Coming One would be the Messiah. The objections raised against the first theory apply equally to this one.

The final hypothesis is that John's doubts were raised when he saw that Jesus was not fulfilling the role of the fierce bringer of judgement about whom he had preached. Unfortunately, this theory also assumes that John expected Jesus to be the central figure in the imminent eschatological event. Not the Messiah this time, but the one who would judge and restore. As has already been established, John expected the arrival of God, who might choose to act through a human agent. If John accepted that God had chosen to send such an agent, then this hypothesis implies that he must have understood Jesus as this person. The objections raised against the second theory apply equally to this one. Moreover, there is nothing in the Gospels or Acts to indicate that John the Baptist ever understood Jesus as the Coming One. Indeed, had John done so, he would not have taken him into his fold, nor appointed him as a baptiser, but would probably have become his disciple instead. This hypothesis must be rejected on the grounds that it does not fit in with what has already been established in this study of the history of the relationship between John the Baptist and Jesus.

It will readily be seen that there are difficulties with John's question. All attempts to explain it have been found to be untenable, except in one case. Here, however, the hypothesis reflects a situation that arose at a time much later than the lifetimes of John and Jesus. Thus, there is as yet no reason to accept the authenticity of Q 7.19.

Suspicions regarding the authenticity of Q 7.19 are strengthened when the passage in which it appears, Q7.19-23, is considered as a whole. It begins with John expressing doubts about Jesus' status as the Coming One. Jesus then justifies himself by means of his answer to John. This alerts the reader to the possibility that John's question serves no other purpose than to set up a scene wherein Jesus is able to 'prove' that he is the Messiah spoken of in Isaiah (29.18-19; 35.5-6; 61.1).

It is more conceivable, therefore, that Q 7.19-23 is an *apophthegm*, or pronouncement story, and so is an invention of the early church. Certainly, it has all the hallmarks of such a form. It has a vague narrative setting, wherein John the Baptist hears about Jesus' activities and sends his disciples to question him (7.18-21). Next, Jesus' answer to John's question forms the expected saying (7.22-3). Moreover, Matthew's reference to the works of 'the Messiah' (11.2) and Luke's reference to Jesus as 'the Lord' (7.19), indicate that this passage reflects a post-resurrection viewpoint.[12]

In view of this, it is important to establish that Q 7.18-23 can, in fact, be regarded as a unity. In favour of its integrity is that fact that Jesus' answer to John reflects other sayings attributed to him (Mt. 13.16; Lk. 10.23-4).[13] On the other hand, it is clear that the words attributed to Jesus in Q 7.20-23 do not answer John's question. Thus, it appears that the compiler of Q has combined a question attributed to John and an independent saying attributed to Jesus to form a single pericope. Interestingly, the messianic sign, 'to proclaim liberty to the captives' (Isa. 61.1) is missing from the list of proofs given by Jesus. There is a very good reason why a redactor would have omitted it. Jesus is supposed to be communicating with John the Baptist. John was not released from gaol; he was executed. Thus, the conclusion must be drawn that the Q 7.19-23 as a whole is a product of the early church.

Jesus goes on to eulogise John (Q 7.24-8), publicly acknowledging him as a prophet, and even 'more than a prophet'. He then tells the crowd that John is no less than the messenger of Mal. 3.1, which passage he quotes. The book of Malachi later identifies this messenger as Elijah (Mal. 4.5). If there are any doubts that Jesus is referring to John the Baptist when he makes this association, they are dispelled when Jesus names John in the next verse. This identification is further clarified in Matthew's redaction of this passage, wherein Jesus gives John his full title, John the Baptist (11.11). This pericope confirms John's prophetic status and identifies him as the messenger of Mal. 3.1, thereby implying that John is to be understood as Elijah *redivivus*.

Quite when and with whom John's association with Elijah began cannot now be known for certain. It might have started with John himself, who would have consciously imitated Elijah and encouraged others to see him as Elijah *redivivus*. Alternatively, John's disciples, Jesus or Jesus' disciples made the association during John's lifetime. Each of these suggestions is possible but doubtful because John's death would have negated the association. Moreover, people could easily have pointed out John's failure to perform the task attributed to Elijah in Mal.4.6 and Sir. 48.10, 'At the appointed time, it is written, you are destined to calm the wrath of God before it breaks out in fury, to turn the hearts of parents to their children, and to restore the tribes of Jacob.'

It is more plausible that the identification originated in the early church, whose purpose it served as it sought to reach an agreement concerning the relationship between John and Jesus. Since it was widely known that John had proclaimed the coming of another figure to follow him, it was easy enough to claim that the one John had announced had been Jesus. The prophecies of Elijah's return were reinterpreted so that John, as the returning Elijah, could give authority to the early church's definition of Jesus.

This view is even more conceivable when it is considered how the Malachi proof text has been altered in Q. Malachi states that God will 'send my messenger to prepare the way before me' (3.1). Q, on the other hand, reads, 'Behold, I send my messenger before thy face, who shall prepare the way before thee' (7.27). The wording changes from first to second person. It is still 'my' (God's) messenger, but instead of being sent before God, he is now being sent before Jesus. The insertion of this altered proof text into a speech of Jesus reflects the early church's discomfort with Jesus' high praise of John and seeks to show him in what it considers to be his proper place. John's place is, of course, as Jesus' forerunner, the one who prepares the way for him. Nevertheless, this is no reason to reject the authenticity of Jesus praise of John as it appears in Q 7.24-6. The fact that Jesus does speak so well of John goes against church tradition, and so can probably be accepted as authentic. Moreover, John was regarded as a prophet during his lifetime. Jesus, a follower of John, would also have regarded him as such and referred to him accordingly.

Jesus notes that John is 'more than a prophet', adding, 'I tell you, among those born of women none is greater than John; yet he who is least in the kingdom of God is greater than he' (Q 7.28). A slightly altered version of this saying also appears in the *Gospel of Thomas* (46.1-2), wherein Jesus praises John, but then qualifies that praise by belittling him. Perhaps Jesus sees John as the 'least' because he did not recognise either Jesus as the eschatological agent of God or the imminent success of his ministry. On the other hand, God did not allow John to witness the dawning of the kingdom; as such, he must be less than Jesus. However, Q, like Luke, views John as belonging to an earlier phase of salvation history, which must be maintained. That includes subordinating John to Jesus. Therefore, that Jesus regarded John as a great prophet cannot be doubted. The early church would not have made up such praise for John. It seems, therefore, that Q 7.28a and its *Thomas* counterpart can be accepted as authentic to Jesus. The disclaimer at Q 7.28b and *Thomas* 46.2 is further evidence of its validity. As such, Q 7.28b must be an invention of the early church, a speech attributed to Jesus in order to lend credibility to it, but also to moderate Jesus' inappropriate praise of the one whose disciple he had chosen to become. Both Q 7.24-28 and *Thomas* 46.1-2 are written from a post-Easter standpoint and cannot be considered authentic to Jesus as they stand.

Jesus' tribute to John the Baptist, including his calling John a prophet, can be accepted as genuine. However, the early church used this acclaim to serve its own christological purpose. It took Jesus' reference to John as a prophet and linked it to the messenger of Mal. 3.1. Since Q 7.27 is not authentic to Jesus, it means that Q 7.24-8, as it appears in its final form, is the creation of the early church. The same must be said of Q's association between John the Baptist and the messenger of Mal. 3.1, who in turn is identified as Elijah.

Jesus' Ministry

The rejection of Q 7.19, in which John expresses concerns about Jesus' identity and role, as authentic to the Baptist holds certain connotations regarding Jesus' mission. Quite simply, it calls into question whether or not Jesus did in fact continue with the mission that John had charged him with. As has been shown, Jesus, in all probability, continued to administer John's baptism. However, this does not mean that his attitude towards the rest of John's message remained the same. It is difficult to imagine that Jesus did not change as he matured, and as his mission unfolded.[14] The fate of John the Baptist must have had a profound effect upon him, which in turn inspired his move from Judaea to Galilee. Clearly, Jesus must have changed. Evidence for it is reflected in the differences between John the Baptist and Jesus as recorded in the Synoptic Gospels.

Major differences between John the Baptist and Jesus are evident in their attitude towards food, fasting, prayer and the performance of miracles. For example, John the Baptist was a renowned ascetic, who came 'eating no bread and drinking no wine' (Lk. 7.33 and par.), choosing instead to live on the wilderness fare of 'locusts and wild honey' (Mk 1.6 and par.). On the other hand, Jesus was known for being 'a glutton and a drunkard' (Lk. 7.34 and par.). Next, John's disciples, and, by extension John, were known to have observed the fast (Mk 2.19 and par.). Jesus' disciples, again presumably following their master's lead, did not. Thirdly, John taught his disciples to pray. In some cases, this was linked to fasting (Lk. 5.33). Jesus appears to have neglected to teach his disciples to pray until they asked him to (Lk. 11.1). This suggests that he had abandoned John's teaching regarding these rites. Finally, it seems that John did not perform miracles (Jn 10.41). Miracle working was a prominent feature in Jesus' ministry, which included healing and the exorcism of demons (Mk 1.32-4 and par.).

There do appear to be radical differences indeed between the ministries of John and Jesus, which might be symptomatic of a complete and irreconcilable parting of the ways between the two men.[15] Advocates of this theory find an explanation in the pivotal passage Lk. 11.20: 'But if it is by the finger of God that I cast out demons, then the kingdom of God has come upon you.' In his version of the same saying, Matthew has altered 'finger' to 'spirit' (12.28). This change probably originated with Matthew, since 'spirit' is more in keeping with Luke (cf. Lk. 4.18).[16] It is doubtful that Luke would have exchanged 'spirit' for a different word if it were original to the saying in which he had found it.

Aside from this small Matthaean redaction, this pericope can be accepted as authentic to Jesus because it conveys the sense of eschatological dynamism that must have been characteristic of Jesus' work.[17] Moreover, Lk. 11.20 differs from early church tradition in that it refers to the kingdom of God in connection with the eschatological activity of God.[18] It also differs from Judaism in its expression of the kingdom as being an already present reality. If Lk 11.20 is read in tandem with 11.19, then that would show that the work of the Jewish exorcists is also a manifestation of the kingdom. This would better support the authenticity of 11.20 because it demonstrates that Jesus is no different from other Jewish exorcists.

Jesus' speech as given in Lk. 11.20 can be accepted as authentic. It is supported by the criterion of dissimilarity because it goes against church belief by showing that Jesus was not unique. It is also supported by the criterion of authentic context since it places Jesus among several Jewish exorcists. The case for accepting its authenticity is strengthened when it is placed in conjunction with Lk. 11.19. The fact that it does not appear in the Markan version of the dispute about the provenance of Jesus' power (3.22-27) suggests that it does not belong in its present context. Thus it is an isolated but authentic saying of Jesus in which he seeks to explain his power of exorcism. This was an important consideration for Jesus because of the connotation his exorcisms, as well as his healing activity and miracles, would have carried.

Like many serious thinkers of his day, Jesus understood the world to be in the grip of satanic powers.[19] Evidence for this abounded in the cruel and blasphemous acts perpetrated by the Roman occupiers of Jesus' homeland. It was also apparent in something that was probably of even greater concern to Jesus: the oppression of the poor and helpless, often at the hands of the very authorities who were supposed to protect them.

Of course, Jesus shared this view with John the Baptist himself (Lk. 3.12-14), and it was probably one of the factors that drew Jesus to John in the beginning. Their shared outlook might have been one of the reasons why Jesus decided to stay with John following his baptism, but at some stage Jesus found that he could heal and exorcise. This new-found power had a profound effect upon him because it made him realise that the imminent kingdom of God proclaimed by John was much closer than either of them had imagined. Moreover, it was through Jesus that it was manifesting itself.

Here, then, is the essence of the difference between John the Baptist and Jesus. For John, the eschaton, although imminent, was still a future event. Jesus, on the other hand, saw it as already manifest to some degree. John expected God to come and fulfil his eschatological purpose. Jesus saw the beginnings of God's work in the miracles he was performing. Thus, he sent out his own disciples to urge people to repent and to heal and exorcise (Mk 6.12-13). Jesus' mission continued along the same lines as John's, but it now took on a greater sense of urgency because Jesus could see the first rays of light that indicated the dawning of the kingdom.

Such a realisation must have had a profound effect upon Jesus. It is probable that he altered his approach to his mission as a result of it. Indeed, it would appear that this was so, since he seems suddenly to have ceased to engage in various rituals such as fasting or praying, and to have altered the slant of his preaching. The hypothetical quality of Lk. 11.20 suggests that Jesus himself was unsure of where the power to exorcise came from.[20] This is understandable. Jesus suddenly found himself experiencing a phenomenon for which nothing he has so far encountered or been taught had prepared him. Certainly, there is nothing to indicate that John had taught Jesus to exorcise and heal, or that he himself engaged in such activities.

Jesus understood, therefore, that the kingdom of God was already present, at least to some extent. The signs that this was so were evident in Jesus' new-found abilities. This affected him so much that he abandoned his Johannine baptising mission and began his own independent ministry. Once Jesus knew that the eschatological event proclaimed by John had all but manifested itself, there was no further need to fast, pray, or even to baptise. After all, such activities had to do with purification in preparation for the kingdom. The emergence of that kingdom rendered such preparation unnecessary.

This, incidentally, is why the Synoptic Gospels never show Jesus as a baptiser. Their accounts unanimously introduce Jesus' ministry in Galilee following the removal of John the Baptist and the temptation story. According to the Fourth Evangelist, Jesus worked alongside John as a co-baptiser who took over his master's mission following his arrest. The Synoptics omit this aspect of Jesus because it does not accord with their interpretation of Jesus. Although much of what is related about Jesus, in terms of his words and activities, can be accepted as historically accurate, the evangelists, including the Fourth, were primarily concerned with presenting a picture of Jesus as they or their respective churches had interpreted him. A baptising ministry does not fit into the historical picture because Jesus abandoned it soon after his arrival in Galilee. It does not fit in with their later interpretation of Jesus simply because it had ceased to be an important component in the ministry of the Christ.

If this interpretation of Jesus' changing approach is correct, then it would certainly account for the differences between John the Baptist and Jesus. Moreover, two Markan passages, 2.19a and 2.21-2, probably reflect an expression of Jesus' need to justify to others, and perhaps even to himself, his sudden change of mission. However, Mk 2.21-2 was formed from two originally separate parables and Mk 2.19a belongs to the same series of associated, but originally separate, parabolic sayings which have been placed in such a way as to link the bridegroom with Jesus.[20] Therefore, while the individual sayings themselves might be authentic to Jesus, the passage as a whole cannot be relied upon to support this hypothesis because the sayings have been lifted out of their original context and placed into an artificial one.

The same critique applies to Jesus' reply to the question attributed to John in Q 7.19-23. It has already been established that John's question to Jesus is inauthentic. On the other hand,

Jesus' reply, while probably authentic, does not belong in its present context.[22] To manipulate the sources so that they might support a hypothesis is to do violence to those sources. There is no evidence that there was a radical parting of the ways between John the Baptist and Jesus. Nevertheless, there are differences in their approach to their respective ministries. Jesus clearly did alter the course of his, and this was accompanied by a change in attitude towards certain practices, such as fasting or prayer. If this does not attest to a rift between John and Jesus, then it could simply indicate a difference in style.

Although Jesus seems not to have engaged in ritual prayer, the operative word is 'ritual'. In fact, Jesus did continue to pray (Mk 1.35; Mt. 6.1-18; Lk. 6.12), albeit in private. As to John, history does not record what form his prayers took or how often he performed them. It can be assumed, however, that they were orthodox enough for them to be seen as inseparable from those of the Pharisees (Lk. 5.33).

Linked to prayer is fasting. It is assumed that Jesus did not fast because the sources say that he did not (Mk 2.18-21 and par.); however, these passages have to do with mourning, and so carry no ascetic import. In fasting, as in prayer, Jesus' disciples were urged not to display their devotion publicly.

The passage in which Jesus is described as a 'glutton and a drunkard, a friend of tax collectors and sinners' (Lk. 7.34 and par.) cannot be used as evidence that Jesus did not fast, nor can it be used to compare Jesus' failure to fast with John's asceticism. Rather, the real point of Lk 7.34 is to show that Jesus' offence lies in his table fellowship with those seen as undesirable from a religious or social point of view. It belongs with such passages as Lk. 13.28-9, which speaks of the table fellowship of the kingdom and its celebratory character. There are no doubts concerning the authenticity of this passage. It is early, noticeably Semitic and translates easily into Aramaic. It places the ministry of John the Baptist on the same level as that of Jesus, which strongly suggests that it is not a product of the early church. Moreover, Jesus' being styled as a 'glutton and a drunkard' probably stems from opposition to Jesus' ministry during his lifetime. Therefore, if Lk 7.34 can be used to underline any difference between John the Baptist and Jesus, it must simply be to show that Jesus was celebrating the dawning of the kingdom that, for John, was still a future event. His friendship with repentant sinners, which includes eating and drinking, anticipates the table fellowship of the kingdom.

The differences between John the Baptist and Jesus are more subtle that they at first appear. As such, it is doubtful that they reflect a serious rift but point instead to differences in style as opposed to mission. Indeed, the only important 'disagreement' between the two men is really nothing more than a question of timing. That which John saw as a future event, Jesus saw as already beginning. The most satisfactory explanation for these differences is that they were recalled as minor divisions between two men who were otherwise in complete accord regarding their commission. This commission was, of course, to prepare people for the coming of God.

Conclusion

Jesus began his ministry in Judaea where John the Baptist had sent him. This phase of his ministry was simply a continuation of that which he had begun under John. Jesus then heard the news that John the Baptist had been arrested, prompting Jesus to take the initiative. As tragic as John's fate was, and despite the danger he himself faced, Jesus realised that he had to go to Galilee because it was the only Jewish province yet to hear John's preaching.

At some stage, Jesus altered the way in which he approached his mission. He conspicuously adopted his own style with regard to such rituals as prayer and fasting. However, it is highly probable that he continued to baptise. Baptism had been the starting point of Jesus' own spiritual journey towards the kingdom of God; he would not have denied the experience to others. He continued to administer it to those who came to him in order that they, too, could join the new community, the remnant of Israel, in readiness for God's coming. Jesus did not alter the focus of his mission. He still endeavoured to turn people back to God. However, something happened to Jesus that caused him to alter his approach: he found that he could heal and exorcise.

These new-found skills signalled to Jesus that the coming of God was closer than he or John had thought. The crucial difference between Jesus and John, which influenced their approach to their ministries, lay in the question of timing. For John, the coming of God and the kingdom was still a future event. He was killed before he could witness the fulfilment of his work. Jesus, on the other hand, lived long enough to see the dawning of the kingdom of God. For him, it was as good as present. This accounts for his change in attitude towards the rituals held sacred by John. However, the character of Jesus' mission did not change. Certainly, he focused upon the positive aspects of the eschaton. He saw God's kingdom manifesting itself in his own healing and exorcising activities. This was proof that God was defeating those satanic powers that had long gripped the earth. On the other hand, John apparently expected the eschaton to be a frightening and dangerous experience. He spoke of a fiery judgement that would sweep away the unrepentant; unfortunately, as was noted in the previous chapter, it cannot now be known what John thought salvation would be like because history has not preserved this aspect of his teaching. It cannot be asserted, therefore, that Jesus radically altered John's message. To do so would be to argue from silence. Of course, to say that Jesus continued to preach John's message exactly as he had heard it would also be an argument from silence. Neither view can be expounded satisfactorily, given such limited knowledge of John the Baptist's preaching. The evidence suggests, however, that Jesus' Galilaean ministry was simply a continuation of John's ministry. Its perspective had shifted from focusing on the future to reacting to what was happening in the present.

6

THE DEATH OF JOHN THE BAPTIST

I want you to give me at once the head of John the Baptiser on a platter (Mk 6.25).

The arrest and subsequent execution of John the Baptist of course endangered his mission of proclamation and baptising. Only the fact that Jesus took over the ministry and carried John's message to the Galilaeans saved it from disaster. Nevertheless, this momentous event is almost passed over by the evangelists. Of the four, only two give it any attention; but even they treat it as a flashback and its historical details are manipulated for the sake of christological concerns.

The aim of this chapter is to make a thorough investigation of the arrest, imprisonment and execution of John the Baptist. It will consider the discrepancies that appear to exist between the Synoptic accounts and that of Josephus. The study will embrace several elements, such as why John was arrested and by whom. Who was responsible for John's execution, and where did it occur? Attempts will be made to clarify other details: the identity of Herodias's former husband, whether Salome was the daughter of Herod or Herodias, whether or not Salome, a daughter of the royal household, would have danced at Herod's birthday party, and how the story might have reached the public domain.

The Sources

The starting point is, of course, an analysis of the primary sources in which John's arrest and death appear. Accounts are to be found in Josephus, Mark and Matthew. The Fourth Gospel makes no reference to the events surrounding the death of John the Baptist. Two passages (5.35; 10.41) imply that John, who is spoken of in the past tense, is dead. However, no attempt is made to elaborate upon the circumstances of the event.

Similarly, Luke does not give details of John the Baptist's death. He does report that John was imprisoned by Herod (3.19) and that Herod had ordered John's arrest because he had rebuked the tetrarch for marrying Herodias. Luke also refers to several unspecified 'evil things that Herod had done' but does not develop the story further. The reason why Luke passed over John's death is due to his understanding that John the Baptist belonged to an earlier phase in salvation history. For Luke, whose account had moved on to the second phase, represented by Jesus' earthly ministry, any reference to John's death, even in flashback, would have been out of place.

Mark (6.17-29) and Matthew (14.3-12) offer accounts of the death of John the Baptist. Like Luke, Matthew (14.3) follows Mark (6.17) in holding Herod responsible for John's arrest and imprisonment, but there are differences. Mark (6.19-20) is anxious to show that Herod wanted to save John's life. Indeed, he implies that Herod imprisoned John in order to protect him from Herodias. Matthew, on the other hand, affirms that Herod wanted to kill John but was afraid of the people, who held John as a prophet (14.5). Matthew then goes on to say that Herod was sorry to have to kill John: he did so only because he was obliged to fulfil his promise to Salome (14.9). Both Mark (6.19, 24) and Matthew (14.8) ultimately attribute John's death to Herodias, although her intrigues are less in evidence in Matthew than in Mark. In fact, Matthew's version suggests that Herodias's scheming simply allows Herod to act as he had wished.

Josephus (*Ant.* 18.116-119) records that Herod had become alarmed because John the Baptist was attracting large crowds. In addition, John's eloquence was having such a profound effect upon his audience that Herod feared they might be roused to sedition, 'for they seemed to do anything he should advise.'

The Arrest of John the Baptist

Josephus attributes John's arrest and execution to political expediency. In contrast, the Synoptics show that Herod ordered John's arrest because John had attacked him for his marriage to Herodias. Luke mentions that Herod had committed other crimes as well, which may or may not have a bearing in the case. The Synoptics highlight a moral dimension that appears to disagree with Josephus's account. However, a closer reading of Matthew reveals that there is a political aspect to his rendering of the story also. Matthew, in agreement with Josephus, places the focus of Herod's fear onto the people rather than John himself (14.5).

The Synoptic Gospels agree that John rebuked Herod for his marriage to his brother's wife, Herodias (Mk 6.17-18; Mt. 3-4; Lk. 3.19). John's rebuke is perfectly in accord with Torah (Lev. 18.16). According to Jewish law, it is perfectly acceptable for a man to divorce his wife (Deut. 24. 1-4). Indeed, Josephus tells his readers that he had divorced his own wife because he was dissatisfied with her behaviour (*Life* 426).

However, that which is acceptable for a man is not always so for a woman. Josephus notes that Herodias had divorced her husband, which went against Jewish Law (*Ant.* 18.136). For someone such as John the Baptist, Herodias's divorce was invalid; as far as he was concerned, she was still married to her first husband. For Herod to 'uncover the nakedness' of Herodias was in violation of Torah (Lev. 18.16), while his marriage to Herodias had rendered him impure according to Torah (Lev. 20.21).

It is easy to see how John, so concerned with right behaviour and purity, would have been outraged at Herod's conduct. As he publicly condemned Herod's new marriage, he was effectively accusing the tetrarch of breaking Torah. This accusation, serious though it is, becomes even more so when it is considered that John made it in an area with a large Jewish population, among whom there was already much discontent. Perhaps his breaking Torah did not unduly concern Herod. However, it would have been a major concern to the people to know that the man ruling over them was both a Torah breaker and impure.

A political dimension to John's arrest is added when it is remembered that one of the functions of his baptism was that it should serve as an initiation rite. To submit to baptism was to become a member of the true Israel. There is no evidence to support a tendency towards sedition in John's message. Nevertheless, his preaching of baptism, which was performed in anticipation of a coming judgement, could be construed as an indictment of the present order.[1] Similarly, John's announcement of a Coming One could have been seen as a threat to the legitimate leadership, since that figure could have been interpreted as a new ruler.[2] When this announcement is placed within the context of discontent among the populace, it is understandable how John could be viewed as a political threat.

This threat becomes stronger when it is considered that John's message spoke of imminent judgement and the removal of unrepentant sinners. There is no doubt that Herod would be counted among this group. Thus, Herod had every reason to be wary of such a gathering in the wilderness. Josephus is correct to point to Herod's great fear that John might instigate a revolt (*Ant.* 18.118). John posed a serious threat to Herod's ability to maintain order in his territory. Seen from Herod's perspective, the removal of John was essential.

There is another factor to be considered. John's choice of location for his ministry, while being symbolic, also brought him into contact with Nabataean traders. The border between Peraea and Nabataea lay less than 20 km to the east of where John spent much of his time preaching and baptising. The traders' reports of John's preaching and his condemnation of Herod must have greatly interested their rulers. This might seem of little consequence, but there is an important political connection. Herod had divorced his first wife in order to marry Herodias, albeit at the latter's request (*Ant.* 18.109-10). Herod's first wife was the daughter of Aretas IV, king of Nabataea.[3] The disastrous consequences of this divorce are related by Josephus (*Ant.* 18.113-15), although some Jews had attributed Herod's fall to his treatment of John the Baptist (*Ant.* 18.16). Herod, then, was attacked on two fronts: by Aretas IV and by own people who should have supported him. In fact, John's rebuke of Herod had turned many people away from the tetrarch at the very time when he needed as much support as possible in order to defend himself against the vengeance of the Nabataean king. Josephus notes that Herod was soundly defeated (*Ant.* 18.109-125).

Josephus's account supports the evangelists' assertion that John's fate was directly linked to Herod's divorce (Mk 6.17-18; Mt. 3-4; Lk. 3.19-20). There is, then, an area of accord between the Synoptic evangelists and Josephus. The accounts of the arrest and death of John the Baptist as presented by Josephus and the Synoptics support rather than contradict each other. The evangelists cite John's rebuke of Herod for his marriage to Herodias. In so doing, they complement John's concern with purity, right behaviour and the upholding of Torah. On the other hand, Josephus's emphasis upon Herod's fear of a popular uprising is entirely consistent with what is known about the fate of wilderness groups of the first century. They were regarded with suspicion by the authorities, who acted swiftly and brutally to remove them. The fact that John attracted large crowds would have made him enough of a threat to Herod. When this is compounded with the political implications of Herod's divorce from Aretas's daughter, then that threat becomes much more serious, especially if Nabataean tradesmen joined the ranks of John's hearers. Finally, John's message of imminent judgement and restoration, with the consequent removal of unrepentant sinners, coupled with his announcement of a Coming One, would probably have stirred the excitement of his audience to dangerous levels. Taking all this into account, Herod's most prudent action was to remove John from the scene.

The Synoptic accounts of the arrest, imprisonment and death of John the Baptist can be reconciled to a large extent with Josephus. However, there are many discrepancies between Mark's account and Matthew's redaction of it that are not so easy to resolve. These discrepancies are so serious that Mark's account has been dismissed as merely a legend with no Christian features.[4] Certainly, the story shares much in common with the Hebrew Bible account of Esther and king Ahasuerus. These inconsistencies threaten to wholly undermine the story as an account of an historical event.[5] Such scepticism can be easily understood when a study of the discrepancies that inspire it is made.

Herod or Herodias?

The most obvious disparity between Mark's account Matthew's is the question of whether Herod or Herodias should ultimately be held responsible for John's execution. Mark (6.19, 24) clearly shows Herodias to be the one influencing events; Matthew (14.8) appears to agree, although his account tends to play down Herodias's intrigues.

In both Gospels, Herodias is seen to be resentful of John for his condemnation of her marriage, and she uses her daughter to bring about his execution. Indeed, it might be inferred from Mark's account that Herod had imprisoned John in order to protect him from Herodias (6.20). More probable, given the circumstances discussed above, is that Mark used the term 'and kept him safe' to mean that Herod was more interested in keeping John out of the public eye.[6] This interpretation also brings Mark more into agreement with Josephus. Mark then goes on to show Herodias standing ready with an answer to her daughter's request for advice. This suggests that Herodias had planned out the entire incident in advance. Mark's portrayal of Herodias is consistent with that of Josephus, who depicts her as an intriguer (*Ant.* 18.110, 240-55). Her opportunity came 'when Herod on his birthday gave a banquet' (Mk 6.21). She took advantage of the celebrations and the rash promise made by her enebriated husband to direct her daughter to ask for John's head as a reward for her dancing (Mk 6.24).

Herodias's guilt seems supportable until it is noted that her influence over John's fate is but singly attested. It is present only in Mark (6.19, 24) and in Matthew's redaction (14.8). However, Mark has contradicted himself. Previously, when showing Herod's reaction to news of Jesus' activities, he records Herod's thoughts, 'John, whom I beheaded, has been raised' (6.16). Herod, by his own admission, is responsible for John's execution. Mark, therefore, agrees with Josephus. Herod's guilt is multiply attested.

This is particularly apparent in Matthew's account of the story, where it is stated that Herod had ordered John's arrest because he was angry that John had condemned his marriage to Herodias (Mt. 14.3). However much he wanted to kill John, Herod was afraid to do so because of his fear of the people. For Matthew, it was not so much the birthday party that provided the opportunity but Herodias's intrigues. Setting her daughter to dance before the company, she knew that the tetrarch would be pleased. He was. In his pleasure, he promised to give the dancer anything she asked for. Prompted by her mother, she asked for John's head. Matthew's Herod is distressed by this. The evangelist describes the scene in such a way that the reader is prompted to think that Herod did not want to kill John, but had been trapped into it by his reckless, drunken oath. After all, Herod had made his promise in front of many important guests; he could not back down without losing face. But Herod had merely taken advantage of his wife's machinations to get his own way. Matthew had simply condensed the account he had found in Mark in order to reach his point more quickly. This was that, while Herodias might have intrigued for John's execution, Herod was ultimately responsible for it.[7]

Herodias's Former Husband

Another problem regarding Herodias cannot be so easily explained. This concerns the discrepancy over whose wife she had previously been. According to Mk 6.17, Herodias was the former wife of Philip. Matthew makes no adjustment to this as he redacts his Markan source (14.3). Luke avoids the problem by omitting the name of Herodias's former husband (3.19). Josephus contradicts Mark, stating that Herodias's first husband was another Herod, who was the half-brother of Herod Antipas (*Ant.* 18.109). No satisfactory explanation has so far been offered for this discrepancy. It has been suggested that Philip might have been called Herod Philip.[8] It is possible also that 'Herod' might have become a dynastic title,[9] 'Philip' would have been used as a personal name. This interesting suggestion, however, has nothing to support it.[10] Perhaps the best solution is to suggest that either Mark or his source has confused Herodias's former husband with her son-in-law; her daughter married Philip the tetrarch.

The Father of Salome

Related to the problem of Herodias's former husband is confusion over who was the father of the dancing daughter, Salome.[11] A textual variant in Mk 6.22 shows that Salome was $\tau\eta\varsigma\ \theta\upsilon\gamma\alpha\tau\rho\varsigma\ \alpha\upsilon\tau\upsilon\ H\rho\omega\delta\iota\alpha\delta\varsigma$. The use of the masculine indicates that the dancer was the daughter of Herod, and that her name was Herodias. Such manuscripts, while few in number, are, nevertheless, important ones: א B D L Δ 238 565.[12] In addition, the fourth edition of the Deutsche Bibelgesellschaft/United Bible Societies' *The Greek New Testament* prints the version in which Herod is shown to be the father. It gives this text a 'C' rating, indicating uncertainty with regard to which version is the correct one.

On the other hand, the greater number of manuscripts give *της θυγατρος αυτης Ηρωδιαδος*, which indicates that Salome is the daughter of Herodias, as Matthew (14.6) makes clear. Matthew, therefore, agrees with the greater number of Markan manuscripts that support the latter version. Matthew's version is not disputed by the Deutsche Bibelgesellschaft's *The Greek New Testament*. That Salome was Herodias's daughter, and not Herod's, finds textual support.

Josephus makes no mention of a daughter being born to Herod Antipas and Herodias, although he does state that Herodias had a daughter named Salome from her previous marriage (*Ant.* 18.136). The feminine pronoun *αυτης*, which is found in the majority of manuscripts of Mark, must be the correct one. Several factors support it. First, the Gospel narrative suggests that Herod and Herodias were recently married. A child born of their union would have been too young to dance at the banquet. Secondly, Mark states that Salome went to her mother for advice when Herod asked her what she wanted as a reward for her dancing (6.24). If Herod had been her father, Herodias could not have been her mother. Thirdly, the use of the feminine pronoun brings Mark into agreement with Matthew (14.6), whose version is undisputed. While it might be argued that Matthew copied from a Markan manuscript that did give the feminine pronoun, Josephus can still be appealed to for support. In fact, Salome was probably Herod's grandniece; Mark was simply misinformed or confused about the complicated relationships of the Herodian dynasty.[13]

Salome's Marital Status and Dance

Another area to be addressed is whether or not Salome was a maiden. Mark (6.22) refers to her as a κορασιον, but is this an appropriate designation for her? Jairus's daughter, who was twelve years of age (Mk 5.42; Lk. 8.42), is also referred to as a κορασιον (Mk 5.41; Mt. 9.24, 25). The implication is that Salome was not a young girl, but rather a woman of, or near, marriageable age.

Josephus (*Ant.* 18.137) records that Salome married Philip the tetrarch, who died in 34 CE (*Ant.* 18.106). On the basis of this, it has been speculated that Salome was actually married to Philip when these events took place.[14] Moreover, she could have been no more than twenty at the time of John's death since, after her widowhood, she went on to marry Aristobolus, with whom she had three children.[15]

Whatever her age and marital status, the account of Salome's dance has been questioned by some scholars. As a princess, it is doubtful that she would have danced at what appears to be a debauched gathering.[16] However, this view of Herod's party is based upon assumptions that Salome's dance was erotic. Such assumptions are thought to have been inspired by Hollywood representations of the story rather than from the Gospels,[17] although a mediaeval sculpture group in Rouen Cathedral suggests that the dance was seen as erotic at a much earlier date. Whatever the case, travellers to Palestine record having witnessed such dances for themselves.[18]

Herod's Promise and the Location of John's Imprisonment and Death

Assuming that Salome did dance at Herod's birthday banquet, would Herod have been able to offer her 'even half my kingdom' (Mk 6.23)? The words used here are the same as those spoken by King Ahasuerus in the story of Esther (5.3). Likewise, the fact that Salome pleased the king reflects Esther 2.9, and the setting of the story at a royal banquet recalls Esther 1.1-22. As a vassal of Rome, Herod had no kingdom of his own to offer. The saying must have been used proverbially, as it probably was in Ahasuerus's time as well.[19] Certainly, it seems to have been a familiar expression (1 Kings 13.8; Lk. 19.8; *Iliad* 9.616) and was probably not taken literally by those who heard Herod's promise. Neither Salome nor Esther are reported to have held their respective rulers to their word. The authenticity of Herod's promise has also been rejected on the grounds that it would have taken too long to send an executioner all the way from Tiberias, where Mark implies that the banquet took place, to Machaerus, where John was held (*Ant.* 18.119).[20] Indeed, such a journey would have necessitated crossing some ninety kilometres of wilderness as well as the Jordan River.

This raises another important question: where was John the Baptist imprisoned and executed? Mark allows his readers to infer that John was imprisoned at Tiberias, since he notes that the banquet was attended by Herod's 'courtiers and officers and the leading men of Galilee' (Mk 6.21). Tiberias was Herod's capital city, making it an obvious choice as the setting for his banquet. On the other hand, Josephus states that John was 'brought in chains to Machaerus ... and was there put to death' (*Ant.* 18.119).

That Machaerus is close to where John preached and baptised makes it more probable that he was held there rather than at Tiberias. Machaerus ties in well with what it known of John's movements, the implications of his preaching, the possibility that Nabataeans were among his hearers, as well as his attack on Herod and his marriage to Herodias. It seems reasonable that John the Baptist was held at Machaerus following his arrest.

Josephus's description of Machaerus (*War* 7.172-7) indicates that it served a dual purpose, that of fortress and palace. Not only were the buildings fortified, but a large stock of weapons was also kept there. Attached to it was a large and beautiful palace that had been built onto the original fortress of Machaerus. Perhaps it was more fortress than palace at the time of the events in question,[21] however, its spacious rooms and constant supply of water suggest that it was meant for people other than soldiers. Moreover, when Herod's first wife, the daughter of Aretas IV, heard of her husband's plans to divorce her, she sought permission to go to Machaerus.[22] Herod granted her request, which he would not have done had the building been no more than a fortress. Since it was also a palace, his suspicions were not aroused.

As previously noted, John conducted part of his ministry in Peraea. Since this province came under the jurisdiction of Herod, the tetrarch was quite within his rights to seize John there, and the most obvious place to hold him would be at Machaerus. Indeed, it would make sense for Herod himself to have been in Peraea, in view of the anticipated vengeance of Aretas IV. Had he stayed at Machaerus, he would have been in a good position to monitor activity along his border. If this reasoning is combined with the fact that no delegation from Peraea is mentioned by Mark, it might logically be concluded that Herod was already in that region.

John's Head on a Platter

Mark (6.28) and Matthew (14.11) add a gruesome detail to the story of the execution of John the Baptist. They observe that John's severed head was handed to the daughter, who then offered it to Herodias. This looks like a piece of sensationalism, but it could have a sound basis in fact. Kings were often shown the severed heads of enemies as proof that they had been killed. This was done in the case of Theudas (*Ant.* 20.97-8), whose head was brought to Jerusalem following his capture and execution.

Similarly, Josephus (*Ant.* 18.115) relates another story, this time directly connected with the activities of John the Baptist and the reasons for his arrest and subsequent execution. As he speaks of Herod's conflict with Aretas IV, Josephus notes that Tiberius, furious that the Nabataean king had begun hostilities, ordered Vitellius to 'declare war and either bring Aretas to him in chains, if he should be captured alive, or, if he should be slain, to send him his head'. In view of this, it is easy to see why Mark and Matthew should include a scene in which Herodias is offered the head of the Baptist. The grisly relic is a trophy of her triumph over her enemy and proof that he had been removed. Considering that both evangelists have shown Herodias to be the victor rather than Herod suggests that this element of the story, while drawing upon an authentic historical detail that has some connection with the events related, should be regarded as embellishment.

The Possible Origins of the Story

It is interesting to note that the confusion and discrepancies found in this account centre mainly upon Herodias and her daughter. This is equally applicable whether Mark is compared with Matthew, or whether Mark and Matthew are compared with Josephus. Where Mark and Matthew focus upon Herod, they find support in Josephus's account. Once they turn their attention to Herodias and Salome, their accounts become confused. The solution to this might lie in the sources used by the evangelists.

It has been noted that the story of the execution of John the Baptist has been dismissed as legendary. This is because it shows some characteristics with other Hellenistic Jewish sources, namely Herodotus 9.108-13; Livy 39.43; Plutarch *Artaxerxes* 17.[23] However, these stories are not close enough to justify this theory.[24] For the same reason, any claim that the story of John's death was influenced by Esther (1.9-11; 5.6) or the attempt upon Elijah's life by Jezebel (1 Kings 19.2) can also be dismissed.[25] Where, then, did the story come from?

An interesting hypothesis is suggested by Lk. 8.3, which mentions a certain 'Joanna, the wife of Chuza, Herod's steward'.[26]

The Greek term interpreted as 'steward' is επιτροπος. The same term is applied to Antipater, the father of Herod the Great (*Ant.* 16.143; *War* 1.199), various procurators (*Ant.* 15.406; *War* 2.117, 223), Thaumastus, the manager of Agrippa I's personal estates (*Ant.* 18.194) and Syllaeus, who managed the estates of King Obedas of Arabia (*War* 1.487). Syllaeus is also mentioned in *Ant.* 16.279-82, 291, 295-6, 343, 353, where he is in charge of Obedas's finances. These functions accord with Mt. 20.8, which suggests that the επιτροπος was in charge of his master's finances and possibly his personal estates. So he was a very important member of the household, and would probably have been present at Herod's banquet.

Another figure, this time mentioned in Acts 13.1, is Manaen, 'a member of the court of Herod the tetrarch'. Manaen is described as a συντροφος, implying that he was brought up or educated with Herod. He might have been a close friend of Herod Antipas,[27] while also enjoying some influential or authoritative position.[28] Chuza and Manaen might, therefore, have been reliable eyewitnesses to the events that took place at Herod's birthday banquet. This suggestion is supported by the fact that Manaen was a member of the Antiochean church (Acts 12.25; 15.37).[29] So their testimony regarding these events might have become known to the author of Matthew, whose Gospel could have been written at Antioch. Even were they not personally present at the banquet, Chuza and Manaen would at least have been in a position to know what had taken place there.

Interestingly, there are several Semitisms in Mark, suggesting a Palestinian origin for this pericope.[30] For example, Mark uses the term βασιλευς four times (6.22, 25, 26, 27), but in a work of Roman origin, one would expect to find the term τετραρχης used for a ruler. Similarly, Matthew uses τετραρχης in 14.1, but βασιλευς in his account of John's death. This shows that both evangelists remained faithful to their source. It also supports the hypothesis that the account of John's death as found in Mark and Matthew has a Palestinian provenance.

Conversely, Mark uses Roman and/or Hellenistic terms for governmental offices and functions. In 6.21, for example, he uses μεγιστασιν, from μεγισταν, which is a late Greek word meaning 'great one' or 'grandee'. The same verse contains πρωτοις της Γαλιλαιας (first of Galilee), a Hellenistic rather than a Palestinian designation. Mark also mentions two military terms: the Greek χιλιαρχοις (6.21) and the Latin loan word σπεκουλατορα (6.27). The latter is a soldier whose duties included carrying out executions. Mark shows a sound knowledge of the correct designations for the personnel to be found in Herod's household and among his guests. It might be argued that his source was Roman or Hellenistic rather than Palestinian. However, it must be remembered that Herod was governing on behalf of Rome in a region steeped in Hellenistic culture. To find such terms being used in his administration is to be expected. The presence of these terms in Mark does not defeat this hypothesis. If anything, it strengthens it.

That Mark and Matthew had access to the testimony of reliable eyewitnesses must, however, remain a tantalising hypothesis. There is little, beyond speculation, to substantiate it. Still, it would have been nice if it could have been said with some degree of certainty that at least one event related by the Gospels could be traced to reliable witnesses who could actually be named. On the other hand, it would be ironic, to say the least, that such would be said of John the Baptist and not the main focus of the Gospels: Jesus.

Conclusion

Several discrepancies that apparently exist between the Synoptic accounts of John the Baptist's death and execution and that of Josephus appear, at first glance, to be quite damning. Such discrepancies have led some scholars to dismiss the Gospel accounts as nothing more than legends with no historical basis. However, closer study reveals that, rather than contradicting each other, the primary sources actually support each other. The Synoptics point to moral and legal reasons why Herod should want to remove John the Baptist. Josephus concentrates upon political motives. These find common ground in the question of Herod's divorce and remarriage.

Herod's divorce had one major implication when looked at in its wider historical context. The wife Herod repudiated in order to marry Herodias was the daughter of Aretas IV, king of Nabataea. This king took full advantage of the circumstances to wage the war that his daughter's marriage to Herod was intended to prevent. The high tension that marked the period between Herod's divorce and the consequent war was exacerbated by John's preaching of judgement and the removal of unrepentant sinners. Herod, as an impure Torah breaker, fitted into this group. However, it was more than simply John's message that caused concern. He attracted large crowds. This in itself would have brought him to the attention of the authorities, who would have acted to remove him. What made John more of a threat was his announcement of a Coming One, who could have been interpreted as a political figure. All this took place within an atmosphere of heightened expectation that the old order would soon be swept away to be replaced by a new age. It was politically essential, therefore, for Herod to remove John.

Herod Antipas must take the blame for the arrest of John the Baptist. He must also be held responsible for John's death. The evangelists prefer to mislead their readers by implying that Herodias was the one influencing the events surrounding John's fate. However, most of the discrepancies that surround the story of John's death centre upon Herodias and her daughter. There is confusion over the identity of Herodias's first husband. Was he Philip (Mk 6.17), or Herod, the half-brother of Herod Antipas

(*Ant.* 18.109)? To whom did the daughter belong: Herod Antipas, as some manuscripts assert, or Herodias, as the greater number of texts suggest? In the former instance, the young woman's name would not be Salome, as Josephus (*Ant.* 18.136) notes, but Herodias. The confusion surrounding the female protagonists in accounts of this event suggests that, if they played a role in it at all, then it must have been a minor one. The historical details that should be present in an authentic account are lacking here. Although Herodias is portrayed by Josephus as an intriguer, there is nothing to support the hypothesis that she had a hand in John's death. Therefore, the Gospel accounts, which blame Herodias for John's death, are unconvincing. Conversely, the accounts in which Herod is shown to be the driving force behind John's fate are acceptable for several reasons. They are multiply attested (Mk 6.16; Mt.14.5; Lk.3.19; *Ant.* 18.119). They are supported by the historical facts surrounding Herod Antipas' divorce from the daughter of Aretas IV and its implications, as well as the wider cultural context surrounding first-century wilderness prophets and their fate at the hands of the authorities. There is only one major discrepancy, and that has to do with the location of John's death. However, this is the result of assumptions based upon Mark's account, which seems to suggest that John was killed at Tiberias. In fact, Mark made no mention of the setting of John's death.

What, then, of the historicity of the story? It is possible to discern a foundation of solid historical fact within the Synoptic accounts of John's death. Also, where their accounts focus upon Herod, they are in accord with Josephus. Once they go beyond Herod's involvement, they fall into uncertainty. Specifically, there is unfamiliarity with the female characters of the story and what role should be assigned to them. While there is a remote possibility that the unadorned details of the tale were originally transmitted by persons present at the celebration, they rapidly became heavily embellished. The fact that some details, such as Salome's dance, Herodias's intrigues and John's head being exhibited before the drunken guests, are credible lends a sense of realism to the adornments.

A study of the account of the death of John the Baptist requires as much care when extracting the historical facts as does any other pericope. Since Josephus's account can be substantiated by history, the researcher would do well to use it as the yardstick for gauging the authenticity of the Gospel accounts. Where the evangelists speak of Herod and his motives for wanting to execute John, their accounts display a sound grasp of history. Where they exceed this boundary, they fall into confusion. The story now becomes redaction, embellishment, and perhaps even political propaganda.

7

MORE THAN A PROPHET

Behold, I send my messenger before thy face... (Mk1.2)

Christianity defines John the Baptist as 'the forerunner of the Christ'.[1] Sometimes he is described as the 'herald of the Christ' or 'the voice in the desert who proclaimed the coming of Jesus'.[2] One dictionary designates him 'the forerunner of Jesus, who was sent to "prepare the way of the Lord"'.[3] This assessment of John is justified by appealing to several texts, including Mt. 3.3; 3.14-15; Lk. 1.41; 3.21; 16.16; Jn 1.29, 36; 3.29; Acts 13.24. In addition, 'John is Elijah [who] must come',[4] with passages such as Mt. 17.10-13 and Lk. 1.76 cited as evidence.

Christianity clearly found it necessary to interpret John the Baptist in relation to Jesus. The presence of John, whose message and mission had influenced Jesus to the degree that he felt he could partake of John's baptism and assist him in his mission, had to be explained in such a way that the uniqueness and superiority of Jesus would be preserved. The solution was simple: John the prophet and baptiser had to be re-interpreted and transformed into the forerunner of the Christ. This chapter, then, will trace the early history and the method of the transformation of John the Baptist.

Forerunner Motifs in Q

The process by which John the Baptist was transformed into the forerunner of Christ is consolidated into Q, the four Gospels and Acts.

In its early form, Q probably consisted almost entirely of wisdom sayings that were remembered as having been uttered by, or were attributed to, Jesus. The Q community appear to have understood Jesus as a Jewish sage, or wise man.[5] Among these saying are the Lord's Prayer (11.2-4), the Beatitudes (6.20b-23) and the Golden Rule (6.31).

Although usually referred to as a sayings Gospel, Q does feature at least two short narratives: an account of Jesus' testing in the wilderness (4.1-13) and a miracle story in which Jesus heels the centurion's slave (7.1-10). Curiously, there are no passion or resurrection narratives, indicating that Q shows no interest in the redemptive significance of Jesus' death and resurrection.

Q also contains some apocalyptic material. This is because the Q community believed that Jesus would return as the apocalyptic Son of Man who would judge those who had rejected his message. The apocalyptic phase probably reflects persecution of the Q community, references for which are to be found throughout Q, often with Jesus offering words of comfort and support (7.31; 11.51; 12. 22-31, 33-34; 16.13). As hostility towards the community increased, the apocalyptic material began to play a much larger role, and it is probably at this stage that John the Baptist was introduced.

Q features several passages that reveal John the Baptist's status as Jesus' forerunner, beginning, as far as can be determined, with his apocalyptic preaching (3.7-9). This speech, in which John addresses himself to a 'brood of vipers', contains fiery warnings of judgement and destruction. The apocalyptic elements of Q are, therefore, apparent from the very beginning. However, this preaching, angry and urgent in tone, is softened by that which follows it. Having frightened those who have come to hear him and threatened those who thought they knew better than he, John next brings hope to his audience by announcing the imminent arrival of the Coming One (3.16-17). This figure is understood by the Q community as the sage Jesus, who will return in judgement as the Son of Man.

Q 3.16-17 appears to be formed from two sources. The information given in Q 3.16 is also found in Mk 1.7-8 and is reflected in Jn 1.26-7. Another parallel is found in Acts 13.25, although since Acts was written by the author of Luke, the reference here is probably dependent upon the same source that was used for the Gospel. John's announcement of the Coming One (Q 3.16) is, therefore, multiply attested, and can be accepted as authentic to him. Q 3.17, however, belongs exclusively to Q. It elaborates upon the task to be performed by the Coming One and offers clues about his ministry, but it reveals nothing about John except to suggest that he should be viewed as the forerunner of this figure.

In Q 7.24-8 Jesus publicly praises John and acknowledges him as a prophet, and even 'more than a prophet'. He then identifies John with the messenger of Mal. 3.1, who in turn is identified as Elijah *redivivus*. (Mal. 4.5).

As has been noted, the Malachi proof text has been altered so that the messenger no longer prepares the way for God, but for Jesus. In the hands of the compiler of Q, Malachi 3.1 now demonstrates John the Baptist's role as the forerunner of Jesus. The reason for its insertion is to soften Jesus' high praise of John and to maintain the Baptist in the position designated to him by the early church.

The same reasoning is behind Q 7.28, where Jesus speaks of John as being 'more than a prophet', adding, that John is less than 'he who is least in the kingdom of God.' Jesus' high regarded of John can be accepted as authentic. The fact that is caused such discomfort to the early church that they felt they had to moderate it is proof enough. Jesus' tribute to John the Baptist also prompted those same authorities to reinterpret John as Elijah, offering an altered proof text of Malachi 3.1, placed onto the lips of Jesus as support. They were motivated by their own view of Jesus as the apocalyptic Son of Man. Since John had emerged prior to the coming of Jesus, it stood to reason that he must be the one spoken of by Malachi's prophecy, Elijah.

Q 16.16 is problematic because it is difficult to know whereabouts in the text it originally belonged. As it now stands, it is very much influenced by the viewpoint of the respective evangelists who used it as their source. As such, Matthew relates Q 16.16 to his theme of the kingdom of heaven: 'from the days of John the Baptist until now in the kingdom of heaven has suffered violence and men of violence take it by force. For all the prophets and the law prophesied until John' (11.12-13). Since this theme was not part of John's original proclamation, as far as the evidence allows such an assertion to be made, it can only be conjectured that Matthew has redacted his Q source so that it calls attention to John's identification as Elijah, which is further clarified in 11.14. Matthew, therefore, uses Q 16.16 to enhance John's forerunner status and strengthen his association with Elijah.

Luke links Q 16.16 to his theme of the separation of salvation history into distant periods: 'the law and the prophets were up until John' since then the good news of the kingdom of God is preached, and everyone enters into it violently (16.16). John the Baptist, of course, belongs to the first period, that of the law and the prophets.

Since Q 16.16 too much reflects the perspective of the individual evangelist, an accurate assessment of how the compiler of Q meant it to be understood cannot now be made. However, Matthew and Luke have used it to portray John as the forerunner of Jesus, in the case of Matthew, or to show that his ministry belonged to the epoch that preceded that of Jesus, in the case of Luke.

Q uses both structure and words attributed to Jesus as it seeks to demonstrate John's role of forerunner of Jesus, which is exemplified by his association with Elijah *redivivus*. As Q opens, the reader anticipates the arrival of Jesus and assumes that he is the Coming One announced by John. Thus Q begins its portrayal of John the Baptist as forerunner.

Probably one of the most striking features of Q's treatment of John the Baptist is that it never refers to him as the Baptist or the Baptiser. It does mention John's baptism, but only once and in passing as part of a general account of John's preaching of repentance and his proclamation of the Coming One. Since the baptism of Jesus is followed by the Temptation in the Synoptics, and Q contains an account of the Temptation, it might be expected to have an account of the baptism as well. However, there is a plausible reason why it should not. A comparable gospel, the *Gospel of Thomas*, makes no mention of John's baptism or his early ministry. Q and the *Gospel of Thomas* are both sayings gospels rather than narratives of Jesus' ministry. As such, an account of Jesus' baptism, and the one who administered it, would be out of place.

More important to Q is John's identification as the forerunner of Jesus, to whom he is carefully subordinated. The sequencing of certain pericopae, specifically 3.7-9, 16-17, which presents John's apocalyptic message and his announcement of the Coming One, allow for no other interpretation of John than that he is to be seen as the forerunner of this figure. Later, the sequence 7.18-23, 7.24-28, which opens with an expression of doubt on the part of John concerning Jesus' identity, provides Jesus with the opportunity to prove his superiority to John. It also further develops John's forerunner status so that he is now implicitly identified with Elijah, the returning eschatological prophet.

Q does not openly state that John should be interpreted as Elijah *redivivus*. Instead, it uses John's announcement of the Coming One as well as speeches placed onto the lips of Jesus to hint that John should be interpreted this way. The readers or hearers of Q are encouraged to associate John's status as Jesus' forerunner with his implicit identification as Elijah.

Forerunner Motifs in Mark

Conversely, the author of Mark makes it clear from the very beginning that his readers should understand Jesus as the Messiah or Christ (1.1). Mark immediately follows the introduction to his Gospel with a quotation from 'Isaiah the prophet' (1.2). In fact, Mark presents two quotations. The first is taken from Mal. 3.1 (Mk 1.2). The second is indeed from Isaiah: 40.3 (Mk 1.3). This combined prophecy introduces Mark's readers to John 'the baptiser' (1.4), who in turn announces the coming of another 'who is mightier than I, the thong of whose sandals I am not worthy to stoop down and untie' (1.7). This coming one would baptise, not with water as John had done, but with 'the Holy Spirit' (1.8). Mark uses John's words as an introduction to Jesus, whom readers already know to be the Christ because Mark told them so in the opening verse of his Gospel.

Mark's four step arrangement of introduction, prophecy, announcement and the appearance of Jesus guides the reader to interpret John as the forerunner whose divinely appointed task is to prepare the way for the Lord. Mark wants to show that in preparing the way for Jesus, John is fulfilling scripture.[6]

Mk 1.2 (= Mal. 3.1) reflects John the Baptist's adoption by the church, which also separates him from his Jewish context.[7] Mark's reference to Mal. 3.1 also shows that he considers John to be the returning Elijah, who is identified as the messenger of Mal. 3.1 in Mal. 4.5-6. That the latter passage is a later addition to the book of Malachi is of no concern here, since the version in which Elijah is identified as the messenger of Mal. 3.1 is that which would have been known in the first century. As such, it was this version of the text that influenced Jewish thinking of the period.[8] Mark's point is to show that John's fulfilment of prophecy legitimises Jesus' ministry.

Mk 1.3 (= Isa. 40.3), on the other hand, could reflect a prophecy that was genuinely associated with John during his own lifetime. John could have used Isaiah as part of his preaching to define his eschatological outlook and to interpret his baptism. Were this so, a tradition might have existed wherein John the Baptist defined his ministry using Isaiah, and especially this particular verse. In favour of this hypothesis is the fact that all four Gospels associate Isa. 40.3 with John the Baptist, though only the Fourth Gospel places the quotation directly onto John's lips. Had John found that this Isaiah passage best explained his purpose and mission, the Fourth Evangelist, by causing him to cite it in his Gospel, could be showing himself to be more aware of this aspect of John's preaching than the Synoptic evangelists. The Fourth Gospel might, therefore, have drawn from a very old tradition surrounding John that was also known to the community for which Mark was writing.

A point to note, however, is that Mark misquotes Isaiah. He alters both the wording and the punctuation of his proof text. No longer is there a voice crying, 'in the wilderness prepare the way of the Lord...,' rather Mark speaks of a voice crying in the wilderness, the message of which is to 'prepare the way of the Lord...' The difference is subtle but essential. He next states that John 'appeared in the wilderness', thus identifying him as the voice. In their redactions of Mark, Matthew and Luke follow Mark's arrangement of Isa. 40.3, rather than the original form of the text found in the Hebrew Bible. The Fourth Evangelist uses a similar arrangement to that found in the Synoptics, but he alters it still further by making John declare himself to be the voice. The fact that John is made to speak these words in the Fourth Gospel shows this to be a dramatic embellishment on the part of the Fourth Evangelist. As such, it is clearly a secondary development. Moreover, it is the altered version that is multiply attested, and not the original version from the book of Isaiah. As such, the presentation of Isa. 40.3 as a part of a speech by John should be regarded with suspicion, though not entirely dismissed. It is possible that John used the passage to explain his ministry or his presence in the wilderness. The evangelists simply took the tradition and presented it in such a way that it now serves their own purposes. They use it to show John as a forerunner preparing the way for Jesus, whom they then go on to show to be the Coming One announced by John. Fulfilment of prophecy is one of the devices used by the evangelists to indicate their belief that Jesus was the figure anticipated by John.

Perhaps Mark was aware of the tradition, also known to the complier of Q, that associated John the Baptist with Elijah. Whatever the case, the result of his redaction of his proof texts is the assertion that John the Baptist is the forerunner of the Lord. However, John is also Elijah. Mark 1.2, which identifies John as a forerunner, can only be seen as a product of the early church. Mk 1.3, as it now stands, is also a product of the early church. Mark has altered the Isaiah passage and combined it with the Malachi prophecy, thus giving prophetic endorsement to Jesus, whom John is made to announce, and his ministry.

Having introduced John the Baptist as the one crying in the wilderness, Mark is now in a position to introduce the man himself (1.6). John is 'clothed with camel's hair, and has a leather girdle around his waist'. John's dress is not multiply attested. Q makes no attempt to offer a description of John's clothes. Matthew simply follows Mark. Luke knows nothing of John's dress or chooses to ignore it, as does the Fourth Evangelist. Josephus makes no mention of John's clothing. How authentic, therefore, is Mark's description of John the Baptist's clothes?

While all versions of Mark agree that John wore camel's hair, not all of them refer to the leather girdle (D and *it* omit this feature). Its appearance in Matthew's redaction of Mark (3.4) means either that his version of Mark contained the leather girdle or that he added it in order to match John more closely to the Elijah of 2 Kings 1.8. In the latter case, a later redactor then 'corrected' Mark's account. Matthew's concern was perhaps to show John to be a genuine prophet. Without the leather girdle, John's dress would reflect the description of the prophets in Zech. 13.4. Here, the prophets are false ones.

The leather girdle is found in by far the vast majority of texts. There is no reason to dismiss it simply because it is missing from only two. It would be more productive to assess whether Mark presents an accurate description of John, or simply his own portrait. This is an important point because of the church's interest in identifying John with Elijah and, as such, any description of John the Baptist wearing clothes that immediately associate him with Elijah should be regarded with suspicion.[9]

However, Mark might simply have tried to highlight John association with the wilderness and his asceticism. In other words, Mark might have invented John's dress to illustrate his evaluation of him. On the other hand, John's garments of camel's hair and leather were the most practical and readily available to a man living in the desert. Camels were of prime importance to the desert nomad, who heavily depended upon them.[10] John's clothing does not necessarily reflect those of Elijah, but rather, might stem from the traditional dress of the Bedouin and other desert dwellers.[11] As such, John was not imitating Elijah, nor did he want to be mistaken for him; his camel's hair and leather girdle were authentic.

To state that there is no symbolism in John's clothing, however, is surely incorrect. Camel hair was used in the making of sackcloth. Such material was worn by those in mourning (Gen. 37.34; 2 Sam. 3.31; Isa. 15.3; 22.12; Jer. 4.8; 6.26; 48.37; 49.3; Ezek. 27.31; Ps 30.12). It indicated repentance (Jonah 3.5-10;

1. Caravaggio depicts John the Baptist using chiaroscuro to great effect: 'He was not the light, but came only to bear witness to the light' (Jn 1.8).

2. The Angel Gabriel announces that the elderly Elizabeth is to have a son: John the Baptist. Like Jesus, John was a miracle baby.

3. The birth of John the Baptist, depicted on an embroidery by Benozzo Gozzoli, 1460–80. (Metropolitan Museum of Art)

4. The Birth and Circumcision of John the Baptist.

5. Even as a child, John is shown to bear witness to Jesus.

Above: 6. Another depiction of John the Baptist bearing witness to Jesus. Here, John is an adult, while Jesus is still a child. Luke's Gospel, however, shows that John was only six months older than his cousin.

Left: 7. The young John the Baptist begins his mission. Wearing his camel hair garments, he already bears witness to the Christ.

8. The desert wastes attracted several prophets, who sought to re-enact important events in which God intervened in history and to look for signs that God would do so again.

9. The prophet, Elijah, with whom John is often associated.

10. John preachers in the wilderness, calling people to repent of their sins and be baptised.

11. *Saint John the Baptist Preaching*, Anton Raphael Mengs.

12. The living waters of the River Jordan provide the setting for John's baptising ministry.

13. Al-Maghtas, putative site of John's ministry.

Above: 14. Guido Reni's *The Baptism of Christ.*

Right: 15. Jan van Scorel's *The Baptism of Christ.*

16. While John urged people to prepare for the coming of God, the Gospels interpreted John's message as preparing the way for Christ.

Right: 17. John the Baptist holds the iconography of Christ, whose forerunner or witness he is.

Below: 18. John's preaching brought him to the attention of Herod Antipas, who ordered his arrest and held him in his palace at Machaerus.

19. *The Arrest of Saint John the Baptist* by Reynaud Levieux.

20. *Herodias with the Head of St John the Baptist*, Paul Delaroche. (Wallraf-Richartz Museum)

Above: 21. Aguste Rodin, *The Severed Head of Saint John the Baptist, c.* 1887.

Left: 22. Salome as depicted by Aubrey Beardsley.

23. *Salome with the Head of Saint John the Baptist*, Andrea Solario, 1507. (Metropolitan Museum of Art)

24. A Byzantine medallion depicting Saint John the Baptist, *c.* 1100. (Metropolitan Museum of Art)

25. Mistletoe – as a saint, John has several plants and flowers associated with him. Mistletoe is perhaps the most important of these.

Above: 26. Thirteenth-century Knights of Saint John of Jerusalem. (Ralph Hammann under Creative Commons)

Left: 27. Philippe, duc d'Orléans depicted as John the Baptist, showing the iconography of the saint.

Q 10.13) and humility before God (1 Kings 21.2-9; Isa. 58.3-5; 69.11; Neh. 9.1-2). Prophets might have taken to wearing sackcloth because of their faith in God and their understanding that they spoke on his behalf.[12]

John's camel-hair garment, therefore, represents the sackcloth of humility and repentance. Uncomfortable clothing was frequently used by ascetics as a means of penance. Josephus speaks of in this context of Bannus (*Life* 11), who wore 'no other clothing than what grew upon trees'. There is good reason to accept that John wore a garment made of camel's hair, whether or not it was fashioned into sackcloth, and that he held it together with a leather belt. He dressed in such a way because he lived the life of a prophet who was also a desert nomad. It was quite simply the most practical and readily available garment for those who would frequent the wilderness wastes.

Nevertheless, that Mark has already primed his readers to think of John the Baptist as Elijah must not be lost sight of. Mark has already indicated that John is the forerunner who would prepare the way. He then interrupts his four-step arrangement of introduction, prophecy, announcement and Jesus' appearance, by giving his readers a description of John's clothes. What John wore is clearly important to Mark, and this is confirmed by the fact that the evangelist does not bother to describe Jesus' clothing.

The significance of John's garments does not lie in Mark's wish to show John as a prophet or a desert nomad. Such people were common enough and usually did not inspire comment. What matters to Mark is that his readers should infer that John is the eschatological prophet: Elijah. Hence, he is anxious to show John wearing the same clothes as Elijah, as described in 2 Kings 1.8. John certainly was a prophet, but for Mark, he was more than a prophet, he was Elijah. Having established this connection in his readers minds, Mark can now bring to centre stage the one for whom John acts as a forerunner, and whose ministry John's announcement served to give endorsement: Jesus.

Prophetic endorsement of Jesus' ministry was of the utmost importance to the early church. Mark returns to this theme in a key passage that again links John with Elijah. In Mk 9.9-13, Jesus returns from his transfiguration. He orders his disciples not to reveal what they have just witnessed 'until the Son of man should have risen from the dead' (Mk 9.9). The disciples then begin to talk among themselves, wondering what rising from the dead could mean. They ask Jesus 'why do the scribes say that first Elijah must come' (Mk 9.11). Jesus answers that Elijah had come already, but he had been made to suffer. Jesus links the suffering of Elijah to the suffering to be expected by the Son of man (Mk 9.12-13). He then closes this subject by implying that Elijah's suffering has been prophesied: 'as it is written of him' (Mk 9.13). Although Mark makes no such statement outright, he makes Jesus imply that John the Baptist, who died at the hands of Herod, should be identified as Elijah *redivivus*.

Mark's reference to the death of John is significant because of his concern to develop a parallel between it and that of Jesus. Thus, Mark allows his readers to believe that John was executed at Herod Antipas's palatial residence at Tiberias, rather than the historically more acceptable location of Machaerus. Jesus, on the other hand, is crucified outside Jerusalem's city walls, on Golgotha. Each of these places is associated with death. Tiberias had been built upon the site of a burial ground, while Golgotha, the name of which comes from the Aramaic *gulgultā*, meaning 'skull.' Furthermore, John's burial (Mk 6.29) will be echoed in Mk 15.45, 46, when it will be Jesus who is buried.

However, Mark's concerns extend beyond even the ministry of Jesus to the Christian community itself. His story is a drama in three acts.[13] In each act, someone preaches and is then 'delivered up'. Act one involves John the Baptist, who 'preaching a baptism...' (1.7) and is then arrested (1.14). In act two, Jesus is 'preaching the Gospel of God' (1.14). He then predicts that he will be 'delivered into the hands of men' (9.31), or 'delivered to the chief priests and the scribes' (10.33). In the third act, the community will preach: 'the Gospel must first be preached to all nations' (13.10). Jesus warns the community that it will, in its turn, be delivered up (13.9-13). The climax of the drama will be the return of Jesus as the Son of man (13.26). Mark, therefore, establishes a link between the fate of John the Baptist, the fate of Jesus and the fate of the church. His account of John's death shows it to be a forerunner of that of Christ but also as a part of a salvation history story, which will find its fulfilment in the *parousia*.

As in Q, Mark portrays John the Baptist as the forerunner of Jesus who, for Mark, is Lord and Christ. Also like Q, Mark links John's role of forerunner to John's association with Elijah.

Mark differs from Q in that he depicts John as 'the baptiser' (4.1). This indicates that Mark regards John's baptising ministry to be at least as important as his prophesying. The reason for this is that it is at Jesus' baptism by John that the reader is made aware of Jesus' true identity (1.10-11). However, only Jesus perceives the heavenly phenomena that accompany his baptism. In this way, Mark is able to introduce his 'messianic secret' motif; that is, Jesus' attempts to preserve the secrecy of his identity and his work.

Mark never makes John's identification with Elijah explicit. Instead, he offers hints, by means of referencing Hebrew Bible proof texts and allusions to Elijah's clothing, that suggest to those of his readers who are aware of the description of Elijah in 2 Kings 1.8 that such an association should be made. Next, he relates a dialogue between Jesus and his disciples wherein reference is made to Elijah, with a suggestion that his mission, although successful, ended tragically. Once again, it is left to the reader to discover a connection between Elijah and John who, at this point in the narrative, is dead. Mark, therefore, constructs an 'Elijianic secret' for John that parallels the 'messianic secret' with which he surrounds Jesus. Finally, Mark includes an account of John's suffering and death, which are to be understood as prefiguring Jesus' own. Having fulfilled his function as the baptiser of Jesus, John is removed from the scene. His death is presented in such a way that the reader should make a connection between this event and the crucifixion of Jesus. John, therefore, becomes the forerunner of Christ in death as well as in life. His death, following a successful ministry, negates questions regarding the success of Jesus' ministry. In short, John could be divinely ordained as the prophet of Christ, yet still die. By the same token, Jesus is able to be Christ, yet still die. Mark, therefore, continues John's association with Elijah, and his role as Jesus' forerunner even to his death.

Forerunner Motifs in Matthew

The Gospel of Matthew sets the scene for John the Baptist by means of the Isa. 40.3 prophecy, first used in Mark. Matthew also retains Mark's description of John's clothing, thus alluding to the now established association between John the Baptist and Elijah. When Matthew introduces John the Baptist, he portrays him as the fiery apocalyptic preacher taken from his Q source. John's announcement of the Coming One is Matthew's cue to introduce Jesus. Matthew, like Mark and, as far as can be ascertained, Q, uses structure as well as dialogue as a literary device as he sets up the presentation of the now adult Jesus, about to embark upon his earthly ministry.

The scene of Jesus' baptism by John is appropriated for the purpose of identifying Jesus to those who witness the event. The heavenly voice no longer speaks to Jesus alone; instead, Matthew's use of the third person indicates that the voice is addressing the crowd. John, however, does not belong to the group so addressed because he already knows who Jesus is.

This is, of course, implied by his announcement of the Coming One, which preceded Jesus' arrival. It is further, and more strongly, indicated by his reaction to Jesus as the latter approaches him to be baptised. John tries to refuse to baptise Jesus, saying, 'I need to be baptised by you, and do you come to me?' (3.14).

John's status as forerunner is enhanced by Matthew's summary of his message (3.1), which is expressed in terms corresponding with summaries of the messages of Jesus (4.17) and his disciples (10.7). Matthew also retains the link, found in both Q and Mark, between John's status of forerunner and his identification as Elijah.

At first, Matthew's identification of John as Elijah is implicit. He suggests it by appropriating Mark's description of John's clothing. To those of his readers who are aware of 2 Kings 1.8, the association should be apparent. Elsewhere, Matthew is less subtle, and offers guidance for those of his readers who might have missed the point by rearranging his sources so that they express more readily what he wants to say. For instance, he inserts Q 16.16 into Q 7.24-28, and adds a passage of his own. The effect of this editing is that, as Jesus eulogises John, he is able to explain to his hearers who they should interpret him to be: 'the law and the prophets prophesied until John; and if you are willing to accept it, he is Elijah who is to come' (11.13-14). That such words are attributed to Jesus gives them greater authority. Similarly, in the scene, taken over from Mark, following the Transfiguration account, Matthew adds 'then the disciples knew that he was speaking to them of John the Baptist' (17.13).

Matthew also makes it clearer than does Mark that John's suffering and death should be seen as the precursor to Jesus' own: 'I tell you that Elijah has come ... but they did to him whatever they pleased. So also the Son of man will suffer at their hands' (17.12). To further emphasise his point, Matthew offers some striking similarities between his accounts of the deaths of John the Baptist and Jesus.[14] Both men were condemned by rulers. In John's case, it was Herod Antipas (14.9), with Jesus, it was Pilate (27.11-26). Both men were seized (John: 14.3; Jesus: 21.46) and bound (John: 14.3; Jesus: 27.2). Herod feared the people because they held John to be a prophet (14.5). The chief priests and Pharisees feared the people because they held Jesus to be a prophet (21.46). Both Herod (14.6-11) and Pilate (27.11-26) were reluctant to kill their respective prisoners. Moreover, just as Herod executed John but let his disciples go free, so would Pilate execute Jesus while sparing his disciples.[15] In contrast, John was buried by his faithful disciples (14.12). Jesus was deserted by his existing disciples (26.56b) and buried by one new disciple (27.57-61).

Clearly, Matthew has adopted and expanded Mark's use of the account of John's death. For Matthew, as well as for Mark, the fate of John foreshadows the fate of Jesus. The connection between the two events is confirmed when John's disciples go to tell Jesus what has become of their master (14.12). By this means, Matthew is able to anchor the event to the fate of his main character, Jesus.[16]

In Matthew, as in Mark, the story of the death of John the Baptist is redacted so that it corresponds with the theological concerns of the evangelist. These concerns are to show the price of discipleship (Mark) and to draw a parallel between the death of John and that of Jesus (Mark and Matthew). It also draws a parallel between the fate of Jesus and that which could await the early missionaries. The conclusion the evangelists wish their readers to draw from their accounts of the death of John the Baptist is a simple one. John the Baptist can be executed, yet still be the forerunner of the Christ. Jesus can be crucified, yet still be the Christ. The church can suffer persecution, yet still be the true, divinely appointed church. The death of John the Baptist, while having a sound historical basis, provided the early church with the means to support and encourage its members. This event, presented as a flashback to the past, would serve to sustain the early church through a difficult and dangerous future.

Matthew, then, portrays John along similar lines as Q and Mark. In his presentation of John's prophetic and baptising ministry, which is drawn from these two sources, Matthew preserves John's role as the forerunner of Jesus.

Matthew has also taken from Q and Mark the implicit suggestion that John the Baptist should be interpreted as Elijah *redivivus*. However, while the two earlier Gospels make such an association implicit, Matthew has made it explicit. Whatever ambiguity Matthew might have discovered in his original sources, he removed as he wrote his own Gospel.

Mark's treatment of the death of John, which he presented in such a way as to provide strong links with that of Jesus, was adopted by Matthew. Here again, Matthew has strengthened the links by removing ambiguity and adding more parallels between the two accounts.

Forerunner Motifs in Luke

Luke's approach of dividing salvation history into three periods influences his treatment of John the Baptist. John, whose ministry belongs to the first period, that of the 'law and the prophets' (16.16), precedes that of Jesus' earthly ministry, which marks the second period. The third period, which is the interval between the Ascension and the *parousia*, is the theme of Acts.

Luke opens his Gospel with two infancy narratives in which the events surrounding the births of John the Baptist and Jesus respectively are recorded. That of John the Baptist opens with an angelic announcement and is provided with a setting in time and place: 'In the days of Herod ... in Judaea' (1.5). It also introduces the characters of John's parents, who are Zechariah, a priest, and Elizabeth, who is 'of the daughters of Aaron' (1.6). Luke foes on to explain that this couple are childless and have no hope of having a child because both are old, and Elizabeth is barren (1.7).

As Zechariah performs his priestly duties (1.8-10), he is confronted by 'an angel of the Lord standing on the right side of the altar of incense' (1.11). Zechariah is afraid, but the angel reassures him (1.12), and this sets the stage for the announcement proper: Zechariah's wife Elizabeth will have a child (1.13-17). Zechariah protests, asking the angel how such miracle could come about, given the circumstances of the couple (1.18). The angel answers, but also punishes Zechariah for his incredulity by silencing him (1.19-20). The people, who are waiting outside for Zechariah to bless them, witness his muteness (1.21-22). Then, his time of service having come to an end, Zechariah returns home to his wife, who subsequently conceives (1.23-24). Elizabeth acknowledges that her pregnancy is the result of divine intervention (1.25).

This is the basic structure of the announcement of John's birth as given by Luke. Its legendary character, the motifs of which are immediately obvious, firmly belongs in Jewish tradition.[17] All the elements are present. There is the announcement of the birth, including the name the child is to be given (cf. Gen. 16.11; 17.19). It is noted that the mother is unable to have children (cf. Gen. 15.2; Judg. 13.5; 2 Kings 4.14). There is disbelief, sometimes accompanied by a request for a sign (Gen. 15.8; Judg. 6.36-38; 1 Sam. 1.2; 2 Kings 20.8-11; Isa. 7.10) and angelic reassurance (Gen. 15.1). Indeed, the entire angelic announcement follows an established Hebrew Bible five-element pattern.[18] 1, an angel appears to the mother or the father. 2, the person so confronted is afraid. 3, the angel makes his announcement, which is often stereotyped. 4, the person hearing the message objects or asks for a sign. 5, the sign, or some reassurance, is given. This pattern features in the birth announcements of Ishmael (Gen. 7-13), Isaac (Gen. 17.1-21) and Samson (Judg. 13.3-20).

The first two chapters of Luke, then, represent the evangelist's pietistic reflection upon Hebrew Bible themes. Specifically, Luke wanted to expand Matthew's birth account of Jesus and certain elements therein, the most prominent of which is its focus upon the book of Genesis. Luke has woven, as it were, a tapestry using Genesis colours, which forms his Baptist Infancy Narrative: just as the old Israel began with Abraham and Sarah, so the new Israel begins with Zechariah and Elizabeth, the parents of John the Baptist. The parallels are obvious. Elizabeth is barren (Lk.1.17), as was Sarah (Gen. 11.30). Like Abraham and Sarah, Zechariah and Elizabeth are old (Lk. 1.7; Gen. 13.11). Both Abraham (Gen. 17.16) and Zechariah (Lk. 1.13) receive a divine message that their respective wives will give them a son. Both are told the name the child should be given (Lk. 1.13; Gen.17.19). The sequence is interrupted only when Elizabeth uses Rachel's words in response to her pregnancy, rather than Sarah's (Lk. 1.25; Gen. 30.23; cf. Gen. 18.12).

Luke sees Zechariah as the new Abraham. He is the one with whom the new redemption begins because he is the father of John the Baptist. As such, he chose the name of this new Abraham with care. Gabriel uses words taken from Malachi (4.6) to explain John's purpose (Lk. 1.17). Since the Book of Zechariah immediately precedes Malachi in the Hebrew canon, Zechariah is the most appropriate name for John's father.[19] Moreover, Zechariah begins with the words: 'In the eighth month, in the second year of Darius, the word of the Lord came to Zechariah the son of Berechiah, son of Iddo, the prophet, saying...' (Zech 1.1). Luke, on the other hand, introduces the ministry of John the Baptist in a similar, though expanded, manner:

In the fifteenth year of the reign of Tiberius Caesar, Pontius Pilate being governor of Judaea, and Herod being tetrarch of Galilee, and his brother Philip tetrarch of the region of Ituraea and Trachonitis, and Lysanias tetrarch of Abilene, in the high priesthood of Annas and Caiaphas, the word of God came to John the son of Zechariah in the wilderness... (Lk 3.1-2).

Thus, Luke is able to show that the new covenant will begin with the herald of Malachi, succeeded by a new Zechariah and that 'the Law and the Prophets were until John' (Lk.16.16).[20] Still more parallels can be found. Zechariah is the name of the last martyr of the Old Covenant (2 Chron. 24.21-2). He was also a priest and a prophet (2 Chron. 24.20). This gave Luke his precedent for the priestly origins of John (Lk. 1.5), who was also a prophet (Lk. 3.2).

There is, therefore, a logical reason why Luke should choose Zechariah as the name of John the Baptist's father. However, Luke also appears to have taken John's mother's name, Elizabeth, from the Hebrew Bible, having borrowed it from Aaron's wife (Ex. 6.23). It is an appropriate name because John's mother is shown to belong to the 'daughters of Aaron' (1.5). However, perhaps more significantly, Elizabeth had an apparently more worthy sister-in-law, Miriam or Mary (Ex. 15.20; Num. 12.1-15; 20.1). The contrast between the less important Elizabeth and the more important Mary,[21] echoes Luke 1.36-45. Here, the significance, in relation to each other, of the children each woman is carrying is revealed. Even before he is born, Elizabeth's child, John, reacts to the presence of the superior Jesus, whom Mary is carrying.

Zechariah belongs to the priestly division of Abijah, which is the eighth priestly division according to 1 Chron. 24.10. The same source states that the next course, the ninth, is that of Jeshua, or Jesus. It is reasonable, therefore, that the forerunner of Jesus should belong to the priestly course that precedes that of Jesus. It naturally follows that Luke should give John priestly origins, and so he has (Lk. 1.5);[22] this is in order to reinforce his position as forerunner. Luke was aware that the tribe of Judah, to which Jesus belongs, (Mt. 1.20; 2.6), was preceded by that of Levi, to which John belongs (1.5). Moreover, the priesthood of Aaron is considered to be imperfect in contrast to that of Christ (Heb. 5.4; 7.11).

Every element of the Baptist Infancy Narrative can be attributed to Luke's gifted creativity. Zechariah's name was taken from the

Hebrew Bible prophetic book of that name. It was chosen because this book preceded Malachi, a book which is so significant in Christian interpretation of John the Baptist. Malachi foretells the coming of Elijah, with whom John is associated in Lk 1.17, as well as in the pre-Lukan traditions of Q (7.27) and Mark (1.2). Zechariah also shares two characteristics with another man of the same name: priest and prophet. Elizabeth was chosen as the name of John's mother because is it the name of Aaron's wife, who is overshadowed by her sister-in-law, Miriam. Nevertheless, Elizabeth is of the tribe of Aaron, which belongs to Levi. This tribe goes before that of Judah. Finally, Zechariah is of the priestly course, Abijah, which precedes that of Jeshua. There is, then, a clear connection between the Baptist Infancy Narrative and Genesis, the beginning of the new order and that of the old. Moreover, a strong forerunner motif runs through Luke's choice of names for his characters, their tribes and their priestly courses.

On the other hand, it is possible that Luke's Baptist Infancy Narrative was inspired by traditions that originated with the Jewish worshippers of John the Baptist.[23] In favour of this hypothesis is the fact that the work has a highly Jewish quality. There is a distinct absence of any inferiority of John; no attempt is made in this section of the gospel to portray him as Jesus' forerunner. The fact that Gabriel was sent by God to announce John's birth and future role (1.19) underlines the miraculous nature of John's birth and shows that his ministry is divinely ordained. Certainly, John the Baptist is held in particularly high esteem in the first chapter of Luke. However, the narrative does conform to the traditional Christian view of John as a prophet (cf. 1.76) and the new Elijah (1.17), whose role is to preach repentance.

Whatever the origins of the underlying traditions behind it, in Luke's Baptist Infancy Narrative, the announcement, birth, circumcision, naming and upbringing of John parallel those of Jesus in Luke's hands. The pivotal passage is 1.36, wherein Luke shows that the mothers of John and Jesus are related. Mary has an excuse to visit Elizabeth, which provides the baby John with the opportunity to leap in his mother's womb in what is his first witness to Jesus (1.41). Even before he is born, then, John's success as a witness to Jesus is demonstrated when his mother becomes filled with the Holy Spirit and recognises the divinity of Mary's child (1.44-45).

John is biologically Jesus' forerunner, since he is the eldest by six months. However, he is also Jesus' forerunner theologically. John, Luke states, will be 'filled with the Holy Spirit even from his mother's womb' (1.15), and he will be called 'the prophet of the Most High' (1.76). Jesus, on the other hand, is conceived by the Holy Spirit (1.35), and so is 'the Son of the Most High' (1.32), called 'holy, the Son of God' (1.36).[24]

John's status as a prophet is demonstrated in the way Luke introduces his ministry. He announces that 'the word of God came to John the son of Zechariah in the wilderness' (3.2). Luke's account of John's call to prophecy recalls similar patterns found within the Hebrew Bible (Isa. 38.4; Jer. 1.1; 13.3). Luke also includes the Q passage, wherein Jesus confirms John as a prophet, and indeed, 'more than a prophet' (7.26). In Luke, John is still associated with the prophet of Mal. 3.1, and so, Elijah. However, Luke does not assert John's identification with Elijah, as does Matthew (11.13-14). Even in the infancy narrative, the reader is told that John will be endowed with 'the spirit and power of Elijah', and that his future task will reflect that of Elijah (1.17; cf. Mal. 4.6; Sir. 48.10). However, elsewhere Luke omits any indication, implicit or otherwise, that John should be associated with this figure. For example, he does not describe John's dress. He also omits the dialogue, found in Mk 9.9-13 and taken over by Matthew (17.9-13), wherein John is implicitly (Mark) or explicitly (Matthew) associated with Elijah.

Luke is eager to separate John the Baptist from Jesus. For example, he does not show Jesus being baptised by John. Rather, he makes it clear that John is in prison before he relates his account of Jesus' baptism (3.20-21). Luke offers no account of the Transfiguration story, and so is unable to follow it with the statement, attributed to Jesus', that draws links between John's fate and that of Jesus. Luke also fails to give an account of John's imprisonment and execution, thereby removing any suggestion that John's suffering and death prefigure Jesus' own. Although he does mention Herod's involvement, there is nothing to link John's fate with that of Jesus in the reader's mind (3.19-20). This approach is influenced by Luke's separation of salvation history into three stages or periods.

Luke continues the forerunner motif into Acts, where both Peter (1.21-2; 10.34-8) and Paul (13.23-5) speak of John as having gone before Jesus. The theme is also extended to John's baptism. Specifically, John's water baptism is compared and contrasted with Jesus' spirit baptism (1.4-5) and is understood to be a preparation for it (11.15-17). However, Jesus' spirit baptism supersedes John's water baptism (19-1.7). These passages might also imply John's subordination to Jesus. Although Luke does not seem to make a theme of this motif, he does preserve the Q passage wherein John's position in the kingdom of God is devalued (7.28).

In summary, Luke maintains John the Baptist's status as forerunner to Jesus. However, perhaps more important to Luke is that John's ministry should be understood as the predecessor of that of Jesus. Luke divides salvation history into three phases or periods. John the Baptist belongs to the first period, while Jesus' earthy ministry is the second. Luke achieves his aim by the subtle and clever use of Hebrew Bible motifs contained within the birth narratives of other great figures in Jewish history. Much of this material is drawn from Genesis, so that the beginning of the new order reflects that of the old. In this way, Luke is able to introduce his theme, which will be developed later in the Gospel, of the separation of salvation history into three distinct periods.

Luke retains John's association with Elijah, albeit somewhat loosely; he makes John Elijah-like rather than explicitly depicting him as Elijah *redivivus*. Luke also shows John engaging in eschatological preaching (3.7-9), adding that he taught as well (3.10-14; 11.1). Still, Luke's primary concern is to separate John the Baptist and Jesus, especially in salvation history.

Forerunner Motifs in the Fourth Gospel

So far, the evangelists have been fairly consistent in their evaluation of John the Baptist. Reading through the Gospels as they appear in the New Testament, the reader might think that he or she has learned how to assess John in terms of who he is and what his role is understood to be. Quite simply, John the Baptist is the forerunner of Christ who has some association with the prophet, Elijah. The Fourth Gospel, however, presents a radical departure from this viewpoint. John's role in this Gospel can be summarised in one word: witness.

The Fourth Evangelist's principal reason for writing his Gospel is 'that you may believe that Jesus is the Christ, the Son of God' (20.31). This is also, as far as the Fourth Evangelist is concerned, John's *raison d'être*. By making him the supreme witness to Jesus, the Fourth Evangelist presents John as the archetypical Christian evangelist, whose sole mission is to proclaim the Christ to whom he is both subordinate and humble. In other words, the Fourth Evangelist takes it upon himself to make a Christian of John the Baptist.

John the Baptist's role of witness is obvious from the very beginning of the Fourth Gospel. The prologue, which, like Luke's Baptist Infancy Narrative, contains allusions to Genesis (1.1; cf. Gen. 1.1), is interrupted so that John might be introduced. John came 'for testimony, to bear witness to the light' (1.7). He proclaims that Jesus 'ranks before me, for he was before me' (1.15, cf. 30). John denies that he is the Christ, Elijah or the prophet (1.20-1). Rather, he is 'the voice of one crying in the wilderness, "Make straight the way of the Lord"...' (1.23). John now actually speaks the words of prophecy that are merely brought into association with him in the Synoptics (Mk 1 3 and par.).

The Baptist's denial that he is Elijah is significant because, like Luke, the Fourth Evangelist has no need to connect the two men. In the Synoptics, Elijah is associated with John's status of forerunner. However, in another departure from the Synoptic viewpoint, the Fourth Evangelist's John does not announce the one who is to come, but one who is already present though as yet unknown (1.26-7). The difference arises because the Fourth Evangelist portrays Jesus, the Christ, as an eternal being. He has existed from the beginning (1.1-5). Consequently, John cannot be the forerunner of someone who is already present. Since the Fourth Evangelist does not equate John with Elijah, he is able to dispense with the description of John's clothing as found in Mark and Matthew. Since John is not Jesus' forerunner, there is no need to include an account of John's death and execution. Parallels between this event and Jesus' arrest and crucifixion are of no use to the Fourth Evangelist, and John is allowed simply to disappear from view (5.35).

It would, however, be wrong to state that the Fourth Gospel ignores John's role of forerunner completely. Two passages, 1.15 and 1.30, contain a speech, placed upon John's lips, which assert that John was sent ahead of Christ: 'He who comes after me...' This can be read as a hint of John's forerunner status, a position that is affirmed when he is depicted as saying: 'I have been sent before him' (3.28).

The Fourth Evangelist's John has not always known Jesus' true identity. Only as he was baptising him did John come to realise who Jesus really was. This differs from Luke, whose John recognises Jesus while still in the womb (1.41), and Matthew, whose John goes so far as to ask Jesus to baptise him. Moreover, the dove and the heavenly voice, apparently only seen and heard by Jesus in Mark (1.10-11), though also observed by the crowds in Matthew (3.16-17), appear to be for John alone in the Fourth Gospel (1.32-34). Here, Jesus' baptism seems to have been intended solely to identify Jesus to John, so that John can bear witness to Jesus and proclaim to Israel that Jesus is 'the Son of God' (1.34).

John's sudden, though quiet, departure from the Fourth Gospel is, in fact, a necessary part of his role, 'he must increase, but I must decrease' (3.30). However, his success as a witness is demonstrated when John's own disciples go over to Jesus (1.35-42). Jesus himself confirms the truth of John's testimony (5.31-3), as do the many who came to Jesus. 'John did no sign,' they said, 'but everything that John said about this man was true' (10.41). It should be noted, however, that not everyone believed after hearing John's testimony. There were those who continued to look elsewhere for eternal life (5.39), or to misinterpret Jesus (6.14).

To summarise, the Fourth Evangelist, in common with Q and the Synoptics, retains John's function as a baptiser. However, as in Q, he never calls John 'the baptiser' or refers to him as 'the Baptist'.

The Fourth Gospel does not explicitly show John as the forerunner of Jesus. For the Fourth Evangelist, this would be impossible. Jesus has existed from the very beginning and, by definition, can have no forerunner. This approach allows the Fourth Evangelist to attribute the reiterated 'he who comes after me ranks before me' (1.15, cf. 30) to John. For the same reason, he refutes any suggestion that John might be Elijah *redivivus*. Elijah, the eschatological prophet, has no place in a Gospel that concerns itself with the Word who was with God and who was God. John, therefore, is primarily a witness. His sole purpose is to testify to Jesus and to identify him to Israel. John bears witness to Jesus, evangelising others and leading them to the Light, while remaining in the shadows and allowing the glory to fall upon Jesus. This is a task in which John is successful, though not universally so.

Conclusion

While the evangelists draw from history or early tradition surrounding John the Baptist, they always evaluate him and interpret his mission in terms of his relationship with Jesus. In the Synoptics, John is an eschatological preacher concerned with the coming kingdom of God. His mission involves the proclamation of, and the preparation for, the Coming One. Once the early church had reinterpreted John's message so that the Coming One now refers to Jesus, John's role as his forerunner was established. Only in the Fourth Gospel is a departure from this assessment of John to be seen. The Fourth Evangelist attributes eternal existence to Jesus and substitutes eternal life for the kingdom of God. Christ is no longer in need of a forerunner and John's mission is modified to accommodate this. Having no coming kingdom of God to proclaim, John becomes the witness *par excellence* to the Christ.

All four canonical Gospels include an account of John baptising Jesus. This event, which was impossible for them to ignore due to its historicity, was treated according to the theology of each evangelist. For Mark and Matthew, it is the occasion upon which the Holy Spirit enters Jesus of Nazareth and he becomes the Christ. This is a personal and private experience for Jesus according to Mark. Matthew makes it more public, using it to identify Jesus to the crowds. Luke also understands Jesus' baptism as the inauguration of his messianic ministry; however, John's role in this is deliberately rendered ambiguous so that his ministry and that of Jesus can be shown to be entirely separate. For Luke, John's baptising ministry is of secondary importance to his main function as forerunner. Yet even here, it is in John's mission, rather than in the man himself, that Luke places the greatest emphasis. John's mission marks the end of the first period of salvation history and is the starting point of the second period, which is Jesus' earthly mission. The Fourth Evangelist uses John's baptism of Jesus to identify Jesus as the Word to John. John is then able to proclaim Christ in fulfilment of his role of witness.

Two sources, Q and Mark, hint at John the Baptist's identification as Elijah *redivivus*. Mark uses a description of John's clothing to guide his readers into making an association between the two prophets. Both Q and Mark carefully insert Hebrew Bible proof texts into strategic points of their accounts, such as a speech of Jesus (Q and Mark) or an opening passage (Mark). This subtle device allows the reader to make the connection between John the Baptist and Elijah in his or her own mind. Matthew has no time for such subtlety; he adds a remark here or a line there in order to make explicit that which was formerly implied.

The Elijah connection appears to have reached its apogee with Matthew. Luke has no use of it since it does not fit into his three-fold structure of salvation history. John's role of forerunner is enough for Luke to get his point across. He is content to make John Elijah-like, an eschatological prophet endowed with the Spirit, and who will go 'in the spirit and power of Elijah' (1.17a) rather than to depict him as Elijah returned. The Fourth Evangelist also has no need to present John as Elijah, implicitly or explicitly. Indeed, he even makes John deny that he is Elijah. The reason for this is simple: Elijah, whether or not one finds him returned in the guise of John the Baptist, is largely portrayed as the prophet who will return to herald the Lord at the eschaton. Since the Fourth Evangelist understands Jesus as the Christ, who was with God and who was God and, most importantly, is pre-existent, he has no need of a forerunner. The Fourth Evangelist, therefore, suppresses this aspect of John's ministry in favour of one that is more suitable to his objective. He makes John a witness to Christ.

John the Baptist, having successfully completed his ministry as the proclaimer or witness to Christ, and having baptised Jesus, is no longer required. Mark and Matthew offer accounts of his death, the details of which are embellished so that readers of the Gospels are able find links between this event and the crucifixion of Jesus. The evangelists elaborate upon the account of John's death for one key purpose: it shows that John's mission could remain a success even though John died. By extension, Jesus could die on the cross and still be the Messiah. Further, the early church could undergo persecution and still survive. Luke mentions John's death, but its significance is much reduced because it is merely part of John's fate as the last of the prophets of the first stage of salvation history. The inauguration of Jesus' ministry heralds the dawning of the second stage, in which there is no further role for John. Similarly, the Fourth Evangelist's representation of John as witness removes the need for him to include John any further in Jesus' ministry. John bore witness to Jesus, many went to Jesus as a result, and so John, having fulfilled his role, is allowed to decrease, fading into the background until he disappears from view.

INTO THE UNDERWORLD

[John the Baptist] was in advance also with those in Hades to announce joyful tidings (De Christo et Antichristo 45)

Death was not the end for John the Baptist. This tragic and brutal event provided the evangelists with much material as they sought to justify Jesus' status in spite of his crucifixion. As they interpreted it, if John could die and still be the divinely appointed forerunner to Christ, then Jesus could die and still be Christ. However, John's death served a purpose in addition to this one, when early Christians came to see it as a continuation of his ministry as forerunner. The execution of John the Baptist was, like his earthly ministry, viewed as also divinely appointed. God's objective was to allow John to descend into the underworld where he could proclaim the coming of Christ to the people there.

Extending John's forerunner status to his death, therefore, includes him in a Jesus tradition that had originated with the early church. Early Christians presented this tradition as part of an apologetic drive that led to the composition and circulation of the passion narratives, which themselves formed the basis of the Gospels. However, this was not the only tradition that would emerge surrounding John the Baptist.

Certain extra-canonical texts reveal a little-known concealment tradition that deserves to be highlighted and evaluated. The starting point, however, is a study of John's descent into the underworld, which is an extension of the tradition as it applies to Christ.

The Sources

One of the earliest occurrences of the tradition concerning Christ's descent into the underworld occurs in the Gospel of Matthew. Other versions are found in Ephesians, where it might be hinted at, and 1 Peter and the *Gospel of Peter*.

The passages containing the descent tradition are special to Matthew and are embedded within the crucifixion account. When separated from their surrounding passages and read concurrently, they form a coherent narrative. Following the tearing of the Temple curtain (27.51), the tombs are opened and the bodies of many of the saints are raised (27-52). After the resurrection, the saints go to the holy city, where they appear to many (27.53). Having witnessed these signs, a centurion becomes a believer (27.54). Next day, the 'chief priests and the Pharisees' go to Pilate to ask for permission to mount a guard at the tomb (27.62-66). Pilate grants their request, but such precautions prove useless because Jesus is raised from the dead (28.2-4).

In Ephesians, it is implied that Christ went into hell to preach to the righteous dead: 'he had also descended into the lower parts of the earth' (4.9). Admittedly, this passage is ambiguous, since 'lower parts of the earth' could refer to earth itself as opposed to the heavens, rather than the underworld. This would give it Gnostic connotations and would reflect a similar doctrine to that found in the Fourth Gospel, where Christ is the Word who came to earth as a man (Jn 1.1, 14).

Turning to 1 Peter, we note that it is influenced by accounts of the suffering of Christians. Its purpose is to encourage strength and resolve through Christ's passion as they suffer and are martyred. I Peter 3.19-20 states that Christ, as part of his mission, preached to the spirits 'in prison'. These spirits might be the souls of the righteous dead, who are presently imprisoned in hell. Equally, they could be angels who had sinned (cf. 2 Peter 2.4) or who had abandoned their sphere (cf. Jude 6). The author's position is clarified in I Peter 4.6, where it is stated that the gospel was read to the dead, 'that though judged in the flesh like men, they might live in the spirit like God.' The message of Christ, therefore, is given to the dead as the means of salvation.

The *Gospel of Peter* consists of four narratives, a passion narrative, an epiphany, an empty tomb story and a resurrection account. It is in the story of the empty tomb (8.28-49), which has many similarities with Matthew's account, that the descent tradition is encountered. According to this account, 'the people' came to believe in Jesus because of signs that accompanied his death (8.28; cf. Mt. 27.54). The 'scribes and Pharisees and elders' then go to Pilate to ask for a guard for the tomb, to which Pilate agrees (8.28, 29-31; cf. Mt. 27.62-6). As an added precaution, a stone is rolled across the entrance of the tomb, which is then sealed (8.32-3; cf. Mt. 28.2-4). Such precautions, however, prove useless. The guards see Christ accompanied by two men, with all three of them being followed by a cross (8.39). A voice from heaven cries out, '"Thou hast preached to them that sleep," and from the cross there was heard the answer, "Yea"' (8.41-2).

There is, then, a development in the tradition surrounding Jesus' mission to the underworld. It seems to have emerged in response to the death of Christ. At first it was necessary to show that the crucifixion, in reality the consequence of the failure of Jesus' prophetic mission, was fully in accord with God's will as it was worked through the actions of Jesus and his followers. Upon death, Jesus descended to the underworld to bring salvation to the righteous dead or to the sinful angels. As Christians began to suffer persecution for their faith, Christ's passion was used as an example to those undergoing persecution and martyrdom for their faith.

The Patristic Interpretation of John's Underworld Mission

Once the tradition of the descent had been established, it was elaborated in order to enhance its interrelation with Christ's earthly mission. Origen believed that, just as the living required prophets to prepare them for the coming of Christ, so too did the dead. Prophets, having completed their work upon earth, would continue their mission in the underworld.

In his *Comment on Matthew* (12.43), Origen states that Moses and Elijah, after conversing with Jesus at the Transfiguration, took the news of their meeting to their fellow prisoners in Hades. As the last of the prophets, John the Baptist is not excluded from this duty, 'and John ... saying, "Do not be afraid" because he has come down into Hades proclaiming the Lord to us, so that he might speak of him who is coming'.[1]

Origen's writings upon this subject are influenced by those of Hippolytus, who tells of how John the Baptist went ahead to Hades, where he announced the joyful news of the coming of Christ, who would save the souls of the righteous through his death.[2] Hippolytus suggests that John's death, which occurred prior to that of Jesus, was intended and timed so that John could act as forerunner to Christ in the lower world. Thus, John's mission in the underworld is a continuation of his earthly one. He goes into the lower regions to preach the coming of Christ and to prepare the way for him.

John's earthly mission was accompanied by a baptism of repentance for the forgiveness of sins. Indeed, as Acts 1.21-2 suggests, John's water baptism was a prerequisite for all those who would become followers of Christ. A second century text, Hermas' *Shepherd*, implies that the dead must also receive water baptism if they are to enter the kingdom of God. Only through baptism could they set aside their deadness and resume life (16.2-3). For Hermas, water represents the waters of the underworld, as well as the waters of baptism. However, it was not John who baptised, but the apostles and teachers, who had preached in the name of God during life. Now dead, they carry on their preaching in the underworld (16.5-7). In contrast, the *Epistula Apostolorum* (26-7)[3] assigns the task of baptism to Jesus.

There is, then, some discrepancy regarding who would baptise the righteous in the underworld: was it Jesus or the apostles and teachers? It can readily be seen why the apostles and teachers should have the task, since Jesus had sent them into the world to baptise as part of the evangelistic commission (Mt. 28.18-20). On the other hand, Jesus might baptise because, historically, he was a baptiser. This aspect of Jesus' mission had by now been suppressed in favour of the more traditional function of bestowing the Holy Spirit. The baptism in the underworld is clearly a water baptism, that is to say, John's baptism, yet there is no mention of John the Baptist. His role of preparing the inhabitants of this realm is restricted to preaching. He who had baptised, and who had unwittingly established the rite as a major sacrament in the Christian church, has lost his function as baptiser in the lower world.

The doctrine of John the Baptist's descent into the underworld closely mirrors the Christian interpretation of him as it was formed in the earliest days, and which is clearly presented in the Synoptic Gospels: John is the forerunner of Jesus. When the Apostolic Fathers extended the theology of the descent to include a baptism for the righteous in the underworld, John had no place in it. His role of baptiser had been taken over by the apostles and teachers, or by Jesus himself. As a result, later Greek authors, such as Theodore Studita (859-826), are able to refer to him, not as 'John the Baptist' or 'John the Baptiser', but rather 'John the Forerunner'.[4]

The Extra-Canonical Interpretation of John

The reason for the change in John's status is difficult to account for, but it is possible to discover an explanation by studying the four extra-canonical Gospels in which John the Baptist is mentioned: the *Gospel of Thomas*, the *Gospel of the Ebionites*, the *Gospel of the Nazoraeans* and the *Protevangelium of James*.

The *Gospel of Thomas* refers to John by name only once: in Jesus' statement that John is exalted above all those born of women, but that those who become as a child will know the Kingdom and will be superior to John.[5] This, then, parallels Jesus' praise of John as given in Q 7.28. It also recalls Mk 10.13-16 (and par.), wherein Jesus states that one must become as a child in order to enter the Kingdom (cf. Jn 3.3).

Elsewhere, Thomas omits reference to John even though he is present in the canonical parallels. Thomas 47.2-5, which immediately follows 46.1-2 but without revealing continuity of thought, speaks of the difficulty of serving two masters, with allusion also to the old and the new wine and wineskins. This can be compared with Mk 2.18-22 and par., which is nevertheless introduced with a reference to John. A similar approach is taken with Thomas 104.1-2, which speaks about fasting (cf. Mk 2.18), yet does not mention John.

On the other hand, Thomas 52.1-2 shows Jesus' disciples speaking of twenty-four prophets of Israel, all of whom were said to have spoken in Jesus. In answer, Jesus tells them that they had overlooked the one still living among them, and that they had spoken only of those who were dead. This living prophet might be John, since John and Jesus had worked alongside, or in conjunction with, each other until John was arrested. However, Thomas 52.1-2 is an isolated saying, and its original context cannot now be discerned.

One final saying reveals much about the *Gospel of Thomas'* attitude towards John: Jesus asked his audience why they came out to the country. Perhaps it was to see a reed shaken by the wind, he suggests, or to see a man dressed in finery like kings and other great men? However, although they are dressed exquisitely, they do not know the truth.[6] This passage should contain explicit reference to John, yet it does not. Instead, it seems to appropriate Q 7.24-8 and apply it to Jesus. Clearly, the *Gospel of Thomas* shows little interest in John the Baptist except perhaps as a prophet, and in one passage in which he is exalted only to be reduced. Considering the form of this Gospel, as a collection of wisdom and prophetic sayings, this is hardly surprising. It is not concerned with actions, and so any reference to John's baptising ministry would be out of place. Moreover, it portrays Jesus as a teacher of wisdom, and even gnosis, and so he does not require a forerunner.

Extant fragments of the *Gospel of the Ebionites* speak only of John's baptising ministry and describe his clothing. Without the surrounding fragments, however, it cannot be determined whether or not the sect wished to associate John with Elijah, as in the Synoptics (Mk 1.6 and par.).

In agreement with Luke 1.5, the *Gospel of the Ebionites* gives the names of John's parents as Zechariah and Elizabeth. It also retains John's priestly lineage. As a priest, John is an authority figure. In contrast to traditions found in the canonical Gospels, John does not appear to proclaim the coming of another, although he does preach a baptism of repentance. In an account predominantly drawn from Matthew (1.13-15), but which is extended by the three-fold repetition of the heavenly voice, Jesus comes to John to be baptised. Unlike the Matthaean account, that of the Ebionites shows that John did not recognise Jesus until the latter was indicated by the descent of a dove and the heavenly voice. As such, it more strongly reflects the Fourth Gospel (1.31-3) at this point.

In the *Gospel of the Ebionites*, John the Baptist is not a forerunner because he does not preach the coming of another, whether Jesus or any other figure. Instead, he is portrayed as a priestly desert preacher whose ministry includes teaching and the performance of a baptism of repentance. The culmination of his career is the baptism of Jesus, which acts as a catalyst for the revelation of Jesus and his identification both to himself and to John.

The *Gospel of the Nazaraeans* mentions John the Baptist once, and this is in the context of Jesus' baptism. Jesus' mother and brothers tell him that John baptises for the remission of sins and suggest that they all go to be baptised. However, Jesus asks what sin he has committed that he should be baptised by John, unless it is that, by asking this question, he is in ignorance. Like the Matthaean passage to which it corresponds (3.13-15), the *Gospel of the Nazoraeans* is concerned to preserve Jesus' sinlessness, which could be questioned by his submission to a baptism designed for repentance. Moreover, it betrays the church's continued unease with Jesus' submission to baptism because of the implication that Jesus became John's disciple, and so inferior to him. As such, the Baptist passage in this text is less about John than it is about Jesus. John is mentioned because he and his baptism appeared in Matthew, the text's original source.

The *Protevangelium of James* (*Prot. Jas*) purports to have been written by James, the half-brother of Jesus. In this second century text, Zechariah is depicted as a high priest (*Prot. Jas* 8.2-3), as opposed to his more humble rank in Luke (1.8-9). When the lot falls to Mary to weave purple and scarlet colours into the veil, Zechariah is struck dumb (*Prot. Jas* 10.1-2; cf. Lk. 1.20-2). John, as yet unborn, leaps in the presence of the pregnant Mary, who has come to visit Elizabeth (*Prot. Jas* 12.2; cf. Lk. 1.39-45). Later, Herod orders the slaughter of all children under two years old (*Prot. Jas* 22.1; cf Mt. 2.13). Elizabeth flees with the young John into the 'hill-country' (*Prot. Jas* 22.3); a rather vague area that nevertheless has traditional associations with John (Lk. 1.39). When she finds nowhere to hide, a mountain miraculously opens up, allowing Elizabeth and the baby to escape Herod's men. Thwarted in his attempt to kill John, Herod sends soldiers to Zechariah, who denies knowledge of his son's whereabouts, even when threatened. Herod's men murder Zechariah on the forecourt of the Temple (*Prot. Jas* 22.1-3; cf. Mt 23.35).

The *Protevangelium of James* says little about John the Baptist. He is not a baptiser. It makes no mention of his future role of forerunner. Indeed, the only hint of his forerunner status is his leaping in his mother's womb when Mary visits her. Even here, however, the allusion is slight.

Much of the material contained within the extra-canonical Gospels about John the Baptist is second hand, drawn as it is from their canonical counterparts. There is very little of John's traditional role of forerunner in any of them. The *Gospel of Thomas* presents him as a prophet, and so reflects that text's status as wisdom and prophetic literature. The *Gospel of the Ebionites* portrays him as a priestly desert figure who baptises Jesus, whose true identity is revealed to John at this event. The *Gospel of the Nazaraeans* merely repeats that which it finds in its source, Matthew. Attention is focused upon John's baptism of Jesus, and the text is careful to show that Jesus was not required to submit to it because he was without sin.

From the accounts of John presented in the extra-canonical literature, it can be deduced that John's position as forerunner of Christ was not universally accepted during the first few centuries of Christianity. The extension of John's role to the underworld was probably in response to continuing quarrels over the relative status of John and Jesus. In particular, a continuing unease with the fact that Jesus submitted to John's baptism for repentance and the forgiveness of sins can be discerned. The unease stems from the implication that Jesus must have sinned. Also, by submitting to John's baptism, Jesus could be seen as inferior to John. This last point is reinforced when traditions of John's priestly status, which would make him an authority figure, are taken into account.

Perhaps more importantly, the *raison d'être* of John's baptism, for repentance and forgiveness, conflicts with Christian interpretation of Jesus' redemptive death on the cross. As John himself is made to say in the Fourth Gospel (1.29), Jesus would take away the sin of the world. This uncomfortable position might have been the driving force behind John's relegation from the bringer of a redemptive baptism to the forerunner of Christ. The negative connotations associated with Jesus' baptism by John were thus counter-balanced by making Jesus, and not John, the baptiser in the underworld.

The Concealment Tradition

John's loss of status as a baptiser is perhaps one of the most unexpected outcomes of his adoption by Christianity. This is more so because he has continued to be referred to as 'John the Baptist' in Christian texts and catechises. However, a survey of the extra-canonical literature reveals a still more unexpected tradition surrounding John the Baptist, a concealment tradition. Hints of this tradition appear in the Pseudo-Clementine Literature, but it is most prominent in the *Protevangelium of James*.

The *Pseudo-Clementine Recognitions* tells of John's disciples separating themselves from the people and speaking to John as though he were concealed, or that they had said that their master was, so to speak, concealed.[7] This suggests a concealment tradition surrounding John. The tradition might have been inspired by the 'Elijahnic secret' found in Mark. However, Mark has a specific reason to invent such a secret: as a literary device to parallel to the Messianic secret with which he surrounds Jesus and his mission.

Another early allusion to the tradition of concealment concerning John occurs in Luke (1.24), and speaks of John's mother, Elizabeth, of whom we are told, 'For five months she hid herself'. However, Elizabeth's seclusion is also a literary device, this time allowing the secret of her pregnancy to be kept until it is revealed to Mary by Gabriel (Lk. 1.36).[8] Elizabeth's pregnancy, serves to prove the truth of God's plan and the authenticity of Gabriel's message. Allusions in Mark and Luke to John the Baptist's concealment are readily explained in theological terms.

The *Protevangelium of James* contains another version of the concealment tradition of John that is not so easily explained. Here, John is hidden by his mother in order to save him from Herod's slaughter of the children (*Prot. Jas* 22.1). A mountain miraculously opens, allowing John and Elizabeth to hide (*Prot. Jas* 22.8). Later, John is protected by his father when he is specifically targeted by Herod (*Prot. Jas* 23.1-3).

This part of the *Protevangelium of James* is concerned with the story of Herod's slaughter of the innocents (Mt. 2.13-18). In a comparable account of this tradition, Matthew (2.13-18) makes no mention of John the Baptist, even though he is only six months older than Jesus (Lk. 1.36), and so would probably have been included among the victims. The compilers of the *Protevangelium of James* might, therefore, have wanted to address this lacuna in John's infancy narrative. Yet, there is no reason why anyone should bother to include John in a writing that is concerned primarily with Mary and Jesus. An explanation can be found if it is remembered that John's status of forerunner is based upon his association with Elijah.

The story of Elijah as presented in 1 Kings reveals several interesting parallels to John's story as given in the *Protevangelium of James*. 1 Kings tells of Jezebel's desire to exterminate all the prophets of Yahweh (18.4, 13). The prophets, however, are saved by Ahab's servant, Obadiah, who hides them in caves and feeds them. Elijah, one of those who managed to escape, is then purposely hunted out by Jezebel (19.1-2). In order to escape, he hides again, this time finding the hiding place himself (19.1-3). Thus, the lives of both John and Elijah are threatened by a person in power, respectively Herod and Jezebel. Both are concealed twice. John is hidden first by his mother and then by his father. Elijah is saved first by a servant, and then by his own initiative. Both manage to escape.

As noted earlier, the *Protevangelium of James* does not depict John as the forerunner of Christ. In view of the concealment tradition embedded into it, however, this assessment should, perhaps, be modified. The *Protevangelium of James* does seem to acknowledge John's by now traditional role of forerunner by associating him with Elijah in a most subtle and original way. There is no open declaration as with Luke (1.17), nor is there any attempt to explain his future role (cf. Lk 1.16-18; 2.76-7). Rather, the *Protevangelium of James* appears to take a story of Elijah and apply it to John in a way that requires the reader to be familiar with the Elijah story and to have the wherewithal to understand the connection between Elijah and John the Baptist. As such, the concealment tradition of John the Baptist is probably an aspect of his role of forerunner of Christ.

Conclusion

The early church established and then consolidated the role of John the Baptist as the forerunner of Christ. His prophetic status and role of baptiser continued to be acknowledged. However, those aspects of John's mission gradually lost their importance in church doctrine concerning John. Persistent attempts to promote John as a figure of authority were doomed to failure in the face of burgeoning orthodoxy, which extended John's role of precursor to the underworld and guaranteed his place within salvation history as interpreted according to Christian values. John, the fiery Jewish apocalyptic preacher, became the first Christian. Now as meek as the Lamb whose coming he is said to have foretold, John the Baptist's place within Christianity is assured as the baptiser, but more importantly, the forerunner of Christ.

9

SAINT JOHN THE BAPTIST

John the Baptist became firmly established as forerunner from the earliest times. He performed this role within the world of the living, and then in that of the dead. John's status as forerunner in the underworld coincided with his loss of status as a baptiser. John the Baptiser, now John the Forerunner, was tamed and embraced by the church with honour, and his altered status brought with it still another attribute, sainthood.

In its early usage, the term 'saint' referred to those who had become members of the church by receiving the Gospel, rejecting sin and living righteously, and they are referred to as such in the New Testament (Acts 26.10; Rom. 12.13; 1 Cor. 6.2). Gradually, the term came to be applied to all those who had died as Christians, and who now dwelled in heaven and were able to intercede on behalf of the living. Finally, 'saint' described someone deemed worthy of special honour and veneration. Such people were observed only in the town in which they lived or the order to which they belonged.

In the early church, the bishop was responsible for the control of the cult of saints in his diocese. Occasionally, however, the veneration of a saint would cross diocesan borders and caused problems which required the need for papal intervention and control.

The first historically attested papal canonisation was that of
St Ulrich of Augsburg, who was canonised by John XV in 993.
However, it was not until the papacy of Gregory IX (1227-41)
that the cult of saints came formally under the jurisdiction of the
Roman Catholic Church. The majority of the saints affected by
this control were local saints, the sanctity of many of whom is
undergoing review to this day. Among those whose feasts have
been reduced in recent years are St Valentine, St Christopher and
St Nicholas. The cult of John the Baptist, however, is not simply
that of a local saint, nor is it subject to review. The precise dating
of John's canonisation cannot now be established, but his cult
is mentioned in the 'Canon of the Mass', which was known to
Ambrose (c. 339-97) in an early form, and again in its virtually
fixed form under the papacy of Gregory I (591-604). John's
canonisation, therefore, occurred prior to the fourth century.

Why John the Baptist should be a saint at all is, at first, difficult
to determine. This man, whom the church was so careful to assess
according to its own interpretation of Jesus of Nazareth and his
mission, would appear to merit no such exalted position within its
ranks as sainthood. However, once it had re-evaluated John to its
own satisfaction and had established him as the forerunner of the
Christ, thus removing from him any threat of superseding Jesus'
significance and role in salvation history, the church was free to
extol him according to the status it had imposed upon him. It
became appropriate to venerate John the Baptist as a major player
in God's plan of salvation and to canonise him as a saint.

Canonisation is a solemn proclamation that the person
nominated for sainthood has practiced heroic virtue and lived in
faith to the grace of God. Grace is God's supernatural support,
which is given to a rational being with a view to sanctification.[1]
Grace is bestowed in order that the person so favoured can work
in harmony with the divine will. In other words, a person is
chosen by God to fulfil a task or to dedicate their lives to serving
God and, in return, they will receive sanctification.

Working in harmony with the divine will can be defined as living a life of humility or exemplary conduct, sometimes it can include the founding of an order or dying as a martyr. Since John the Baptist had accepted his divinely appointed office and carried it out so effectively and selflessly that it led to his death, his sacrifice is acknowledged with gratitude by the church. His martyr's death, and his life devoted to God and to Christ, and which was filled with holy deeds, according to the Christian viewpoint, ensured his acceptance as a saint by the church. The church made John the Baptist a saint because it saw his life as one of dedication to God and to Christ, and his death as that of a martyr to his beliefs.

The Nativity of Saint John the Baptist

Because so much significance had been given to the birth of John the Baptist, one of his feast days was celebrated on the supposed anniversary of his nativity, 24 June. As the thirteenth-century Dominican teacher and preacher, Voragine (1993a:335), noted, John's birthday was worthy of celebration because Gabriel had sanctioned it as a day for rejoicing: 'and you will have joy and gladness, and many will rejoice at his birth' (Lk 1.14). The birth of John the Baptist has been observed since the fourth century, in contrast with the church's usual practice of celebrating the feast day of a saint upon the anniversary of his or her death, or the translation of their relics.

The respective births of John and Jesus are celebrated on days that diametrically oppose one another on the calendar. John's birthday is six months earlier than that of Jesus. Moreover, they coincide with the two great pagan fire festivals of midsummer and midwinter respectively. The church's imposition of the festival of the birth of John the Baptist onto Midsummer's Day could cynically be interpreted as a deliberate attempt to usurp the event for its own purpose. Certainly, the church imposed many of its festivals onto already existing pagan celebrations in an attempt to

'Christianise' pagans by subterfuge. Both Christmas and Easter are examples of this practice. However, the dating of St John's Day was calculated from the dating of Christmas. The six-month interval is dictated not by devious calculation on the part of the church, but by Lk 1.36: 'And behold your kinswoman Elizabeth in her old age has also conceived a son; and this is the sixth month with her who was called barren'. As such, the church can appeal to scriptural sanction. Since St John's Day relies for its dating upon Christmas.

When the church came to establish the feast days for the nativities of its holy persons, first in order of importance was that of Jesus: the Christ-Mass, or Christmas. The earliest mention of Christmas being celebrated on 25 December occurs in the Liberian Catalogue or Philocalian Calendar, which details Roman practice in 336. Once Christmas had been fixed at midwinter, the timing of John's nativity, six months before that of Jesus, naturally fell at midsummer.

If the birth of Christ is celebrated on 25 December, then it follows that John's birth should be celebrated on the preceding 25 June; but John's nativity is celebrated on the previous day, the 24 June. This is not due to bad mathematics on the part of the church. Rather, it is attributed to the fact that the nativity of Christ was deliberately set according to the pagan celebrations that took place about the time of the winter solstice. It is probable that the date was chosen to oppose the pagan feast of the *Natalis Solis Invicti*, or the birth of the unconquered sun. The winter solstice saw the celebration of many pagan gods, such as the Star Child, or Light Bringer, but especially Mithras, who is also known as the Unconquered Sun. The winter solstice falls about 22 December and coincides with the sun's crossing of the ecliptic, but the consequent lengthening of the days is not immediately perceptible. It is not until three days after this time, that the effect upon daylight can be visibly discerned.

In the case of Midsummer, which is observed on 24 June and falls three days after the summer solstice on the 21 June, the reverse of this process is seen. The shortening of the days does not immediately become apparent; but, with a lapse of three days, the gradual reduction in daylight becomes noticeable. This phenomenon was not lost upon the church. As Augustine (*Tractate XIV; Sermon* 287.4) noted, it is reflected in the words attributed to John the Baptist himself in Jn 3.30: 'he must increase, but I must decrease'.

The Decollation of Saint John the Baptist

Once the church had established the date of Jesus' nativity, that of John became obvious, but the anniversary of John's death is also celebrated. The death of a saint is commemorated because it marks his or her entry into heaven. Because the church understood John's death to have been that of a martyr, it added to its calendar the Decollation of St John the Baptist, sometimes called the Passion of St John the Baptist, on 29 August. This feast, which is mentioned in the fifth century *Martyrologium Hieronymianum*, gives John the rare privilege of being celebrated by two feast days rather than one. He shares this honour only with Jesus and Mary.

While the dating of John's nativity is easy to explain, that of his death is less so. Setting the date at 29 August seems to contradict a statement made by Baring-Gould that John's death was 'supposed to have occurred just before the third Passover, in the course of the Lord's ministry, AD 30.'[2] Since Passover occurs during the month of Nisan, which falls in March-April, a reason must be sought for why the anniversary of John's death was moved to 29 August. An explanation is offered by Augustine, who notes that the dating of John's death had to be changed because Easter is the Passion of Jesus, and the 'less ought to give way to the more and greater'.[3] According to the church, therefore, John is lesser than Jesus, who has increased while John has decreased (cf. Jn 3.30).

The church moved the feast of the Decollation of St John the Baptist in order to give precedence to the passion of Jesus.

Nevertheless, this does not explain why August was chosen. An answer can be found in the Martyrology of Ado (c. 800-75), where it is revealed that the celebration was originally in commemoration of the translation of John's head from the monastery near Emesa to the church of the city, a story that will be discussed below. Setting the feast of the Decollation at this date was simply the most logical course of action.

Minor Feast Days

The observation of both the nativity and the death of John the Baptist constitute major feast days within the church calendar. However, certain other days are noted within the church as minor feast days of John the Baptist, the first significant of which is 7 January. This day is kept as a memorial day for John in the Greek and Russian churches and has is basis in the fact that John's nativity was originally celebrated in connection with Epiphany, 6 January. Observance of Epiphany originated in the East and commemorated the day of Jesus' baptism by John. By the fourth century, it had become an important feast, second only to Easter and Pentecost. The fourth century also saw its introduction to the West. However, while the day retained its connection with the baptism of Christ in the East, this was rapidly lost in the West, where it became associated with the visit of the Magi and Christ's manifestation to the Gentiles.

The next date in the calendar of John the Baptist falls on 24 February when The Invention of the Head of the Baptist at Jerusalem is commemorated. A similar celebration occurs on 25 May to mark The Invention of the Head of the Baptist at Comana according to the Greek and Russian calendar, and the Arabic Synaxarium. The story of the Invention is interconnected to that of the translation of John's head from the monastery near Emesa, which will be related below.

Finally, 24 September commemorates the conception of John. Since this falls exactly nine months before 24 June, it is the most appropriate date for the celebration of this event. However, September also coincides with one of the greatest of the Jewish festivals: Tabernacles, which commemorates the Israelites' wanderings in the desert following the flight from Egypt, as described in Exodus 35-6. The exodus meant freedom and salvation and was the endorsement of Israel as God's chosen people. John's mission was also one of salvation.

The Legend of Saint John the Baptist

As a saint, John has a 'legend' or life story, otherwise known as a hagiography, of which there are usually several versions. The oldest hagiography of John the Baptist, although incomplete, is that gleaned from the oral and written traditions used by the evangelists. Tantalising details of John are to be found scattered throughout the Gospels, and it is left to the reader to piece them together. Luke devoted the first chapter of his Gospel to the nativity of John, and this forms the longest narrative of John in the Gospels. Q (3.2-20) and Mark (1.4-14) offer rare glimpses of John as a man, accompanied by what, to them at least, was the most significant part of his teaching. Mark (6.17-29) and Matthew (14.3-12) speak of John's death and the events surrounding it. Josephus also mentions John (*Ant.* 18.116-19), although this can no more be considered a biography than can the Gospel accounts. Later, in the fifth century, Chrysippus of Cappadocia (d.479) wrote an *encomium* or panegyric of John the Baptist.

Perhaps the earliest attempt at a legend proper of John the Baptist in the Christian tradition appeared between 1255 and 1266 in Jacob de Voragine's *The Golden Legend*. Two centuries later, in 1483-5, the English printer, Caxton, offered his version of *The Golden Legend*, which purports to be an English translation of Voragine's work. This is true with regard to the accounts of the death of John, where there is no difference between the two versions. However, Caxton's account of John's nativity is markedly different. Voragine offers a very short account of John's life, focusing upon the angelic announcement, Mary's visit to Elizabeth, and the birth of John. Caxton provides a fuller legend of John the Baptist. These versions as well as a laconic rendering by the twentieth-century theologian and art historian, Jöckle, will now be discussed in order to highlight the different means by which hagiographies are approached.

Hagiographers usually arrange their work according to the order in which the feast days of the saint in question appear in the calendar. The legend of the birth of the Baptist will often appear in a separate volume from that of his death since they are celebrated upon different dates. As though to prove the rule, Jöckle approaches his legend in a different manner. He does not present a narrative, as does Voragine, albeit to a limited extent, and Caxton. Instead, he summarises the embellishments to a story that is familiar to his readers from the Gospel accounts. Moreover, he arranges his study of saints in alphabetical order according to name, rather than according to the dating of the relevant feast days.

Voragine devotes most of his time to justifying the sainthood of John the Baptist, but he does offer a concise account of John's legend. He begins with the establishment of Zechariah's priestly lineage so as to confirm Zechariah's piety and explain his presence in the Temple. He then paraphrases of the Lukan account of the announcement of the birth of John and the role he is to play. Of Gabriel's announcement that John is to go 'in the spirit and power of Elijah' (Lk. 1.17), Voragine[4] offers the following exegesis, to which the appropriate references are added. He notes that John is called Elijah because both are associated with the wilderness by the Jordan (2 Kings 1.6-12; cf. Mk 1.5). John and Elijah ate very little. Elijah ate 'bread and meat ... and he drank from the brook' (1 Kings 17.6), was fed water, meal made into cakes and oil by a widow (1 Kings 17.8-16) and was given 'a cake baked on hot stones and a jar of water' by an angel

(1 Kings 19.6), while John ate 'locusts and wild honey' (Mk 1.7). Their external appearance is another factor in common: John the Baptist was 'clothed with camel's hair, and had a leather girdle around his waist' (Mk 1.6), while Elijah 'wore a garment of haircloth, with a girdle of leather about his loins' (2 Kings 1.8). John and Elijah are both forerunners. Voragine (1993a:329) explains that Elijah was to precede someone named 'the Judge'. This can only refer to the prophecies of Malachi, which speaks of a messenger to come (3.1), who is later revealed to be Elijah (4.5). Elijah is the forerunner of the one who announces: 'I will draw near to you for judgment' (3.5). John, on the other hand, is the forerunner of the Saviour. Finally, John is called Elijah because both shared a common zeal. Voragine draws attention to the impact made by the speeches of each man. This might refer to 1 Kings 19.10, where Elijah tells God, 'I have been very jealous for the Lord, the God of Israel...' Later, Elijah challenges the 'captain of the fifty', saying, '"if I am a man of God, let fire come down from heaven and consume you and your fifty". Then fire came down from heaven and consumed him and his fifty' (2 Kings 1.10-11). Thus, there are references to Elijah's zeal and the burning torch quality of his words. Similar references can be found for John. His zeal for God is revealed in his observance of prayer (Lk. 11.1) and fasting (Mk 2.18), and his willingness to obey the word of God (Mk 1.2-3; Lk. 3.2; Jn 1.33). His words burn as fiercely as the fire of which he speaks: 'You brood of vipers! Who warned you to flee from the wrath to come...? Even now the axe is laid to the root of the trees; every tree therefore that does not bear good fruit is cut down and thrown into the fire' (Q 3.7-9). The Fourth Evangelist attributes to Jesus the declaration that John 'was a burning and shining lamp' (Jn 5.35).

Voragine[5] next turns his attention to why Zechariah should be punished for doubting. In the ensuing discussion, he refers to Bede, who offers several reasons why Zechariah should be silenced. First, Zechariah voiced his doubt, and so was punished by having his voice taken away. Second, he was struck dumb so that the miracle of John's birth would be doubled by the restoration of Zechariah's voice. Third, it was appropriate for Zechariah to lose his voice at a time when a voice was being born and the Law silenced. Lastly, Zechariah's silence served as the sign he had asked for and as a signal to the crowd at the Temple that something miraculous was occurring. Voragine[6] further elaborates upon the 'voice' theme, noting that the baby John leapt in his mother's womb, and that his dance was a salute to the one he could not welcome in voice. Voragine cleverly draws together these points, which are so intimately connected with John the Baptist and his mission. The Synoptics tell us that John was the voice who cried in the wilderness, a forerunner preparing for the coming of Christ (Mk 1.3 and par.). In the Fourth Gospel, John is not even a forerunner, he is not the Light, nor Elijah nor the Christ; he simply declares himself as a voice (1.23), a witness and nothing more.

Voragine continues his story as far as the birth of John and states that Mary stayed with Elizabeth until John was born, when she acted as a midwife.[7] That Mary assisted at the birth of John appears to be an eisegesis of Lk 1.56, where Luke writes that Mary 'remained with her about three months, and returned to her home'. Although Luke does not say that Mary assisted at the birth of John, simple maths would support such an assumption. Since Elizabeth had been carrying her baby for six months by the time of Mary's visit (Lk 1.36), the three months Mary stayed with her would see Elizabeth at full-term and ready to give birth. The difficulty with this is that Luke asserts that Elizabeth's time to be delivered came after Mary had left (1.57). Since Voragine leaves the legend of John's nativity at this point, we turn to Caxton.

As he approaches his account of the nativity of John the Baptist in *The Golden Legend*, Caxton,[8] like Voragine, draws from the first chapter of Luke. Unlike Voragine, Caxton continues the narrative to the point at which John baptises Jesus. Here, we shall concentrate upon the embellishments Caxton made to the Lukan account as he tells John's story.

Caxton declares that John's mother, Elizabeth, was the daughter of Esmeria, whose sister, Anne, was the mother of Mary (cf. Lk. 1.36). John's parents wished for a son that he might 'be a bishop of the law by succession of lineage after Zacharias [sic]'. Rather than depicting Zechariah as a lowly priest, therefore, Caxton shows him to be a bishop of the law, a man holding an exalted office. He goes on to explain that Elizabeth hid for five months (cf. Lk. 1.24) because she was ashamed of her pregnancy: she 'waxed great, and when she perceived it she was shamefaced and kept in her house well five months'.[9] Like Voragine, Caxton,[10] suggests that Mary assisted at the delivery of the baby John. He adds that Zechariah lived in the mountains two miles from Jerusalem, and that this is where John was born,[11] an allusion to Lk. 1.39, where it is stated that John's family lived in 'the hill country'.

In keeping with his representation of Zechariah as a bishop, Caxton[12] adds that John 'was nourished as a child of a noble and rich man and a son of great dignity'. This contrasts markedly with the meagre diet of 'locusts and wild honey' (Mk. 1.6) that John would follow later. Caxton also reminds us of the speech made by Jesus, in which he asks the people what they came out into the wilderness to see (Q 7.24): 'a man in soft raiment?' (Q 7.25), he suggests, answering his own question by pointing out that such people are only to be found in king's courts. Jesus' words are ironic, since a king's court was exactly where John is to be found at that moment, albeit in a prison-dungeon. However, were Zechariah a bishop, he would probably have moved in rich and courtly circles. Caxton does not name his source for this part of his *Golden Legend*, and it is not found in Voragine. Perhaps this poignant speech had entered tradition in some way, leading to speculation that John might have had loftier origins than is generally supposed. However that may be, at the 'age of fifteen years accomplished, and others say he departed at twelve years of age',[13] John left the family home and embarked upon his life in the desert.

Now a child of the wilderness, John exchanges his soft raiment for rough camel skins, and his fine cuisine for locusts and wild honey. Caxton considers what 'locusts' could mean. 'Not such as we have here that we call honeysuckles'[14] he asserts. It is interesting to note, in connection with this, is that, according to the English physician Nicholas Culpeper, honeysuckle is a 'hot martial plant', which is warming, good for cramp and the nerves, and is governed by the zodiac sign of Cancer, in which the supposed birthday of John the Baptist, 24 June, fall. Caxton goes on to speculate that locusts might refer to the flesh of certain animals roaming the area where John baptised. Caxton's suggestion would have horrified the Ebionites who, in their Gospel, made John a vegetarian who ate cake. This change of diet reflects the Ebionites' own vegetarianism, and subtly associates them with the Baptist.

The isolation of John's desert existence continued until 'he was about twenty-nine years old'. Following Luke, Caxton[15] shows John being coaxed out of his sojourn by a message. In Luke, this came as 'the word of God' (3.2), which sent John back to the people to preach his 'baptism of repentance for the forgiveness of sins' (Lk. 3.3). According to Luke, therefore, John's preaching and baptising ministry is the will of God. This is consistent with the miraculous nature of his birth, the wonders that surrounded it, and the predictions that were made regarding the future of the baby John.

Now a man, John, who has communed with God for his entire adult life so far, embarks upon the next stage of his divinely appointed mission. Caxton describes him being approached by an angel who instructs him to 'purge them that were baptised, in accustoming the baptism of our Lord Jesu Christ'. As in the Gospels, John's mission is to prepare the people for the baptism that Jesus will bring, but part of the angel's message is to prepare John himself for the coming of Christ, and to help him identify the Saviour when he arrives: 'Jesus Christ, Saviour of the world, should come to him for to be baptised, and it should be he on whom the Holy Ghost should descend in semblance of a dove'. Here, Caxton draws from Jn 1.32-3, 'I saw the Spirit descend as a dove from heaven, and it remained on him. I myself did not know him; but he who sent me to baptise with water said to me, "He on whom you see the Spirit descend and remain, this is he who baptises with the Holy Spirit."' The Fourth Evangelist relates that John was unaware of Jesus' true identity until it was indicated to him by the dove.

Having shown how John was impelled to return to the world of men, Caxton next presents his baptising ministry.[16] Those whom John addresses as 'ye children of serpents' (cf. Q 3.7), are described by Caxton as 'religious men of evil life'. Caxton, therefore, agrees with Matthew (3.7), wherein the Pharisees and Sadducees are so addressed, against Luke, who shows John to be speaking to 'the multitudes' (3.7). According to Caxton,[17] John preached for a year prior to the coming of Jesus, during which time he was approached by the religious authorities and questioned. Their questions as well as John's answers, come directly from Jn 1.19-27. However, Caxton alters the identity of those who come to question John from 'priests and Levites' (Jn 1.19) to Pharisees, thereby strengthening the implied association with the Matthaean text.

John next speaks of Jesus, whom he precedes. Here, Caxton and Jn 1.27 agree. However, due to his fidelity to the Matthaean version, Caxton shows John describing Jesus' baptism to the Pharisees, rather than to the anonymous hearers of Jn 1.33. Moreover, Caxton elaborates on the form and purpose of the rite. In Jn 1.33, it is a baptism 'with the Holy Spirit', while Caxton's John describes it as 'in the virtue of the Holy Ghost, in water and fire of penance'. That Jesus' baptism should be with the Holy

Spirit (Mk 1.8; Jn 1.33) or the Holy Spirit and fire (Q 3.16) is consistent with the Gospel accounts, even though they themselves are at variance over the details. By adding water to Jesus' baptism, Caxton may be attempting to explain Jn 4.1, which suggests that Jesus administered John's baptism.

As the first year of John the Baptist's mission nears its end, Jesus approaches him to be baptised. The angel had told John that he would recognise Jesus as the Christ by means of the Holy Spirit descending upon him in the form of a dove. However, finally confronted by Jesus, John has no need of such a sign. Drawing from Matthew 3.13-17, Caxton portrays John pointing out the inappropriateness of his baptising Jesus: 'Sir, thou comest to me, which art pure and clean, and to be baptised and washed of me that am foul and wasted, which ought to be baptised of thee and washed, how dare I lay on thee my hands.'[18] At Jesus' insistence, in order 'to fulfil all justice and to humble and give ensample of baptism to all people',[19] John baptises him, whereupon the dove descends and the voice of the Father speaks in the familiar scene of Mk 1.10-11 and par. Caxton dates Jesus' baptism to when 'our Lord was thirty years old from his nativity and thirteen days beginning of the thirty-first year'. This dating brings us to 7 January, which as has been noted, was traditionally associated with Jesus' baptism, and is still kept as a day of memorial for John the Baptist in the Greek and Russian churches.

The baptism of Jesus is the point at which Caxton's *The Golden Legend* concludes the story of John the Baptist's nativity. What stands out about this story is its reliance upon the Gospel accounts, although it uses these accounts somewhat indiscriminately. It places Q in conjunction with the Fourth Gospel, combining the elements of Jesus' baptism with that of John, so that it now includes Holy Spirit, fire and water. Caxton, therefore, has felt free to embellish the story as he wished. Thus, John the Baptist, the son of a poor rural priest, has become transformed into the son of a wealthy and highly placed bishop.

His parents' home is that of a noble family, and John was brought up with all the privileges of his parent's social standing.

Why John should be accorded this dignity is uncertain, although several suggestions might be offered. First, *The Golden Legend* maintains the blood tie between Elizabeth and Mary. Coming from the same family, they probably belong to the same social class, with John's elevated social position perhaps being attributed to the 'Lordship' of Jesus. On the other hand, Jesus, according to Mt. 1.1, 17, 20; 2.2, is of royal blood. If Jesus is of such high dignity, it is fitting that his cousin should at least be born of nobility. On a more metaphysical level, the spiritual position of Jesus may be reflected in the earthly position of John the Baptist. That is to say, John's exalted social rank may be a metaphor for the spiritual rank of Jesus, which is the highest possible. Alternatively, John's exalted social position might be a metaphor for his own spiritual wealth.

Finally, in an elaboration taken from Voragine, Caxton speaks of Mary staying with Elizabeth until John is born, and that she assisted at the birth. This tradition could not have been drawn from Luke, since the evangelist clearly states that Elizabeth gave birth after Mary's departure.

The Legend of the Death of John the Baptist is featured as part of Voragine's *The Golden Legend*. Caxton's version is a direct translation of this. The death of John the Baptist, as given in *The Golden Legend*[20] and Caxton's translation of it,[21] opens with an account of Herod's marriage to Herodias as it is presented by Josephus (*Ant.* 18.109-115). John rebukes Herod for marrying Herodias since, by doing so, he has violated Torah. As a result, Herod imprisons John. Both Herod and Herodias want to kill John but are afraid to act because he is beloved of the people. However, an opportunity arises upon the occasion of Herod's birthday. Herod and Herodias form a plan. Herodias' daughter should dance before the guests. Herod would be so pleased by her dance that he would offer to grant the girl anything she should desire. At this point, her mother would tell her to ask for the Baptist's head. Herod, pretending to be aggrieved by her request, but unable to abjure in front of so important an assembly, would reluctantly acquiesce. A headsman would be sent to kill John, whose head would then be given to the daughter who would show it before the guests. The day of the feast having arrived, the plan worked exactly as Herod and Herodias had intended. The death of the Baptist is achieved.

The Golden Legend, therefore, presents the death of John the Baptist in a manner that stays faithful to the Gospel accounts. The one area in which it diverges is that both Herod and Herodias are anxious to kill John. It should be noted, however, the Gospels are also divided upon this point. Mark (6.19) shows that Herodias wanted to kill John. Matthew (14.5) asserts that Herod was to blame. The reasons why Herod or Herodias do not act also differ. Mark (6.20) attributes Herodias' failure to proceed to Herod's fear of John. Herod saw John as a 'righteous and holy man, and he protected him.' In Matthew (14.5), Herod is afraid to kill John for fear of how the people, who love John, would react. *The Golden Legend* agrees with Matthew in this respect.

As noted earlier, Jöckle does not offer a narrative. Rather, he attempts to complete John's life story by adding elements excluded by the evangelists. It is, therefore, a tradition based upon lacunae. Moreover, Jöckle gives no account of John's death. Rather, he simply notes two events that occurred after it, and leaves it at that.

Jöckle[22] begins by stating that Elizabeth and John visit Mary and the baby Jesus. This is a pretext for what follows, which is that Elizabeth and John flee from the massacre of the innocents. Desperate to save her child, Elizabeth searches for a hiding place, but finds none. At this point, a rock opens up, revealing a cave. They go inside, and the cave closes behind them, offering them safe refuge from Herod's men. John's father, Zechariah, refuses to disclose the hiding place of his wife and child, is murdered.

It can immediately be seen that Jöckle has drawn his account from *The Protevangelium of James* 22.3-23.3, which he has condensed. This part of the legend addresses to a certain extent the question of what became of John's parents. It states that Herod's soldiers killed his father, although the fate of his mother remains unknown. She could have died of old age, or she might have given her life to save her son, as did Zechariah. Next, Jöckle reveals that the angel Uriel takes the young John into the desert, where he clothes the child in garments that will grow as he does.

The choice of Uriel as the angel who leads John into the wilderness is interesting, especially since one might have expected the angel to have been Gabriel. Of prime interest are the coincidences that exist between traditions surrounding Uriel and certain aspects of the life and work of John the Baptist. Uriel's primary function, as given in 1 Enoch 20.1, is to govern the army of angels in the underworld. This reinforces the link with John, whose task in death is to preach to the righteous in that place.

Uriel is also associated with the Temple sacrifice. The angel is variously depicted as an eagle or a lion that crouches upon the altar (*Zohar* 1.6b; 3.32b, 211a). If he devours the sacrifice, it is an indication that God has accepted it. Those who saw Uriel upon the altar would undergo a change of heart and repent of their sins. This provides an interesting parallel with John's baptism. It is generally understood that the baptism offered by John was intended, in part, as a replacement for Temple sacrifice. Provided the penitent submitted to it with sincerity, his repentance would be accepted by God, who would then forgive his sins.

In another parallel, Uriel was overcome by the burden of Israel's sins. His strength left him, and he was no longer able to come to the altar. John, too, was overcome by sin: that of Herod and Herodias. Imprisoned, he was unable to continue his baptising ministry.

The *Zohar* shows Uriel and Nuriel to be two aspects of the same angel. As Uriel, he is merciful, as Nuriel, he is severe and rigorous. These two qualities were manifest in John the Baptist. His speech, given in Lk 3.10-14, shows him to be merciful. His rebuke, as presented in Q 3 7-9, shows severity and harshness.

Finally, 2 Esdras 4 contains some correlations between Uriel's actions and the Baptist's preaching. Uriel, for example, presents various visions to Ezra, in which Ezra learns God's plan for the world and for his people of Israel. Thus, Uriel, like John, is a messenger of God, who imparts information about the present age and the new one to come. Their methods, however, are different. Uriel divulges his message in the form of visions. John, appropriately for one who is called 'a voice', preaches. In order to prove his worthiness to receive Uriel's message, Ezra is required to perform a task set by the angel. This task is to 'weigh for me the weight of fire, or measure for me a measure of wind, or call back for me the day that is past' (2 Esdras 4.5). Curiously, Uriel mentions the two elements of Jesus' baptism as it is described by John: Holy Spirit, which is often spoken of as wind, and fire.

Further on, Uriel describes the end time as 'the time of threshing' (4.30, 39; cf. Q 3.17). In 4.35, the general resurrection of the righteous is seen as a harvest (cf. Q 3.17). These references have to do with the point in time at which the 'time of the threshing' will occur. 2 Esdras 4.48-50 shows that the end is drawing near. John also thought that the eschaton was imminent: 'even now the axe is laid to the root of the trees' (Q 3.9). These correspondences are puzzling and require explanation. It could be that John the Baptist, as he planned the content of his preaching, studied 2 Esdras and was inspired by Uriel's speech. However, this cannot be, since 2 Esdras originates at a time post 70 CE. Perhaps John's preaching was the inspiration for 2 Esdras. Again, this would be wrong. The preaching of John the Baptist and the speeches of Uriel are drawn from metaphors and analogies that are to be found in several places throughout the Hebrew Bible. The themes are entirely Jewish, and their appeal to the early church can be attributed to the fact that the earliest Christians were Jews. It is more probable that the choice of Uriel as the angel who led John into the wilderness and clothed him in his special garments, was inspired by his correspondence to John; the two sharing similarities in word and deed.

While in the wilderness, John encounters Jesus, who is being brought home from Egypt by his parents. Since Jesus is still a boy at this point, 'rise, take the child and his mother, and go to the land of Israel' (Mt. 2.20), John must also be a child, since he was only six months older than Jesus. What occurs next in John's life is, as in Luke, not mentioned. Luke states only that John 'grew and became strong in spirit, and he was in the wilderness till the day of his manifestation to Israel' (1.80). Jöckle asserts that 'an angel', this time unnamed, summons John to the Jordan.

The main observation to be made concerning Jöckle's version of the legend is that it makes much use of *The Protevangelium of James* 22.3-23.3. This extra-canonical Gospel is dated to the middle of the second century and is believed to have used a combination of the Hebrew Bible, oral and written traditions, some of which were probably known to the evangelists. It adds nothing to our knowledge of the historical John the Baptist. As far as tradition goes, it reveals little more. As noted earlier, its inclusion in Jöckle's legend hints at what happened to John's father, although it still leaves the question of the fate of his mother unanswered. *The Protevangelium of James* shows John and Elizabeth being watched over by an angel (22.3). In Jöckle's account of the legend, John encounters several angels. Uriel takes him into the desert and gives him clothes. These clothes grow as the child does. Possibly, it symbolises that John's wants will be catered for and that he would have no need to return to society until the appointed time. Finally, another angel summons John to the Jordan to begin his baptising ministry. While in the desert, John encountered Jesus and his parents, who were returning home after their sojourn in Egypt. Jesus is still in the care of his earthly parents. John is, in all probability, an orphan. At this point, Jöckle goes straight to the events following John's execution, in which John appears to St Frances of Rome as she lay dying, and that Julian the Apostate orders John's bones to be burned.

Hagiography or legend represents the life of a saint in story form. There are several means of approach. One is to contradict that which is found in the Gospel accounts. This was noted in the case of Caxton who, for example, gave John a rich background. Both Caxton and Voragine depict Mary assisting at the birth of John. This challenges Luke (1.56-7), who notes that Mary returned home prior to the birth of John. Another approach is to conflate two conflicting elements in the Gospels accounts. Caxton achieves this by showing both Herod and Herodias planning John's death. In this way he resolves the apparent disagreement between Mark and Matthew, who attribute this event to either Herodias (Mk 6.19, 24) or Herod (Mt. 14.5). A third approach is to build upon lacunae or gaps in the Gospel accounts. This was especially notable in the legend by Jöckle, which drew primarily upon the *Protevangelium of James*.

Iconography of Saint John the Baptist

Most saints have an iconography, which is the representation of Christian ideas, figures and history in pictures and symbols.[23] When applied to saints, it refers to the symbols that are associated with them, and by which they are identified.

In art, John the Baptist is often represented wearing sheepskin, which alludes to his life in the desert. He usually holds either a wooden cross bearing the words *ecce Agnus Dei*, a book upon which sits a lamb, or a lamb surrounded by a halo and bearing a cross on the right foot. The lamb refers to the speech in which John points to Jesus and announces, 'Behold the Lamb of God, who takes away the sins of the world' (Jn 1.29). Occasionally, he holds a reed in reference to his not being a 'reed shaken by the wind' (Q 7.24).

Such images are based upon depictions of John the Baptist as given by the evangelists, and they represent the traditional western image of John as a saint. However, another image of John is unique to the eastern tradition. Making its first appearance upon a fresco in Serbia is a depiction of John the Baptist bearing the wings of an angel. This portrayal, which is inspired by Mal. 3.1, is based upon the etymological link between the Hebrew words for both 'messenger' and 'angel', מלאך. By the sixteenth century, such an image of John had become common throughout the area influenced by Eastern Orthodox customs.

There is probably no better example of the iconography of John the Baptist as it is depicted in the western tradition than an anonymous portrait dating from c.1680. (See plate section.) This painting depicts Philippe d'Orléans, the brother of Louis XIV, as John the Baptist. Although the portrait is that of a prince, it nevertheless contains more John the Baptist symbolism than any other image of the saint. As such, it is well worth a close study. While the portrait is of Monsieur, its subject shall continue to be referred to as John the Baptist.

John sits in front of a tree in a lush landscape. The tree is that at whose roots the axe is poised in Q 3.9. A deciduous tree, as this one appears to be, symbolises the world in constant renewal and regeneration. That is to say, 'dying in order to live', as in resurrection.[24] John, as a saint and martyr, would be resurrected in the last days. It is possible that the tree also signifies the Tree of Knowledge, which was the reason for the Fall and the need for redemption.[25]

The grass upon which John sits represents submission. The lamb, as has been noted, represents the Lamb of God, Christ, who died for the sins of the world (Jn 1.29). However, the lamb can also represent the redeemed Christian, probably from Lk. 15.3-7 in which the Good Shepherd seeks the lost sheep which represents the penitent returned to the fold. John could be seen as a redeemed Christian, in that this Jewish apocalyptic preacher has been transformed into the messenger of God and the herald of Christ.

John's mantle is a symbol of refuge and safety for humanity. His baptism sheltered the repentant from the wrath of God. It also identifies John with Elijah, who wore a mantle (2 Kings 2.8). The mantle can also signify concealment, mysteriousness, power and hints at a specific task.[26] This recalls the 'concealment tradition' surrounding John, which is based upon his association with Elijah and is an expression of his status as forerunner to Christ. This symbolism applies to John in several ways. Following his arrest, he was concealed in prison. He is mysterious because nothing is known about him from his leaving his parental home (Lk. 1.80) to his re-emergence from the wilderness (Mk 1.1.4 and par.), in fact another concealment. In Mark especially, John mysteriously appears. John is powerful because his ministry attracted many (Mk 1.5), even Christ himself (Mk 1.9). The specific task allocated to John was act as forerunner to Christ.

John's mantle is red with brown fur edging. In Christian art, red represents Christ's passion and the blood shed upon Calvary. Appropriate to John are its attributes of zeal, faith, power, especially priestly power, and intrepidity. It is the colour of martyrdom and cruelty. It is also the colour of blood, a reminder of John's sanguinary end. Brown signifies spiritual death[27] as encountered in the monastic world in which John is an important role model. The colour also represents renunciation. John renounced his birth right, which was to follow in his father's footsteps in the Temple, and the world in favour of a strict asceticism. His questions to Jesus from prison might be interpreted as a renunciation of faith. Brown also signifies penitence, which John demanded of others as well as himself. It represents degradation, and is appropriate due to John's ignoble death, but also his will that Jesus should increase, while he should decrease (Jn 3.30). The fur alludes to John's desert camel hair clothing. As a symbol of repentance, it also represents the garments God made for Adam and Eve upon their expulsion from Paradise (Gen. 3.21).

In the background lies a city, probably symbolising Jerusalem. The staff carried by John represents the staff of pilgrimage and is one of his emblems. Here, the staff is topped by a cross, which represents the acceptance of death, or suffering and sacrifice, and salvation. John's death is, of course, accepted in Christian tradition as a sacrifice, and that led to his martyrdom. Rather than being made of reed, the staff held by John in this representation is golden. Gold signifies the sun, which is fitting for John, one of whose feast days coincides with the pagan sun festival of Midsummer. It also stands for enlightenment and immortality. John enlightened the people to Jesus' coming, and his immortality is assured due to his sainthood.

Coiled round John's staff is a snake or serpent. This creature ties in with John's Q sermon, in which he addresses some of his hearers as 'you brood of vipers' (3.7). However, the serpent wound round a cross, as here, signifies Christ.[28] Its origins lie in Num. 21.8, wherein God tells Moses to put a serpent (or snake) onto a pole to heal the suffering Children of Israel. Its connection with Christ is made in Jn 3.14: 'just as Moses lifted up the snake in the desert, so the Son of man must be lifted up.' The serpent is blue in colour, signifying heaven and heavenly truth, as well as faith and eternity. Especially apt for the Baptist, blue represents baptism in water in the Gnostic tradition. The Mandaeans, a Gnostic sect for whom baptism is of paramount importance, claim to be the descendants of John's original disciples. Conversely, for much of their existence, the Gnostic Cathars rejected John as an evil spirit or an emissary of the devil and saw his water rite as corrupting.

Water flows from John's cross, a reminder of his baptism in living waters. Water also signifies regeneration, since water is the basis of life. It also represents purification, as in baptism and inspired by Ps. 51.2, 'wash me thoroughly from my iniquity, and cleanse me from my sin.'

Lastly, John holds a book. This represents the teaching of the nations by the Apostles (Mt. 28.18), the Gospels. It can also signify the two testaments; the old law or Torah, having passed away, and the birth of the new law of Christ, signifying the new age.

This portrait of Monsieur as John the Baptist contains a very high proportion of symbolism related to John. Ironically, this image, while displaying a remarkable knowledge of John's iconography on the part of its anonymous artist, was nevertheless intended to flatter the prince rather than to venerate the saint.

John the Baptist as Patron Saint

Many saints are adopted as patron saints. This means that, as well as interceding between human beings and heaven on an individual level, they can also intercede on behalf of groups. Many places, trades and organisations claim John the Baptist as its patron saint. Among the places are Burgundy, Malta, Provence, Florence, Amiens, Jordan and additionally, spas.

In most cases, a saint is associated with a particular location because his or her relics are held there. Sometimes the association is linked to an organisation that has adopted John as its patron. For example, in 1530, Charles V granted the Knights of St John of Jerusalem sovereignty of Malta. Occasionally, a location is associated with a saint's activity. That John should be the patron saint of spas is due to his baptism with water, which is seen as health giving in the spiritual sense. He is patron saint of Jordan because he prepared for the coming of Jesus in the area that is now Jordan.

Trades that have adopted John include farriers, tailors, tanners, furriers and shepherds. John's association with farriers is due to the fact that they work with iron, which is forged in fire and is therefore linked to the Baptist's eschatological speech, which made frequent mention of fire (Q 3.9, 17). That tailors should adopt John the Baptist is probably due to the materials from which his garments were made, fur and leather. Also linked with John's clothes are tanners, who work with leather, and furriers, whose material, fur, is represented by the camel's hair worn by John. That John should be associated with shepherds stems from his proclamation of the Lamb of God.

Many churches are dedicated to John the Baptist. Perhaps the most famous is the Lateran Basilica (S. Giovanni in Laterino) in Rome. However, some churches are much older. Prior to the religious revival brought about by Constantine, it was impossible to erect monuments to the sacred persons of Christianity. Once the church had gained liberty, its first priority was to found sanctuaries dedicated to Christ and the Virgin Mary. John the Baptist came next. Antoninus Martyr,[29] travelling through Palestine in 570, reports seeing a small church at Shechem[30] dedicated to John the Baptist. The church itself was built over the supposed site of the well where Jesus asked the Samaritan woman for water (Jn 4.6-7). Inside the church was a water-pot, said to be that from which he drank. Elsewhere, Antoninus notes that he found a monastery of John the Baptist on the spot where Jesus was baptised at the Jordan, roughly opposite Jericho. He describes it as 'a very large building, in which are two hospices.'[31] Legend has it that this monastery was founded by Mary of Egypt in the fifth century. Mary, on the day of her conversion, went to Jerusalem and founded the church of St John the Baptist.[32]

The proximity of a church founded by Mary of Egypt to the River Jordan is significant. From ages past to the modern day, a church built close to a river or stream will often be dedicated to John. This is due to his connection with the Jordan and the fact that he baptised in water. Because of John's baptism, all baptisteries, no matter to which saint the adjoining church is dedicated, are sacred to John.

Within the church, various orders and organisations claim John's patronage. Among these are the Carmelites and various brotherhoods who support the condemned. The Carmelites began life as the Order of Our Lady of Mount Carmel and were founded by St Berthold in Palestine in about 1154 CE. The order claimed continuity with hermits who had settled upon Mount Carmel, hence the name. In another tradition, they laid claim to be descendants of Elijah and the sons of prophets (cf. 2 Kings. 2.5).[33] Exploiting the link between Elijah and John the Baptist, they took John for their patron. They adopted a life of severe austerity and extreme asceticism, of which John was the highest example. The brotherhoods supporting the condemned comprise several groups from diverse churches and confraternities, who organised themselves under the title 'Beheading of John the Baptist'. These groups, which emerged during the Middle Ages, dedicated themselves to looking after those condemned to death. Under their influence, execution became 'almost an act of religion'.[34]

The Monastic Movement and Saint John the Baptist

Perhaps the most important group for whom John the Baptist is patron is the monastic movement. For those who would follow a life of asceticism and devotion there is no better model than John the Baptist. Monasticism adopted John as its mentor, its inspiration and its example. As Lupieri notes, from the very beginning, Christian monasticism saw John as its spiritual father and the model for life.[35] So true was this that some Egyptian monks called themselves, or were referred to by others as, sons of John the Baptist.

John's influence upon early Christian monasticism is vast. Athanasius twice mentions him as a teacher of the spiritual life (*Vita Antonii* 20.7; 36.4). The *S. Pachomii Vita Graeca* 1.2 cites John, Elijah and Elisha as models for Antony. A more elaborate tradition is given in *Vita Sinuthii* 117-18. Here, three monks dressed in pure white garments visit the monastery one night, speak with Shenoute, and then disappear before dawn. Shenoute's night-time visitors were John the Baptist, Elijah and Elisha, who had come to visit John's friends, the monks. Jerome[36] begins all three of his Saint's lives with some mention of John the Baptist, while Cassian, in his Conferences (18.6), states that the monk, whether hermit or coenobite, is a man who wishes, not to escape the world, but to dedicate himself to the further contemplation of God. In order to accomplish this, they retreat into the desert like John the Baptist, Elijah or Elisha.[37]

One monk who was attracted to a mountain is Innocent the Italian. Innocent, formerly a married man and high official at Constantius' court, built a shrine on Olivet (the Mount of Olives) for the relics of John the Baptist. The same love of John can be seen in the works of the Church Fathers, whose writings were influential to early monasticism. For Basil the Great, the desert, where John ate grasshoppers and preached penitence[38] is the ideal monastery. Gregory of Nyssa states succinctly that John was their model.[39] Following the death of Basil the Great, his brother Gregory of Nazianzus declared that Basil had lived his life and behaved like John the Baptist, even having his Herod in the form of the emperor Valens.[40]

Another monk who found himself opposed by secular power was John Chrysostom. His adversary was Eudoxia, the wife of Emperor Arcadius. Finding himself at the mercy of the empress's wrath, he evoked the spirit of the fiery prophet as he bellowed from the pulpit: 'Now Herodias flies into a rage again, now she is dancing again, now she desires again the head of John on a dish.'[41] John Chrysostom, in his most desperate hour, evoked the spirit of John the Baptist, appealing, not to his teaching, but rather to his experience at the hands of Herod and Herodias. That he identified with the Baptist at that point in his life shows how important and influential he was for monks.

Sometimes monks found themselves in disagreement with the church authorities. As seen above, the *Vita Simithii* mentions John the Baptist in the company of Elijah and Elisha. These three figures are, of course, closely connected with the wilderness, the natural home of the monk. However, that the story related in that work appears to be dependent upon the story of the Transfiguration of Jesus led some to ask the monks whether their allegiance to John was not misplaced. Early monks were sometimes forced to defend themselves against accusations that they were not true Christians. Palladius[42] is one such monk spoke on the apparent inconsistency in the examples set by John the Baptist as Jesus. John, as we are told, 'came neither eating nor drinking, and they say, "He hath a demon"; the Son of Man came eating and drinking, and they say, "Behold a glutton and a drunkard, a friend of tax collectors and sinners' (Mt. 11.18). Monks faced the same dilemma, and to solve it, they fasted with John when it was reasonable to do so and drank wine with Jesus when they were thirsty. As such, Palladius, writing in the late fourth century, was able to show that monks are indeed true Christians since they follow the teachings of both John and Jesus.

The reverence in which John the Baptist was held by monks led to the development of legends wherein he is shown to mark or influence the lives of certain monks. Stephen of Muret (c. 1047-1124) provides a good example of this. Traditions concerning Stephen's early life parallel those of John the Baptist.[43] Like Elizabeth and Zechariah, Stephen's own parents, Stephen and Candide, were childless (cf. Lk. 1.7). It seemed that their wish to have children would be denied, since both were elderly (cf. Lk. 1.7). That God had not blessed them with children was all the more bewildering to them because both were deeply pious (cf. Lk. 1.6). In their sadness and desperation, they supplicated God, vowing that any child he would give them would be dedicated to his service. Their prayers were answered. Candide, in spite of her age, went on to bear three sons, the eldest of whom was Stephen.

A similar legend can be seen in the story of Francis of Assisi. The story begins with Francis's mother, the devout Pica,[44] who named her son John in honour of the Baptist. Deep within her, she repeatedly heard the words of Zechariah,

And you, child, will be called the prophet of the Most High;
for you will go before the Lord to prepare his ways, to give
knowledge of salvation to his people in the forgiveness of their
sins, through the tender mercy of our God, when the day shall
dawn upon us from on high to give light to those who sit in
darkness and in the shadow of death, to guide our feet into the
way of peace (Lk 1.76-9)

Upon his return from France, the boy's father, Pietro, was
horrified to learn the name his wife had chosen for their first-
born. In those days, it was believed that a person's name would
have an influence upon his or her life. Pietro, a merchant who
had become rich through trade, did not want his son to be named
after an ascetic prophet who roamed the desert wastes wearing
camel skins and eating locusts and wild honey. Since he had made
his fortune in France and, according to tradition, Pica was French,
Pietro hurriedly changed his son's name to Francesco, which is
Anglicised as Francis.

Although he no longer carried his name, the Baptist nevertheless
appeared to have left his mark upon Francis. John was his
favourite saint. In chapter twenty-three of the First Rule (1221),
which is concerned with prayer, praise and thanksgiving, Francis
places John after the angels and makes him first among the saints.
Bonaventure[45] observes that Francis had a horror of soft clothes
and a love of coarseness, adding that the Baptist had been praised
by God for this very thing (cf. Matt. 11.8; Luke 7.25). Francis
identified himself closely with John. One day, as he was walking
through woods, singing the praises of God, he was beset by
robbers who demanded to know who he was. Francis confidently
replied that he was the forerunner of the great King.[46]

Pica's faith, expressed in the words of Zechariah, was vindicated
in her son. Perhaps this is not surprising, since Pica herself was
said to have possessed the gift of prophecy. Francis, in his turn,
proved also to be blessed with this gift. While John prophesied

from within his mother's womb, Francis prophesied while still a child and unaware of his divine calling.[47] Once more, Zechariah's words, so significant to Pica, turned out to be influential in the life of her son, Francis.

A story concerning a contemporary of Francis, Hugh, abbot of Cluny (1024-1109), shows how the monastic view of John had evolved to the point that it was believed that his spirit could be evoked. Hugh found himself threatened by a certain Bernard, lord of the castrum Rehoterius, whose evil deeds gave Hugh no choice but to reproach him.[48] The more he was rebuked, however, the more Bernard misbehaved, until Hugh finally thought he would be attacked. The abbot called upon John the Baptist for protection. Vengeance was swift. That night, Bernard went mad and had to be tied to his bed. During the night one or two fires broke out in the house, and Bernard had to be rescued on each occasion. Fortunately, Hugh's thirst for vengeance rapidly abated, and in the morning, he not only absolved Bernard but cured him as well.

This tale suggests that John has taken on a potentially destructive quality. Quite why he should be associated with vengeance is difficult to ascertain. It is equally a mystery why Bernard should have gone mad following the evocation of this saint and prophet. There is nothing in the Gospels, Acts or Josephus to suggest why madness should feature in a story about John. Certainly, John speaks of judgment and divine wrath (Q 3.7-9, 17), but that is, by definition, on the part of God and not John himself. Indeed, it is John's task to help people avoid it. However, John is associated with fire, since he spoke of the apocalypse in fiery terms (Q 3.9, 17), and this provides one explanation for the fires that were said to have broken out in the house. Hugh was able to cure Bernard, although there is no suggestion that the cure had anything to do with John the Baptist; it seems to have been affected purely by Hugh. Nevertheless, that Hugh evoked John for protection shows that

John has been fully endowed with the trappings of a saint. John has the ability to protect those who evoke him, an established feature of sainthood.

Another example of a tradition of destruction surrounding John the Baptist concerns a certain Mog Ruith, a druid versed in magic.[49] Said to have lived in the first or third centuries CE, Mog Ruith claims as his tutor no less a personage than Simon Magus (Acts 8). Legend has it that Mog Ruith was the only man prepared to cut off the head of John the Baptist, and that his crime brought cold, famine and sickness upon all the Irish.

Saint John the Baptist: Miracle-worker

Further enquiry into John's links with Christian monasticism uncovers an appealing tradition: miracles. The idea of John the Baptist performing miracles is incompatible with the Johannine tradition where, we are assured, he 'did no sign' (Jn 10.41). This passage has been interpreted as denoting the completion of the Baptist's mission. The people had accepted his message and believed in Jesus as a result.[50] On the other hand, Jn 10.41 can be linked with Mk 6.14, which suggests that the idea of John's return from the dead anticipates the resurrection of Jesus. Jn 10.41 is consistent with Herod's belief that John *redivivus* could perform miracles.[51] Mentioning the place across the Jordan where John had baptised allows the Fourth Evangelist to make a final comparison between Jesus and John: John had not performed miracles, so he could not be the Messiah.[52] It would seem, then, that the Fourth Evangelist was engaging in polemic. That is not all. John is shown to deny that he is the Christ or the 'prophet'; he is also shown to emphatically deny that he was Elijah. There is some sense in this, since Elijah is generally interpreted at the forerunner of Christ, and that John is largely interpreted as Elijah *redivivus*. By extension, therefore, John is Christ's forerunner. The Fourth Evangelist plays down any obvious notion of a forerunner for Christ. However, there is another dimension to Elijah than that of forerunner: that of miracle worker. John, as Elijah *redivivus*, might have been expected to perform miracles as well. Evidence of Elijah's miracle working occurs in the first and second books of Kings. He increases the meat and oil of the widow at Zarephath (1 Kings 17.9-16). He wins a competition between himself and the prophets of Ba'al over who could make it rain (1 Kings 18.18-46). He summons lightning to destroy the companies of the fifty who had been sent against him by Ahaziah, the king of Samaria (2 Kings 1.3-18). The miracle-making aspect of Elijah's tradition might have transferred to John whom, we are told, would go 'in the spirit and power of Elijah' (Lk. 1.17).

In support of a hypothesis of John as a miracle worker, the case of Jesus might be studied. Traditions of Jesus' miracle working activities are not disputed. Among his miracles are those of healing (Mk 1.29-31 and par.; Mt. 8.27-34) and control of the elements (Mk 6.45-52 and par.; Mk 4.35-41 and par.). However, prophets usually passed down their powers to their disciples, for example, Elijah, who passed his powers on to Elisha (2 Kings 2.9). If Jesus had been John's disciple, then it is not unlikely that Jesus would have honed his miracle-making skills under John. After all, it was the miracles of Jesus that recalled John the Baptist to Herod (Mk 6.14; Mt. 14.1-2; Lk. 9.7-9).

As attractive as it might be, support for miraculous activity on the part of John the Baptist cannot be found by appealing directly to the Gospel accounts. It should be noted, however, that had John not been associated with miracle-working, he would have been quite unusual among first century prophets. Josephus recounts the stories of several first-century prophets who claimed to be able to perform miracles. Theudas (*Ant.* 20.97-8) believed he could part the waters of the Jordan. Several unnamed prophets are noted in two works, *War* and *Antiquities*. The latter book speaks of their promise to show those who would follow them 'unmistakable marvels' (20.167-8). The Egyptian, as he appears in *Antiquities*, promises that 'at his command Jerusalem's walls would fall down' (20.167-72). Finally, an unnamed solitary prophet of the Jewish War commanded several people to go to the Temple court to 'receive there tokens of their deliverance' (*War* 6.285).

Traditions quickly arose in which John the Baptist, like his contemporaries, was associated with miracles. A story related by Sanuto[53] involves monks living at 'Babylon in Egypt, seven leagues from Heliopolis'. Each year, monks from a monastery dedicated to John the Baptist would carry a chest containing his relics to another monastery further along the Nile, which was also dedicated to John. The object of the exercise was to allow John to decide in which monastery he wished to rest. Placed in the river, the chest began to drift against the stream back towards the first monastery. This it does so rapidly that 'men riding at full speed on horseback cannot outrun it'. This story associates John with a river, in this case the Nile, rather than the Jordan. The water miracle complements the fire miracle of Hugh of Cluny. As such, John's miracles correspond with elements of his baptism, in water, and the fiery consequences of not heeding his message (Q 3.9, 17).

The Relics of Saint John the Baptist

Sanuto's miracle story of John the Baptist introduces another important factor in the consideration of the miracles of John the Baptist, his relics. The reverence of relics is traced to affection for the dead person, where the living wish to cling to the mortal remains of a loved one, or to visit their place of rest.[54] Christianity adds to this the desire to prevent harm befalling the remains. This is allied to the belief that the body is a temple for the Holy Spirit (cf. 1 Cor. 6.19), and the expectation of a future resurrection. In Epistle 109, Jerome observes that the spirits of saints were understood to hover near their tombs and, later, the shrines in which their relics are held. This, like many Christian beliefs, has its origins in the pagan world.

The veneration of relics led to the belief in miraculous powers associated with them. Much of this belief is grounded in scripture. 1 Kings 13.27-31, for example, speaks of the body of a 'man of God' that the lion would not eat. Sirach 48.13-14 notes that Elijah continued to prophesy even though he was dead. Acts 5.15 speaks of the faithful who believed that even Peter's shadow could heal. Finally, Acts 19.11-12 observes that handkerchiefs and aprons that Paul had touched could cure the sick and dispelled evil spirits. As a saint, John the Baptist is also endowed with such power by means of his relics.

Miracles associated with John do not appear to have played a part in his tradition until 362 CE. In this year, Julian the Apostate, who had abjured Christianity upon the death of his cousin Constantine II, violated the tomb of John the Baptist at Sabaste. John's bones were burned and scattered. However, a miraculous rain extinguished the fire so that some of the relics were saved. Once again water and fire appear in connection with John. Interestingly, Fetellus[55] asserts that John's bones were not saved by rain, but were 'given to the wind'. This forms a connection with the Holy Spirit, often described as wind, or the breath of God (Gen. 1.1; Isa. 11.4; Ps 33.6), with which the figure about whom John preached would baptise. Present, then, are all the elements of John's preaching of salvation: the water in which he baptised, the Holy Spirit and the fire of the baptism of his successor.

Several stories tell of the fate of John's relics, which were gathered and preserved by monks, who soon had remarkable stories to tell of their miraculous powers. One such story is Dionysius Exiguus' dramatic tale, the *History of the Invention of the Head of Saint John the Baptist*.[56] It begins with two monks who, on a visit to Jerusalem, were told in a dream to dig in the ruins of Herod's castle. Upon doing so, they discovered the head of John the Baptist in a rough sack. Elated at their find, they carried it back to their monastery. On the way, they met a poor potter from Emesa, who accompanied them on the journey. The potter also had a dream. In it, John the Baptist told him that he would like to rest at Emesa. In accordance with the Baptist's wishes, the potter stole John's head from the monks, placed it in a vase, and returned home to start a new life, blessed by the saintly relic.

John's head remained with the potter's family for several generations until a man named Eustatius 'a pseudo-monk and heretical priest' received it as an inheritance. He took the vase and buried it in a cave near his home. Forced suddenly to flee by a group described simply as 'the Catholics', the cave was soon inhabited by genuine, holy monks. Some of them experienced strange dreams in which John the Baptist appeared in white accompanied by two other men, similarly dressed. Finally, a star guided the monks to the spot where the head had been buried and the vase was found. The monks summoned the bishop, who arrived at the head of a procession of priests. One of the priests, Malcus, refused to believe that the vase contained the true head of John the Baptist. He placed his hand into the vase, where it became fastened firmly onto the head. Only the fervent prayers of those present allowed Malcus to free himself. Nevertheless, the hand was now paralysed.

The bishop ordered the building of a church in which to shelter the head, which was translated there in a ceremonial procession a few months afterwards. During the procession, Malcus, following the instructions of the Baptist, who had appeared to him in a dream, placed his paralysed hand upon the relic, whereupon the hand was restored.

There is much Christian symbolism in this story. John's head is found in a rough sack, thus recalling the clothing made of camel's hair worn by the Baptist (Mk 1.6). The white garments of John and his companions evoke the Transfiguration (Mk 9.3) and are symbolic of spiritual purity.[57] The star guiding the monks to the burial site of the head is an obvious Christological symbol. It can be an allusion to the Star of Bethlehem (Mt. 2.2, 7, 9-10) or a sign of the messiah (Num. 24.17). Finally, the Malcus sub-plot appears to have been inspired by the story of the midwife in the *Protevangelium of James* 19.

Considering the manner in which John died, it is not surprising that his head should have special reverence attached to it and be preserved as a relic. In fact, John's head appears to have experienced many adventures. Butler[58] tells us that it was carried to Amiens in 1204 by Wallo de Sarton, bishop of that city. Voragine,[59] on the other hand, asserts that the head was taken to Poitiers during the reign of Pepin, where the saint's merits caused many of the dead to be restored to life. Another story, related by Fetellus[60] mentions that John's head was taken to Aquitaine by a monk named Felicius, again during Pepin's reign. Later, it is said that the head restored to life twenty soldiers who had been slain by the Vandals. Thus, France claims the ownership of three heads of John the Baptist, although Amiens insists that its head is the genuine one.

Another relic of John is the finger that he used to point out Christ and to rebuke Herod. The same Fetellus[61] notes that it had been carried to Savoy by the virgin Tygris (Thecla), where it was kept in the church of Maurienne. This story is refuted by Le Braz,[62] who maintains that the finger was taken to an unnamed town in Normandy where it lay in a church especially built for it. During the Hundred Years War, a Breton named Plougeznou, in the service of the lord of this Norman town, left to become a soldier. He desperately wanted the finger, but as a religious man, he refused simply to take it. After several hours of fervent prayer, prostrate in front of the relic, he rose to find himself possessed of a most unusual feeling. The finger had gone into his arm. After several miraculous escapades, Plougeznou returned to Brittany, where the finger shot from his arm through an open but bloodless wound onto the altar of the church where it has stayed ever since. The town, Traoun-Mériadek, adopted John the Baptist as its patron saint, alongside its original saint, Mériadek.

The relics of John the Baptist are all connected with aspects of his life, preaching and rite. His bones were burned by Julian the Apostate, which recalls John's fiery preaching. They were saved from total destruction by rain, thus recalling the water in which he baptised. One relic is his head, the severance of which was the means by which he became a martyr. Also, his finger is preserved because he pointed out Christ with it and wagged it at Herod in rebuke.

Saint John the Baptist, Healer

Perhaps the most significant miracle associated with John the Baptist is that of healing. The story, related by Palladius,[63] of Innocent the Italian is a good example of the healing abilities claimed for John. Innocent, it will be remembered, built a shrine for the relics of John the Baptist upon the Mount of Olives. One day, a woman brought her son, who was paralysed and possessed by a demon, to Palladius and some of his companions for healing. Palladius reproved the woman for bringing the boy, since he doubted that he could be cured. The distraught woman was found by Innocent, who was moved to tears by the plight of the mother and child. Filled with compassion, he took the boy to the shrine in which lay the relics of John the Baptist. Here, he prayed over the child from the third hour to the ninth before returning him to his mother fully cured.

John's connection with healing was later capitalised upon by those who would become healers themselves. The eleventh century saw the foundation of an organisation that become famous worldwide for its devotion to helping the sick and injured. It began as a small group of lay monks living in a monastery at Jerusalem but would soon become known as the Knights of Saint John of Jerusalem, or the Knights Hospitallers.

The Order adopted John the Baptist as their saint because the site upon which the hospice was built had been associated with John from ancient times.[64] It was upon this site that, according to tradition, the archangel Gabriel announced to Zechariah that he was to have a son (Lk. 1.8-23). It was believed that Zechariah had once governed the hospice. His successor was a certain Julian the Roman, a mythical figure who formed a bridge between the Old Testament and New Testament.[65] It was held that Jesus was a frequent visitor to the hospice during Julian's administration.

Hospitaller historians trawled the New Testament for endorsement. When Christ healed the sick, they discovered, he did so at the hospice. The Virgin Mary and the apostles sheltered within its walls during the Passion. Christ's post-resurrection appearances took place here. Thomas doubted (Jn. 20.24-29), Ananias and Sappira were struck down (Acts 5.1-11) and the seven deacons were elected (Acts 6.1-6) at the hospice. Saint Stephen (Acts 6.1-8.4) was once a governor of the Order. The historians had not invented the connection between these events and the hospice, however. They merely claim to have corrected an oversight on the part of the evangelists, who had woefully neglected to identify the location in which they occurred.

As wonderful as the legendary origins of the Order are, they are merely the result of the desire to give the Order a foundation that would anchor it in antiquity and bestow upon it an association with Christianity's most sacred persons and events. The historical truth is, inevitably, less exotic, and has its origins in Italian merchants who wanted to break Muslim monopoly upon trade in the Levant.[66] During the middle part of the eleventh century, the merchants, who hailed from Amalfi, west of Salerno, founded the Benedictine Abbey of St Mary of the Latins at Jerusalem. This they peopled with Italian monks who, like themselves, were probably from Amalfi. Although established by merchants, its chief function was to serve as a hospice, or house of refuge, which catered for pilgrims to the Holy Land.

The Knights of Saint John of Jerusalem, therefore, began as a Benedictine Order, established at Jerusalem upon a site that had a long association with John the Baptist, whom they adopted as their patron saint. Their function was to offer refuge to, and to serve, pilgrims to the Holy Land.

Following the First Crusade, the Order took on the responsibility of caring for the sick and injured. Indeed, Brother Gerard, the first known administrator of the Order, appears to have viewed this duty as his special vocation born of his own personal desire to help those in need. However, this could only have been enhanced by the monastic association between John the Baptist and healing. Such a calling would have been strengthened still further by, on the one hand, the fact that the area in which the Order was established had for so long been associated with John, and on the other, that John was their patron saint. The Order's dedication to the sick is reflected in the vows taken by new members upon their entry into the Order. The novitiate would take the missal in his hands and swear an oath to God, the Virgin and John the Baptist that they would live and die in obedience to the King in chastity, owning no property, and acting as a serf and slave to the sick.[67]

This list of trades, movements, places and organisations of which John the Baptist is a patron is by no means exhaustive. Time will no doubt see John the Baptist being claimed as patron by new associations and applied to an assortment of items. For example, in recent years John has become the patron saint of motorways, which is inspired by his mission statement: to 'prepare the way of the Lord' to 'make his paths straight' (Mk 1.3). John's patronage of motorways is so new that it is not yet officially recognised. Nevertheless, it seems fitting that he who makes the Lord's paths straight should be entrusted with the care of one of the most modern of thoroughfares.

Several places, trades and organisations have adopted John the Baptist as their patron saint. The adoption stems from association. Places are associated with John because he is believed to have lived in the area, or that his relics were carried there. Churches are dedicated to him because they are situated next to a river or stream, or the person who founded them felt an affinity with John, such as Mary of Egypt. The earliest churches were built over sites where he is said to have preached and baptised.

In the case of trades and professions, the association with John sometimes lies with his clothes, which made him attractive to various workers in that industry. It may be more subtle, such as his influence over those who work with fire, such as farriers. This stems from his fiery speech. His words about the Lamb of God attracted him to shepherds.

Finally, groups have associated themselves with John because they were inspired by his teaching and lifestyle, such as the monastic movement. Perhaps their headquarters were established in an area associated with John, such as the Knights of Saint John of Jerusalem. Alternatively, their association may be more 'removed', such as the Carmelites, who were associated with Elijah, who in turn is associated with John. Then there are the movements dedicated to succouring the condemned, who were inspired by John's execution.

Midsummer

John the Baptist's main feast day, that of his nativity, falls at Midsummer. This pagan festival involves the worship of the Earth Mother, from whom springs all life and who controls fertility, and the praise of the Sky Father, whose storms and thunder revive nature. Midsummer is, therefore, ultimately concerned with agriculture and the fertility of the land and all that lives upon it. The festival of Midsummer also marks the crossing of the sun over the ecliptic, with the subsequent shortening of the daylight hours, always an occasion for some sort of feast or celebration.[68] Like Christmas, it is a time when darkness and light battle for supremacy. Light, having been defeated, withdraws,

but only until midwinter, when the contest would begin again.
Midsummer is the turning point in the sun's cycle wherein, having
climbed higher in the sky, it appears momentarily to stop before
descending. In an attempt to stop the sun's downward progress,
people would build bonfires.[69] The Midsummer fires are an
example of sympathetic magic, where a desired result is achieved
by imitation.

Having established the nativities of John and Jesus upon pagan
festivals, the church sought to eradicate the pagan elements of
these feast days. Church bells would ring out on Midsummer
Eve, as a challenge to the pagan gods who took the day for their
own.[70] They met with limited success. As a result, many of the
rituals and practices associated with Midsummer's Day came
to be seen by the church as appropriate to St John's Day and
absorbed into its lore. One example of this is the Midsummer
fires. Primarily meant to encourage the sun's return, they would
also frighten away dragons, which were believed to swoop
down and destroy crops.[71] Although pagan in origin, the ritual
of lighting bonfires is appropriate for one who came to be seen
in Christian tradition as a 'burning and shining light' (Jn 5.35).
Moreover, John's Q speech (3.9, 17) contains references to
fire, thus providing a further justification for his link with the
Midsummer bonfires. One example of the seamless fusion of
pagan and Christian tradition is to be found in Greece where one
St John's Eve custom, apparently observed only by women, was to
leap over a fire while saying 'I leave my sins behind.' Thus, a form
of 'folk-Christianity' began to emerge, in which elements of a new
and foreign cult were found to be compatible with, and absorbed
into, long-held traditions and beliefs.

Fertility Rites

Midsummer has always been strongly associated with fertility,
particularly that of the land. It was once the first proper
celebration of the year, and was occasioned by a successful hay

harvest, which ensured the safekeeping of livestock throughout the winter. The agricultural connection between this and John the Baptist's repentance speech (Q 3.9, 17) appealed to the church. John's proclamation is filled with terms associated with the land and farming: axe, trees, fruit, winnowing fork, threshing floor, wheat, granary, chaff.

As has already been noted in the case of the bonfires in Greece, the boundaries between pagan Midsummer and Christian St John's Day often became blurred. John the Baptist himself came to be seen as a protector of crops. In Estonia, for example, it was believed that those who do not attend the St John's Day fire would see his barley infested with thistles and his oats choked by weeds.[72] Not to evoke the protection of the Baptist while working in the fields could have serious consequences. Gregory of Tours speaks of a woman who had gone to work in her field instead of attending the St John's Day mass. Not having shown the respect due to John, her hands were attacked by a holy fire, her face hot as flames and swollen with boils and blisters.[73] The connection with John and his fiery discourse is unmistakable.

People would perform rituals designed to encourage rain. Often a favourite or local saint was invoked for this purpose, as at Commagny in France, where St Gervais is the 'rain saint'. Similarly, a ritual once observed in certain parts of southern and western Russia, associates John the Baptist with a rain-charm.[74] Here, a crowd of women would bathe on St John's Day. As they did so, they would dip into the water a figure made of branches, grass and herbs, which was meant to represent John the Baptist. Two influences are at work in this ritual, which draws upon sympathetic magic. The first is the association of John the Baptist with Elijah, who performed a rain miracle (1 Kings 17.1-18.46). The second link is with John's baptism. The Russian rite even involves a figure representing the Baptist, and which is 'baptised' in water. The idea of sympathetic magic is not incompatible with John's baptism, its Christian associations notwithstanding. Since rain is desired, the practitioner engages in a ritual that involves water. Since John the Baptist is called upon to affect the desired result, it makes sense to imitate his own ritual of baptism.

A similar ritual corresponds John to the Slavonic deity, Kupala.[75] Kupala's feast day, which is marked in June, is observed by bathing in rivers, or washing in the 'dew of Kupala', and throwing floral crowns into the water. The rites also involve fires over which worshippers jump and which are believed to be purificatory. A straw idol is constructed, which is adorned with necklaces and ribbons. At sunset, the idol is carried in procession to the river, which is believed to be endowed with mystical powers. Kupala has survived Christianisation and is partnered with John the Baptist, so that many Slav countries now celebrate the festival of Ivan-Kupala.

Of course, fertility is not restricted to agriculture. It is equally relevant to couples wanting a child. People finding themselves in this position might leap over the flames of Midsummer fires to ensure fertility.[76] This ritual was believed to work even in the case of women thought to be barren, and might have some connection with John's mother, Elizabeth, who was said to have been beyond childbearing age (Lk. 1.7). If so, it reverses the usual direction of customs, wherein the pagan elements are absorbed and transformed by the church. Here, Christian teaching concerning Elizabeth's barrenness appears to have influenced a purely pagan tenet, combining of the customs of both traditions.

John the 'Marrying Saint'

Closely connected with fertility is marriage. Many Midsummer rituals are designed to help a single girl to 'see' her future husband, or to find out if she would meet him in the near future. In a common ritual, a young lady might pick a rose at midnight on Midsummer Eve, keep it in a sheet of paper until Christmas Day, and then eagerly unwrap it. If the bloom were still fresh, she would place it against her bosom whence the man she would marry would take it from her. In another version of this rite, the rose is substituted with St John's Wort. Similar rituals existed for those who were married or who knew the identity of their intended, but who wanted to know whether or not he would be faithful. That such rituals were performed by women rather than men is probably due to the fact that, in the old days at least, men were largely free to choose whom they would marry. A woman often had little influence over her choice of man.

The connection with fertility, marriage and faithfulness in the pagan celebration became transferred to John the Baptist when Midsummer was adopted as John's feast day. It is strengthened by the fact that St John's Day, like most saints' days, was usually marked by pilgrimages. People from far and wide would gather at market squares, churches or monasteries, and such social interaction afforded participants the opportunity for courtship. St John's Day, then, saw the meeting of two influences: the pagan fertility rites and the Christian saint's day pilgrimages. For this reason, John the Baptist became known, at least in certain areas, as a marrying saint.[77] In Portugal, where belief in John as a marrying saint is particularly strong, unmarried girls will pay particular homage to him in the hope that he will show his appreciation by granting them a husband. If John failed to provide the hoped-for spouse, the girl would often exact retribution by lowering an image of him down a well, turning his face to the wall and breaking a bottle of wine on his back.

That John the Baptist should have evolved into a marrying saint may be due to the pagan rites associated with Midsummer, but there are factors within the Christian tradition that would also support such a designation for John. Although the Gospels never disclose John's marital status, the church generally regards him as having been virgin[78] and so, presumably, single. Caxton's *The Golden Legend* also asserts that 'St John Baptist is named in many manners,' one of which is that of 'friend of the spouse', by virtue of 'noblesse of love'. This view of John is supported by the words attributed to him in the Fourth Gospel, wherein his love for Christ is seen to shine: 'He who has the bride is the bridegroom; the friend of the bridegroom, who stands and hears him, rejoices greatly at the bridegroom's voice; therefore this joy of mine is now full' (3.29). Elsewhere, John is shown to advocate good marriage, a clear reference to the case of Herod and Herodias (Mk 6.17 and par.). John's association with marriage, therefore, forms another link between Midsummer and the feast day appointed by the church for the celebration of John the Baptist, and adds another element to folk-Christianity.

Flowers, Herbs and Plants

A fascinating custom associated with saints is that of dedicating flowers, plants and herbs to them. This may be due to the fact that certain flowers bloom at the time of his or her saint's day. For this reason, the scarlet hychnis and the great candlestick are dedicated to John the Baptist. In the lore surrounding plants, blooming is sometimes referred to as 'lighting up', in a reference to the sun and light.[79] The lighting up of these flowers in time for St John's Day makes them, therefore, doubly appropriate.

Often the association is more complex, not least because one is required to understand how certain properties associated with the plants correspond with the attributes of the saint in question. For example, many flowers that are associated with light and sunshine are dedicated to John the Baptist because of his frequent allusion to fire (Q 3.9, 17), his being described as a 'burning and shining lamp' (Jn 5.35) and his association with the light (Jn 1.8). This, as has been seen, justified the church's adoption of Midsummer fires as part of the St John's Day festivities. The purpose of Midsummer fires is primarily to encourage the sun to return. Thus, there is a link between John the Baptist, fire, the fading sun and Midsummer fires. As a result, all flowers that are associated with fire or the sun, whether because of their shape or their colour, are dedicated to John the Baptist. Perhaps the most well-known example of this is the plant that bears his name: St John's Wort, or *Sol Terrestris*. Its yellow flowers symbolise the sun as well as the Baptist who proclaimed the Light. The association is particularly strong if the flower is sun-shaped, such as the moon-daisy, chrysanthemum, or is of a yellow hue.

Certain plants are dedicated to a saint because of the healing properties attributed to them, which, in turn, are associated with the malady against which the saint is invoked. The association is not always consistent, varying as it does according to location. For instance, at Braga, in Portugal, John the Baptist is associated with basil and leeks, or leek garlic.[80] Traditionally, basil is used to bring wealth,[81] which provides a complete contrast with John the Baptist, whom the Gospels are unanimous in depicting as living in abject poverty, at least as regards material matters. However, wealth can be measured in many ways, and we recall that Caxton's *The Golden Legend* depicts John's family as highly placed and wealthy, the young John being brought up in a rich and noble environment. Here, the spiritual wealth that was John's is depicted as material wealth.

Medicinally, basil is endowed with prophylactic qualities according to the traditions of many peoples; it is also used as an anti-inflammatory, an antiseptic and an antispasmodic. The first quality is particularly interesting in relation to John the Baptist. An anti-inflammatory reduces fever, which in turn is associated with fire, as is John. As an antispasmodic, basil reduces convulsions. The connection between John the Baptist and convulsions is not obvious, but it does exist. John was not a 'reed shaken by the wind' (Q 7.24). Convulsions cause shaking, hence the association. Elsewhere, a story of an epileptic boy is juxtaposed with an account of John (Mk. 9.9-29 and par.). The demon is said to have caused the boy to fall 'into fire and into water' as it convulsed him. Again, there is a connection, albeit a loose one, between John, convulsions and the water in which he baptised. In the case of the antiseptic quality of basil, one has to admit defeat, unless it has to do with John's death by beheading.

Garlic is used as a digestive, an antiseptic and a purifier.[82] The digestive quality is clearly associated with John's simple diet of locusts and wild honey, both of which may be seen as pure and wholesome; locusts are *kosher* according to Lev. 11.21-2. The association between John and the antiseptic properties of garlic is obscure, like that of basil, but it might have to do with John's beheading. The connection with purification is significant because John's baptism was intended, in part, to purify the body after the soul had been cleansed by repentance. Magically, garlic is said to encourage strength (cf. Lk. 1.80) and create family togetherness. John's birth completed Zechariah's family.

The people of Piedmont and Lombardy would search oak leaves for 'oil of St John', which was supposed to heal all wounds made by cutting instruments.[83] The connection with John the Baptist is appropriate. John was beheaded, which obviously required a cutting instrument in the form of a sword or an axe. Thus, there might be a correspondence between oil of St John and the antiseptic qualities of basil and garlic. Oil of St John was probably mistletoe, or a decoction made from it, which, in Holstein, is regarded as a universal remedy for green wounds.

Mistletoe

The link between John the Baptist and mistletoe is particularly fascinating when the many uses of this plant are considered. Principally, it is seen as a cure for epilepsy,[84] a malady against which John is invoked in France and Belgium.[85] In Sweden, people would protect themselves from epilepsy by carrying a knife, the handle of which was made of oak mistletoe. German children were protected from the illness by the placing of pieces of mistletoe about their necks. As noted in the discussion of basil, the connection between John and convulsions is appropriate.

Moreover, the Celts believed that mistletoe was efficacious against barrenness.[86] Once again we find a connection with John's birth, to elderly parents and a barren mother (Lk. 1.1.7).

Mistletoe has strong associations with John the Baptist because of the illnesses it cures and the association of these illnesses with John. However, it would appear that John's connection with the plant ultimately derives from ancient customs relating to Midsummer. Druids would honour the annual sacrifice of the Oak King[87] at Midsummer. According to the second-century philosopher Maximus of Tyre, the ancient Celts worshipped Zeus, who is represented as a tall oak in Celtic imagery. The Oak King is a variant of this deity.[88] The fire, which formed part of the celebration, was built of oak wood. Oak is sacred to Druids, and mistletoe grows mainly upon oak. When Midsummer was taken over by the church and turned into St John's Day, the martyred Baptist replaced the sacrificed Oak King, with the ancient associations and qualities attached to mistletoe and the Oak King transferring to John. Appropriately, oak was regarded as special because its roots go so deep into the earth that they are believed to reach the underworld. This is especially significant for the church, wherein John's mission is to preach the salvation of Christ to the people in that lower region. Also significant is the belief, prevalent in Sweden, that mistletoe is a safeguard against fire. Once again, there is a connection with the Baptist. Finally, mistletoe is also known as the 'Golden Bough', because of the golden tints in its berries and leaves. Golden plants, as previously noted, are dedicated to John.

Conclusion

There are two approaches to the study of the sainthood of John the Baptist, the first of which is fixed within the formal setting of the church. Here the dating of John's feast days, hagiographical exegesis and iconography are to be found. The second approach dips into the realm of pagan custom and tradition into which

John the Baptist has become absorbed, and which relates to the customs surrounding the feast day for John's nativity.

The first question to be addressed is why John the Baptist should be a saint. We find that, according to Christian interpretation, John had lived a pious life, one that was dedicated to the service of God and Christ. He had also died a martyr's death. These two factors more than satisfied the church's requirements for sainthood; nevertheless, certain exegetes were moved to elaborate upon John's saintliness and several themes emerged. John was endowed with pre-natal grace. He was born without Original Sin. His life was marked by prophecy. He was showered with gifts from God, such as his ability to preach, his sanctification, and his miraculous birth. These special privileges were not prerequisites to sainthood: John was elevated to that status by virtue of his pious and dedicated life and his death as a martyr. Rather, they were designed to enhance John's position as forerunner and prophet of Christ.

Having established why John should become a saint, the next step is to investigate the dating of his feast days and the reasons for it. John was celebrated within the church by two feast days: 24 June and 29 August. These days observed his Nativity and Decollation respectively. This was highly unusual, and a privilege John shares only with Jesus and the Virgin Mary. Moreover, the main celebration was to be held at the anniversary of his birth, in marked contrast with Christian tradition wherein saints are honoured upon the anniversary of their death or the translation of their relics. The saint is, therefore, usually commemorated upon the day associated with his or her martyrdom, not birth. This is not to say that the day of John's martyrdom was not commemorated. It was. Rather, his nativity is seen as a more important feast day on account of Gabriel's words: 'you will have joy and gladness, and many will rejoice at his birth' (Lk. 1.14). The dating of John's nativity was calculated from that of Jesus, which had been set three days after the winter solstice. Allowing for the six-month interval suggested by Lk. 1.36, John's nativity was set at 24 June, three days after the summer solstice.

An investigation into hagiography involves the study of three legends of John the Baptist, those of Voragine, Caxton and Jöckle, each of whom had a choice of at least three different approaches. One approach is to present a narrative the details of which might contradict that which is found in the Gospel accounts, another is to conflate two contradictory elements in the Gospels accounts, while a third is to build upon lacunae or gaps in those accounts.

A legend serves to inspire the reader by presenting an image of a saint's life and showing how God had intervened in it. Another purpose is to bring the saint alive to the reader, making him or her more accessible. An alternative way to achieve this is to present the believer with an image of a saint, which includes symbols, or icons, that represent the reasons why he or she was selected for sainthood and recalls events within the life of that saint. In discussing John the Baptist's iconography, we find that the Western tradition drew largely from portrayals of John as presented by the evangelists. The Eastern tradition, however, added the wings of an angel to John's image, thus reflecting his status as a messenger or angel, as described in Mal. 3.1.

Several places, trades and organisations adopted John the Baptist as a patron saint. The factors influencing his adoption were varied. In the case of places, it is often because the location lays claim to being the resting place of some of his relics. Florence and Amiens are examples of this. Perhaps it was the scene in which many of the events of his life were played out. This was especially so in the case of early churches. Similarly, churches built close to a river or stream will often be dedicated to John because of his connection with the River Jordan. A trade might adopt John because it works with materials that are associated with him, or have links with elements found in his discourses. For instance, furriers see a connection between their trade and John's camel hair garments. Farriers link themselves to the fiery elements of John's Q speech (3.9, 17). An organisation might embrace John as its patron if it is located in a spot that has a strong association with him, as is the case with the Knights of Saint John of Jerusalem. Alternatively, as with the monastic movement, it may be because it sees him as the ideal model for its chosen way of life.

Each of these facets of John's sainthood, the justification for it, the dating of his feast days, the legends, iconography and his rank as a patron saint belong specifically to the Christian tradition as it pertains to John. The church is able to control what is said and accepted about John in this realm because it largely invented it. The Saint John the Baptist of Christianity is the result of church interpretation of John as it was made in the earliest times. However, there is a second approach to the study of John's sainthood.

Many of the customs surrounding the feast day of John's Nativity have their roots firmly planted in ancient pagan belief. This comes as no surprise since the church's setting of St John's Day coincides with the great pagan festival of Midsummer. This festival, marked as it is by bonfires, was seen as appropriate by the church because the fires were interpreted to represent John's fiery discourse. Midsummer is mainly concerned with agriculture and fertility. This came to be transferred to John by means of the agricultural metaphors that are to be found in his Q speech (3.9, 17). John became linked with fertility because he was himself the fruit of an infertile marriage. Childless couples would leap over the flames of Midsummer fires to ensure fertility. This ritual was believed to work even when the woman was thought to be barren, and so this marks a connection with John's mother, Elizabeth, who was beyond childbearing age (Lk. 1.7). As such, it reverses the usual direction of customs, wherein the pagan elements are absorbed and transformed by the church. John's association with Elijah and, perhaps more strongly, his baptism in water ensured he would be invoked as a rain charm.

John's stance concerning marriage caused him to be adopted in certain areas as a marrying saint. This designation for John is aided by the fact that saints' days are usually celebrated by pilgrimages. Such occasions afforded ample opportunity for people to meet, families to unload a superfluous daughter and relationships to be established. In addition, young ladies who wished to know the identity of their future husbands would invoke John, or engage in rituals associated with his feast day. Betrothed or married ladies would sometimes follow similar rites to see if their intended or spouse would remain faithful.

John the Baptist is associated with various flowers, plants and herbs. The link may be due to the coincidental timing of the blossoming of a flower and his feast day. Sometimes the influencing factor is the colour or shape of the flower or plant, which symbolises John. In other cases, it can be ascribed to correspondences between John and certain attributes that are associated with him, such as wealth, or a condition such as an illness or an injury. John is associated with herbs that are understood to cure epilepsy, since he was not a 'reed shaken by the wind' (Q 7.24) and he has tentative links with an epileptic boy cured by Jesus. Many of John's herbs are used to control fever, an association influenced by his many references to fire. Some of his plants are antiseptic, and so are used to heal wounds in a strong association with John's death by beheading. Others reflect aspects of John's life. Garlic finds a correspondence with John's strength (Lk 1.80) and the fact that he completed Zechariah's family.

One plant in particular, mistletoe, has more associations with John than any other: it is believed to cure epilepsy and it is yellow in colour. Its correspondences even extend to John's role in the underworld: mistletoe grows mainly upon oak and the roots of these trees run so deeply into the earth that they are said to reach that lower realm. Interesting also is the correlation between mistletoe, the Oak King and John the Baptist.

In druidic mythology, mistletoe represents the Oak King, who was sacrificed; the church transformed this deity into the martyred John the Baptist. Here is a perfect illustration of how pagan belief was adopted and adapted by the church but never completely eradicated.

This study of John the Baptist as a saint has yielded some fascinating results. It has revealed how John and his feast days are honoured. Observances of John follow a sliding scale from purely Christian theology expressed within the formal setting of church interpretation to pagan belief, only slightly tinged with Christian overtones and observed in the customs and rituals of common folk. Christianity has taken John into its fold by moulding him into the desired image of the prophet and forerunner of Christ. Occasionally, his status as a baptiser is remembered, but only insofar as his rite is understood to have been the means by which Jesus of Nazareth became Christ. As though to compensate for this, Christianity has made John a healing saint. Paganism too, has taken John the Baptist to its heart by making him a virtual deity. It has endowed him with the magic and mystery of its deepest beliefs and made him a healer. Although usually at odds, in this respect, Christianity and paganism are in perfect agreement.

SUMMATION

John the Baptist was a Jewish wilderness prophet who conducted his ministry in the area surrounding the Jordan River during the first century CE. His choice of location was significant. The desert held powerful historical and religious connotations for Jews, of which John was acutely aware. For example, it was to one of the demonic entities that inhabited the desert wastes that priests would send the sacrificial goat bearing the sins of the people at the Day of Atonement. On the other hand, for centuries, prophets such as John had been drawn into the desert, where they encountered the dynamic force of God, whose messages they would relay to his chosen people.

The prophets urged their hearers to live righteously and piously, to live in peace and harmony with their neighbours and to give right worship to God. The oppression under which the people lived was understood to be the result of their refusal to obey these simple rules. Were they to return to God's ways, the prophets taught, they would be restored. However, God's wrath awaited those who continued their self-seeking, impious ways. The wilderness, therefore, so closely connected with God, sin and atonement, came to acquire powerful eschatological associations. Such associations were heightened by the fact that the desert had been the setting for Israel's deliverance by God and the establishment of the covenant.

The period of Roman rule that marked the first century brought with it a new flowering of prophecy. Drawn once more into the desert, men such as Judas the Galilaean, Theudas, several unnamed prophets, the Egyptian and John the Baptist were heirs to a tradition that had continued since the days of old. They saw themselves as the new recipients of God's word, which they passed on to the followers with varying degrees of success. Although they differed markedly in their approach, such men found common ground in their respective messages, which were entirely eschatological. This factor was, of course, common to all prophets, whatever century they lived in. However, while the ancient prophets were content simply to preach their message, the majority of first-century prophets chose to reinforce their message by deeds. Thus, the people witnessed the rise of a new type of prophet, the prophets of action. Judas the Galilaean favoured the militant, revolutionary approach. Theudas, several unnamed prophets and the Egyptian directed their ministries in such a way that they came across as re-enactments of certain significant biblical events. The events they chose to imitate were selected specifically because of their association with God's intervention in the salvation of his people and their release from oppression. The Exodus and the Conquest, events so prominent in the minds of Jews, became avenues of renewed hope for the people. It seemed that all one had to do was to remind God of his previous intervention in order to press him into action once again. Whether their methods were peaceful, or whether they sought to hasten God's hand by more violent means, the Roman authorities viewed each of these groups with suspicion. Seeing them as a threat to peace and stability, they put them down in the harshest way possible.

This, then, is the milieu in which John the Baptist lived. He might, like his contemporaries, have sought to re-enact the

Exodus by causing people to cross the desert and the Jordan, just as their forebears had done so long ago. However, the most important element of his message was not the exploitation of wilderness symbolism. John's approach was unconventional, as was his message. He saw the oppression under which his fellow Jews were living as a sign that the old order was coming to an end. God would come, bringing fiery judgement and damnation. There was but one way to survive the wrath and attain salvation. This was to submit to a 'baptism of repentance for the forgiveness of sins'.

Baptism was a predominant feature of John the Baptist's ministry, but immersion in water was not unknown to Jews. Water rituals were prescribed in the Torah, where they restored the individual to ritual purity and rendered them worthy to serve God again. However, John's baptism differed from these forms of ablutions. Unlike the prescribed immersions and washings, which were designed to be taken whenever the need arose, John's baptism was meant to be taken only once. With rare exceptions, Jewish lustration rites were self-administered. John administered his baptism himself. The Torah rites and that of John did find common ground in that they were concerned with physical purity. However, John knew that this alone would not prepare people for the coming judgement. People had to meet the eschatological event with a pure heart. John, like the prophets of the classical period, knew that rituals designed to restore the body to ritual purity could do nothing to cleanse a heart rendered impure by immoral behaviour, so he called upon people to change within their innermost being. He urged them to reject sin and return to God. In a word, he asked them to repent. It was imperative that the people were sincerely penitent. They had to ask forgiveness for their sins, resolve to act justly towards their neighbours and show piety towards God. Only then could they submit to baptism. Serving fundamentally as a penitential ritual, John's baptism was acceptable to God because the penitent had truly and sincerely changed his or her ways. Now God bestowed his forgiveness upon the penitent through baptism, with John performing the rite in the role of a priest. The penitents, now purified in their inner and outer being, were prepared for the imminent judgement.

John, therefore, conducted a ministry that was entirely in accord with Jewish tradition. It functioned as a purification ritual in accordance with Torah and reflected the teachings of the prophets of the classical era, who spoke of the necessity to return to God in sincere repentance. However, it contained several revolutionary aspects. It removed ritual from the Temple and brought it into the midst of the people. John brought the people into the wilderness, to him a more holy place because it was the natural dwelling place of God and the scene of the Covenant. John did not ask for sacrifices. Instead, he baptised in living water; this water had not been collected by people but had been given to them by God in the form of rivers and springs. John prepared the people for imminent judgement using a water rite that made him unique in comparison with the prophets of old, as well as his own contemporaries.

Another area in which John the Baptist was unique among the latter is his proclamation of a figure who was to come; a Coming One. Although he appears not to have identified this person, he did define the mission he expected him to perform. Among the figures, human or supernatural, who were expected to come to judge and restore at the end of days, were many who fitted some of the criteria outlined by John. Only one fulfilled them all: God. Nevertheless, John was probably receptive to the idea that God would appoint a human agent to continue his work in much the same way as John himself had been used as a prophet and baptiser. It was even possible that such a person might emerge from the ranks of John's followers.

Among the followers of John the Baptist was Jesus of Nazareth. Jesus had come of his own accord to hear John. He then submitted to John's baptism. He did so because he agreed with John's message and wanted to show his commitment to live in righteousness and piety. Although most of those baptised by John returned to their homes, purified and prepared for the judgement to come, Jesus remained with John. At some stage, his position within this emerging sect changed when John appointed him as a baptiser. The relationship between John the Baptist began as one of master and disciple.

John's appointment of Jesus as an assistant arose from his need to proclaim his message while there was still time to do so. Jesus, therefore, preached John's message, which included the proclamation of the Coming One, and offered John's baptism. He, too, warned of the imminent eschaton and the judgement that it would bring. He exhorted, as strongly as did John, the people to repent while they still had a chance to do so. Due to the urgency of the task, Jesus also took helpers, some of whom were probably assigned to him by John, others he would have called himself. These people were to become his disciples.

In the beginning, Jesus' baptising ministry ran in conjunction with that of John. Although it cannot be known how long John and Jesus worked together, it was probably a significant length of time. Then Jesus began to follow a different path. He moved his mission to Galilee, where he appears to have become the leader of what had by now grown into a movement. The catalyst for Jesus' change of locale was the arrest of John the Baptist. His move to Galilee was the only logical step because that was the only province that had not yet heard John's message.

At approximately the same time as he changed the setting of his ministry, Jesus altered his approach to his mission. He adopted a new attitude towards praying and fasting, but not to baptising, which he continued to perform. The reason for the change was that he found that he could heal and exorcise, and he interpreted his ability to perform miracles as a sign that the coming of God was closer than he or John had imagined. Jesus was forced to shift the perspective of the mission he had inherited from John so that it focused on the present rather than the future.

John the Baptist had been arrested by Herod Antipas and taken to the fortress-palace of Machaerus in Peraea. The reasons why Herod ordered the arrest were entirely political. John had preached repentance, urged sinners to change their ways and submit to baptism. He had singled out Herod as an example of sinfulness due to the tetrarch's adulterous marriage to Herodias.

Herod found himself under attack from two fronts: the first came from John, whose preaching humiliated him; the second resulted from the serious political implications arising from his divorce. The wife he had repudiated in order to marry Herodias was the daughter of Aretas IV, king of Nabataea, whose kingdom bordered upon Herod's province of Peraea, and whose traders would have heard and spread the preaching of John the Baptist. Herod would, in time, pay the price of this insult to the king, which also involved reneging upon a peace treaty.

Meanwhile, John the Baptist, the voice in the wilderness, had to be removed and silenced because he was attracting large crowds. This in itself was a cause for concern to the authorities. However, John had announced another figure to come. The Coming One could have been interpreted as a political figure. This, and the fact that John worked within an atmosphere of heightened eschatological expectation, left Herod Antipas with no alternative but to act. John the Baptist was taken prisoner to Machaerus, where he was subsequently condemned to be beheaded at Herod Antipas's order. John the Baptist suffered the fate of many of his contemporaries when he was executed within the walls of a fortress-palace, far from the open spaces in which he had encountered God.

Such is the history of John the Baptist. He was a prophet who lived, preached, baptised and died in the desert regions where he encountered God, whose message he carried to the masses. However, the end of history marks the beginning of tradition.

John the Baptist, his identity, purpose and mission took on a new dimension as followers of Jesus, John's former disciple and co-baptiser, reinterpreted their master in accordance with a new theology. They had come to see Jesus as more than an eschatological prophet and preacher, one who discovered that he could heal, exorcise demons and hold sway over nature. John the Baptist, who had initiated Jesus into his new career, had to be reinterpreted so that he would fit into this new viewpoint.

There was no real consensus among those who presented the mission of Jesus to their respective churches as consolidated in the four Gospels and the extra-canonical literature. This meant that differences in the various interpretations of Jesus were reflected in differences in the representation and portrayal of John the Baptist. Beginning with Q, John's historical persona as an apocalyptic preacher was largely preserved. Accounts of his baptism were offered with varying degrees of emphasis. More importantly, his announcement of the Coming One was included, with the evangelists making it clear in various ways that they understood this figure to be none other than Jesus, now the Christ. John's preaching of the Coming One sealed his fate in tradition as the forerunner of Christ. Only in the Fourth Gospel does he deviate from this path. Here, he is the witness to Christ, a figure who had existed from the very beginning, and so could have no forerunner.

John's role of forerunner was closely allied to his identification as Elijah *redivivus*. However, here also, the evangelists differ as to their degree of acceptance of this connection. Of the Synoptics, only Matthew makes it explicit by showing that a speech of Jesus' regarding Elijah actually refers to John. Q and Mark simply imply it, although Mark is a little more forthcoming, with references to Mal. 3.1, later taken up by Matthew and, to a lesser extent, Luke. This Hebrew Bible proof text speaks of 'my messenger' later identified as Elijah (4.5). Mark invents for John an 'Elijahnic secret', which parallels the 'messianic secret' with which he shrouds Jesus. Luke's position is ambiguous. For him, John is

Elijah-like, rather than Elijah *redivivus*. Luke seeks to separate John the Baptist from Jesus in salvation history. For him, John belongs to an earlier period, that of the Law and the prophets. Jesus belongs to the new period, ushered in by his own ministry. The relative positions of John and Jesus in salvation history being a natural progression, there is no need for insinuations or elaborate explanations, but simply statements of the facts as Luke sees them. In the Fourth Gospel, John is entirely separated from any idea that he should be identified as Elijah. This stems once again from the Fourth Evangelist's portrayal of Christ as an eternal, pre-existent being.

John, having fulfilled his function of forerunner in life, however it might be portrayed, reprises his role in death. His execution is presented in such a way that the reader should make a connection between it and the crucifixion of Jesus. John's death, following a successful ministry, negates questions regarding the success of Jesus' ministry. In short, John could be a divinely ordained prophet of Christ, yet still die. By the same token, Jesus could be Christ, yet still die.

John's death also allowed his role of forerunner to be extended to the underworld. This was, in a way, a necessary development stemming from the need to explain the crucifixion as being part of God's plan of salvation. If Jesus must die, then Christ must rise up in fulfilment of his mission. The period between the death on the cross and the resurrection was shown to be part of Christ's ministry of salvation to the righteous dead. Christ went to those who would have been his followers had they not died prior to the Incarnation. Just as Christ required a precursor on earth, so, too, did he have a precursor in the underworld. That function in both locations was fulfilled by John the Baptist.

As it was, John's status as forerunner did not appear to be universally accepted. The extra-canonical literature largely ignores a forerunner tradition. Instead, it places much emphasis upon John's baptism and an uneasiness with the implications associated with Jesus' submission to it. Primarily, it is used as a means of conveying the message that Jesus was without sin.

The relegation of John's role as baptiser to minor importance is a continuation of a phenomenon that can be traced throughout the Gospels. In the earliest written Gospel, Mark, John plays an important part in what appears to be the 'initiation' of Christ. Matthew includes the baptism but feels he must qualify Jesus' submission to a rite that was presented as 'repentance for the forgiveness of sins'. Luke shows that Jesus was baptised after John's imprisonment. The Fourth Gospel presents John's baptism of Jesus merely as a memory of John's.

In the hands of the Church Fathers, John's baptism would become the responsibility of the apostles and teachers, and even of Christ himself. The apostles and teachers might have been given the task of baptising in the lower world because Jesus had sent them out to baptise as part of the evangelistic commission (Mt. 28.18-20). Their mission in the underworld would be an extension of that commission. On the other hand, Jesus had bestowed the Holy Spirit and, according to the Fourth Evangelist, had baptised in water. There was, therefore, no longer any need for John to baptise in the underworld; indeed, the *raison d'être* of John's baptism meant that it no longer had a place within salvation history. John – attempts to Christianise him notwithstanding – remained part of Judaism and belonged to an earlier period of salvation history. Here, then, is another reason for his being excluded from baptising. As one who bestows baptism, John no longer has a place in Christianity. As one who points the way to the Christ, who led the people to the Light, John's status in Christianity is assured. Despite the epithet that will always be attached to his name, John the Baptist has officially and formally become John the Forerunner.

Now that the fiery preacher of the desert wastes has been tamed and redefined by the early church, John can be accepted into it ranks as a saint. He can now be worshipped and appealed to, his birth and death are marked by celebration, feasting and prayer. Various movements and groups adopt him as their patron, and he becomes associated with various locations and trades. Imagery from the pagan world is pressed into service, as John's iconography emerged to mix with symbols inspired by the Gospels and Extra-Canonical literature. As a saint, John had relics, he worked miracles and could fulfil the wishes of those looking for a suitable and faithful marriage partner, and he could heal. Plants and herbs became associated with him, reflecting the iconography that had applied to him. Perhaps more than any other saint, the imagery and association of John the Baptist most successfully combine elements of the pagan and the Christian world. In this respect, John is truly a saint for all seasons, a baptiser and a forerunner who introduced a message and a ritual that has endured up to the present day.

NOTES

Introduction

1. Summaries of Life of Jesus Research can be found in Telford (1994), pp.33-74; Webb (1991b), pp.19-23; Stanton, pp.285-90.
2. Webb (1991b), pp.20-22
3. Sanders, p.11.
4. Webb (1991b), pp.23-4.

Chapter 1: The Wilderness

1. See Wilkinson *More than a Prophet: John the Baptist in Tradition, Art, Literature and Film* (unpublished PhD thesis; University of Newcastle upon Tyne, 2003).
2. Tatum, p115.
3. See Scobie (1964), pp.41-48; Kraeling, pp.1-32; Thyen, p.150.
4. Sometimes translated as 'impostor', the word used by Josephus is γόης, meaning a wizard or sorcerer. Either way, Josephus's assessment of Theudas is clear.
5. See Brandon, p.101.
6. See Trumbower, p.30); Barnett, p.681; Horsley, p.457.
7. See Barnett, p.688; Rhoads, p.83.
8. Trumbower, p.32.
9. Horsley, p.437.

10. See Stern, p.238; Harvey, p.420.
11. See Harvey, p.420.
12. Martin, p.20.
13. See Rhoads, p.75-76.
14. Horsley, pp.455-56.
15. See Vermes (1997), pp.84-90; Horsley, pp.455-56.
16. See Rhoads, p.90.
17. Heard, p.689.
18. Aenon, near Salim suggests that John took his mission to Samaria.
19. Cf. Webb (1991b), pp.363-4.

Chapter 2: Baptism

1. Tatum, pp.122-23.
2. Guyénot, p.67.
3. Kraeling, p.112.
4. Barclay, J.M.G, p.32.
5. Webb (1991b), p.57.
6. However, the perception that there were the two types of repentance is not unique to John. It was known to Judaism as a whole and is derived from the Hebrew Bible. See Webb (1991b), pp.184-89.
7. Cited in Charles, p.135). Although it is difficult to date this text, it is used here because it provides an important example of 'penitential repentance'.
8. In one exception, Neh. 9.29, people are required to return to Torah.
9. Cited in Charles, p.396.
10. Taylor, J., p.89.
11. See Josephus, *Jewish War*, 2.164, 3.374; *Apion* 2.218; Dan. 12.1-3.
12. BDB 3824.
13. BDB 1320.
14. Taylor, J, p.88-89.

15. Tatum, p.122.
16. Conzelmann, p.102.
17. Lüzemann, p.277.
18. Bultmann (1963), p.145). His conclusion is based upon the fact that the profession of a soldier is taken for granted. Thyen, pp.136-37 agrees that this passage is Hellenistic in origin, and also that it was probably constructed by Luke. He adds that, given the imminence of the judgement, John had no time to concern himself with 'such social teaching or its preservation'.
19. Tatum, pp.134-35.
20. Lüzemann, p.278.
21. This hypothesis was discussed by the delegates of the Jesus Seminar and given an average of 52% in favour, see Tatum, pp.123-24.
22. Murphy, p.53.
23. See pp.65–66.
24. This was discussed by the Jesus Seminar and awarded an average of 52% in favour see Tatum, p.125.
25. See pp.22, 26, 36, 38, 58, 66, 101, 119, 133.
26. Tatum, p.126.
27. Those who do not accept this hypothesis are Kraeling (p.119) and Becker (pp.39-40). Those who support it are Webb (1991b, pp.197-202); Webb (1994, pp.194-96) and Tatum, (pp.125-26).
28. Webb (1994), p.195.
29. Scobie (1964), pp.114-15 cites the multitudes, tax collectors and soldiers mentioned in the special Luke passage 3.10-14.
30. Webb (1994), p.195.
31. Webb (1991b), p.199.
32. Webb (1991b), p.200.
33. Hollenback (1992), p.893.
34. Tatum, p.133.
35. Tuckett (1996), p.116.

36. Webb (1991b), p.176; Kraeling, p.49.
37. Webb (1991b), p.177 n.43.
38. See pp.52–53.
39. Tatum, p.136.
40. Miq. 8.5. Although a late text, possibly reflects concerns that might have been current in John's day.
41. A similar phenomenon occurs at Ephesus (Acts 19.1-7).
42. Discussions recorded in the Mishnah (Miq. 9.1) suggest that the question of what was acceptable for people to wear during immersion was the subject of much debate.

Chapter 3: The Coming One

1. This figure will henceforth be referred to as the Coming One.
2. The delegates of the Jesus Seminar supported the authenticity of John's proclamation of the Coming One by a vote of 51% in favour, see Tatum, p.129. This relatively low vote reflects the delegates' concern that the announcement of the Coming One is combined with John's assertion of his unworthiness to carry, or untie, this person's sandals. The Fourth Gospel (1.26-27) and Acts (13.25) report John's unworthiness without the announcement of the Coming One.
3. Webb (1994), p.199.
4. Or 'winnowing shovel', to give the literal translation of πτυον.
5. The Coming One is a masculine figure; Mk 1.8 and par. use αυτος.
6. Webb (1994), pp.198-99.
7. Guyénot, pp.70-76.
8. Best, p.237.
9. Scobie (1964), p.67.
10. Dunn, pp.83-84.
11. Hollenbach (1992), p.896.
12. See pp.54–55.
13. However, God is not a personified element like Agni, the

Indian fire-god. Rather, he is a majestic being who embraces both grace and judgement, see Lang, p.937.

14. Webb (1991b), p.273.
15. See Webb (1994), p.274; cf. Scobie (1964), p.73n.1; Dunn, p.87; Robinson, J.A.T (1957). pp.277-78n.4.
16. Telford (1999), p.14-15; Scobie (1964), p.73n.1.
17. Brown, R.E. (1965), p.136.
18. Scobie (1964), p.62.
19. Webb (1994), p.202.
20. Collins, p.75.
21. Collins, pp.75-77.
22. Webb (1991b), pp.237-39.
23. Collins, p.173; Vermes (1997), p.85.
24. Guyénot, pp.130-31.
25. Cf. Scobie (1958), p.41.
26. Webb (1991a), p.107.
27. Cited in Charles, p.315.
28. Cited in Charles, p.649.
29. This was the conclusion of the delegates of the Jesus Seminar, see Tatum, p.135. The hypothesis that the 'Lamb of God' speech was authentic to John the Baptist was awarded a vote of 100% against since it represented too much the evangelist's own creativity.

Chapter 4: Jesus the Baptiser

1. Elsewhere, the Fourth Gospel (5.35) speaks of John in the past tense, from which the reader infers that he is dead.
2. Murphy-O'Connor, p363.
3. Jeremias, p.182.
4. See pp.23–24.
5. Guyénot, p168.
6. Guyénot, p.168.
7. See Conzelmann, p.21); Duling and Perrin (1994), p.381.
8. Dodd (1963), pp.272-74.

9. See Meyer (1992), p.5.

10. Murphy-O'Connor, p.363.

11. Meyer (1979), p.283 n.23.

12. Murphy-O'Connor, p.362.

13. Murphy-O'Connor, p.362.

14. Webb (1994), p.221.

15. Meyer (1979), pp.283-84, n.23.

16. Murphy-O'Connor, p.365.

17. Murphy-O'Connor, p.362.

18. Brown (1978b), p.169.

19. Dodd (1963), p.236. Brown, R.E. (1978b), p.175-77 also allows that there might be an element of tradition underpinning this material.

20. Murphy-O'Connor, p.364-65.

21. Murphy-O'Connor, p.364-65; Brown, R.E. (1978b), pp.183-84); Scobie (1964), pp.175-6.

22. Brown, R.E. (1978b), pp.179-80.

23. Lohse, pp.271-72.

24. Jacobsen Buckley, p.361, Rudolph, p.363; Tatum, p.101.

25. A study of John's connection with the Mandaeans is made in Wilkinson *More than a Prophet: John the Baptist in Tradition, Art, Literature and Film* (unpublished PhD thesis; University of Newcastle upon Tyne, 2003).

26. Scobie (1964), pp. 95, 154.

27. Webb (1994), p.222.

28. Guyénot, pp.204-205.

29. Dodd (1963), pp.223-28.

30. Guyénot, pp.204-205.

31. Dodd, pp.174-80.

32. Dodd, p.174.

Chapter 5: The Kingdom of God

1. Murphy-O'Connor, p.371.

2. Dunn, p.640.

3. However, this did not prevent the development of a miracle tradition associated with John the Baptist, see pp.222–31.
4. See Chilton (1988), p.2); Bultmann (1963), p.171.
5. Rodd (1987), p.292.
6. France (1994), p.105.
7. Fitzmyer (1981), p.664.
8. Cf. John Chrysostom *Hom. xxxvi in Matt.* 11.2; PG. 57. 413-15; Augustine *Sermones de scripturis* 66.3-4; PL. 38 432-3.
9. Loisy (1907), p.660.
10. Goguel (1928), pp.64-65).
11. Tertullian *Adversus Marcionem* 4.18.4-6; CC. 1.589-90.
12. Dunn, p.56.
13. Dunn, p.57.
14. Hollenbach (1982), p.202.
15. Kraeling, p.151; Jeremias, p.48; Hollenbach (1982), p.209.
16. Perrin (1967), p.63.
17. Bultmann (1963), p.162.
18. Perrin (1967), p.64.
19. See Lohse, pp.57-65).
20. Hollenbach (1982), pp.209-211.
21. Telford (1999), p.62.
22. Bultmann (1963), p.23.

Chapter 6: The Death of John the Baptist
1. Tatum, p.160.
2. Webb (1991b), p.368.
3. Richardson, pp.42, 307.
4. Bultmann (1963), p.301.
5. See Enslin (1975), p.13; Tatum, p.161.
6. Harrington, p.610.
7. Hoehner, p.158.
8. Scobie (1964), p.181; Hoehner, p.135.
9. Hoehner, p.135.

10. Richardson, pp.307-308 n.59.
11. The name of Herodias's dancing daughter is given by Josephus (*Ant.* 18.136).
12. Taylor, V., p.314.
13. Taylor, V., p.314.
14. Kraeling, p.87.
15. Taylor, V., p.314.
16. See Kraeling, p.87; Enslin (1975), p.13.
17. Tatum, p.161.
18. Dalman, cited in Hoehner, p.157.
19. Hoehner, p.151.
20. Enslin (1975), p.13.
21. Richardson, p.181.
22. Hoehner, p.148.
23. See Bultmann (1963), p.301.
24. Cf. Hoehner, pp.117-18).
25. See Enslin (1975), p.13); cf. Harrington, p.610.
26. Scobie (1964), p.180.
27. Hoehner, p.305.
28. Scobie (1964), p.180.
29. Hoehner, p.306.
30. Hoehner, pp.118-19.

Chapter 7: More than a Prophet

1. Livingston, p.276.
2. Jones, p.152.
3. Cooper, p.139.
4. *Catechism of the Catholic Church*, p.166.
5. Duling and Perrin (1994), p.115.
6. Webb (1991b), p.55.
7. Taylor, J., p.12.
8. Webb (1991b), p.252; Telford (1999), p.195.
9. See Wink, p.3; Tatum, pp.116-17.
10. Kraeling, pp.14-15.

11. Pesch (1976), pp.80-82.
12. See Taylor, J., p.37.
13. Duling and Perrin (1994), pp.322-23.
14. Davies and Allison, p.476.
15. Taylor, J, p.249.
16. Viviano, p.657.
17. Bultmann (1963), p.295.
18. Fitzmyer (1981), p.318.
19. Goulder and Sanderson, pp.15-16.
20. Goulder and Sanderson, p.16.
21. The name Mary is a variant of the Hebrew name, Miriam.
22. Goulder and Sanderson, p.17.
23. See Kraeling, p.17); Dibelius (1953), p.8; Scobie (1964), pp.52-53.
24. Tatum, p.69.

Chapter 8: Into the Underworld

1. Origen, Homily on 1 Kings 28.9, *Patrologia Graecae* 12.1024.
2. *De Christo et Antichristo* 45 (translated from Sheerin (1976), p.5).
3. Cited in Cameron, pp.147-48; see also p.133.
4. 'In decollationem S. Joannis Baptistae', *Patrologia Graecae* 107.196B; 197D-200.
5. *Thomas* 46.
6. *Thomas* 78.1-3.
7. *Rec.* 54.8.
8. Fitzmyer (1981), p.329; Brown (1978a), p.282.

Chapter 9: Saint John the Baptist

1. *Catechism of the Catholic Church*, p.192; Livingstone, p.219.
2. Baring-Gould, p.331.
3. Augustine cited in Caxton, vol 5, pp.69-70.
4. Voragine, vol 1, p.329.

5. Voragine, vol 1, pp.329-30.
6. Voragine, vol 1, p.330.
7. Voragine, vol 1, p.330.
8. Caxton, vol 3, p.254.
9. Caxton, vol 3, p.256.
10. Caxton, vol 3, p.258.
11. Caxton, vol 3, p.257.
12. Caxton, vol 3, p.257.
13. Caxton, vol 3, p.258
14. Culpeper, p.76. Many plants and herbs are associated with John, either through his feast days or by the medicinal or magical properties of the plants themselves, which correspond to conditions associated with him by virtue of events in his life and aspects of his teaching.
15. Caxton, vol 3, p.259
16. Caxton, vol 3, p.259
17. Caxton, vol 3, p.260
18. Caxton, vol 3, pp.260-1
19. Caxton, vol 3, p.261
20. Caxton, vol 1, pp.132-40
21. Caxton, vol 3, pp.67-8
22. Jöckle, pp.241-2
23. Cross and Livingstone, p.688
24. Cooper (1978), p.176
25. Metford, p.246
26. Cooper (1978), p.104
27. Cooper (1978), p.40
28. Metford, p.224
29. Martyr, p.5
30. In fact, Antoninus Martyr states that the church was built at Samaria. His editor/annotator, C. W. Wilson, corrects the mistake.
31. Martyr, p.12
32. Buzy, p.269

33. McGreal, p.19
34. Schuster, p.84
35. Lupieri, p.14
36. Jerome, pp.17, 30, 56
37. Cited in Chadwick, pp.267-8
38. Basil the Great, 1.42, 5
39. *De Virginitate*, cited in Lupieri, p.14
40. Gregory of Nazianzus, 42.75
41. Socrates, p.328
42. Palladius, p.27
43. Hutchison, p.28
44. Fortini, p.87
45. Bonaventure, p.219
46. Thomas of Celano, p.242
47. Thomas of Celano, p.364
48. Smith, pp.231-2
49. Maier, pp.196-7
50. Perkins, p.969
51. Harrington, p.609
52. Keiffer, p.981
53. Sanuto, pp.58-60. This story was written in 1321
54. MacCulloch, p.653
55. Fetellus, pp.132-3
56. Cited in Lupieri, pp.18-20
57. John the Baptist does not appear in the Transfiguration story. However, he features in the dialogue following it.
58. Walsh, p.312
59. Voragine, vol 1, p.138
60. Fetellus, pp.132-33
61. Fetellus, pp.132-33
62. Le Braz, p.132
63. Palladius, p.121
64. Sire, p.3
65. Riley-Smith, p.32

66. Sire, p.3
67. Riley-Smith, p.233. In connection with healing, it should be noted that a saint is often associated with certain illnesses or injuries, against which he or she can be invoked
68. Demdike, p.23
69. Frazer, pp.814-28
70. Taylor, B. p.43
71. Sinker, p.885
72. Frazer, p.822
73. Gregory of Tours cited in Van Dam, pp.256-7
74. Frazer, p.92
75. Alexinsky, pp.296, 298. Kupala is a deity of joy. The name comes from the root kupat, to bathe
76. Wilson (1989), p.59.
77. Wilson (1983), p.272
78. Caxton, vol 3, p.253
79. Taylor, G., p.65
80. Wilson (1983), p.263.
81. Medici, p.115
82. Medici, p.115
83. Frazer, p.866
84. Culpeper, p.98
85. Baring-Gould, p.334
86. Green, p.151
87. Wilson (1989), p.59
88. See Maier, p.211

BIBLIOGRAPHY

Alexinsky, A., 'Slavonic Mythology' in F. Guirand (ed.) *The New Larousse Encyclopaedia of Mythology* (London: Book Club Associates, 1973).

Allison, D.C., 'A Plea for Thoroughgoing Eschatology', *Journal of Biblical Literature*, 113 (1994).

Augsburger, M.S., *The Communicator's Commentary: Matthew* (Waco: Word Books, 1982).

Bammel, E., 'The Baptist in Early Christian Tradition', *New Testament Studies*, 18 (1971).

Barclay, J.M G. (ed.), *Frequently Asked Questions on The Dead Sea Scrolls* (Glasgow: Trinity St. Mungo Press, 1998).

Barclay, W., *The Gospel of Mark* (Edinburgh: The Saint Andrew Press, 1975).

Baring-Gould, S., *The Lives of the Saints* (Edinburgh: John Grant, 1914).

Barnett, P.W., 'The Jewish Sign Prophets – AD40-70: Their Intentions and Origins', *New Testament Studies*, 27 (1981).

Basil the Great, *Epistle* 1.42, 5 (*Patrologiae Graecae*, 32; Turnhout: Typographi Brepols Editores Pontifici, J.P. Migne, no date).

Becker, J., *Johannes der Täufer und Jesus von Nazareth* (Biblische Studien 63; Zurich: Neukirchener, 1972).

Best, E., 'Spirit Baptism', *Novum Testamentum*, 4 (1960).

Bonaventure, *The Soul's Journey into God. The Tree of Life. The Life of St Francis* (London: SPCK, 1978).

Brandon, S.G.F., *Jesus and the Zealots* (Manchester: Manchester University Press, 1967).

Brown, R.E., 'Three Quotations from John the Baptist in the Gospel of John', *New Testament Essays* (London: Geoffrey Chapman, 1965).

Brown, R.E., 'Jesus and Elisha', *Perspective*, 12 (1971).

Brown, R.E., *The Birth of the Messiah* (London: Geoffrey Chapman, 1978a).

Brown, R.E., *The Gospel According to John*, vol. 1 I-XII (London: Geoffrey Chapman, 1978b).

Brown, R., *Bible Guide* (Glasgow: HarperCollins Publishers, 1993).

Brownlee, W.H., 'John the Baptist in the New Light of Ancient Scrolls', in K. Stendahl (ed.) *The Scrolls and the New Testament* (London: SCM Press, 1958).

Bultmann, R., *Jesus and the Word*, translated by L. P. Smith and E. Huntress (London: Ivor Nicholson and Watson; New York: Scribner's, 1935).

Bultmann, R., *The History of the Synoptic Tradition*, translated by John Marsh (Oxford: Basil Blackwell, 1963).

Buzy, D., *The Life of S. John the Baptist the Forerunner of Our Lord*, adapted by J. M. T. Barton (London: Burns Oates & Washbourne, Ltd., 1933).

Cameron, R. (ed.), *The Other Gospels: The Non-Canonical Gospel Texts* (Cambridge: Lutterworth Press, 1982).

Catchpole, D.R., *The Quest for Q* (Edinburgh: T. & T. Clark Ltd, 1993).

Catechism of the Catholic Church (Geoffrey Chapman, 1994).

Caxton, W., *The Golden Legend or the Lives of the Saints as Englished by William Caxton*, vol. five (London: J. M. Dent, 1900b).

Caxton, W., *The Golden Legend or Lives of the Saints as Englished by William Caxton,* vol. three (London: J. M. Dent, 1900a).

Chadwick, O., *Western Asceticism* (London: SCM Press, 1958).

Charles, R.H., *The Apocrypha and Pseudepigrapha of the Old Testament in English,* vol. 2: *Pseudepigapha* (Oxford: Clarendon Press, 1913).

Charlesworth, J.H., *Jesus within Judaism* (New York: Doubleday, 1988).

Chilton, B.D., 'Jesus and the Repentance of E. P. Sanders', *Tyndale Bulletin,* 39 (1988).

Chilton, B.D., 'The Kingdom of God in Recent Discussion', in B.D. Chilton and C.A. Evans (eds.), *Studying the Historical Jesus: Evaluations of the State of Current Research* (New Testament Tools and Studies 19; Leiden: Brill, 1994).

Cohn-Sherbok, D., *The Hebrew Bible* (London and New York: Cassell, 1996).

Collins, J.J., *The Scepter and the Star. The Messiahs of the Dead Sea Scrolls and Other Ancient Literature* (Garden City, NY: Doubleday, 1995).

Conzelmann, H., *The Theology of St Luke* (London: SCM Press, 1960).

Cooper, J.C., *Cassell Dictionary of Christianity* (London; New York: Cassell, 1996).

Cooper, J.C., (ed.) *An Illustrated Encyclopaedia of Traditional Symbols* (London: Thames and Hudson, 1978).

Cope, L., 'The Death of John the Baptist in the Gospel of Matthew; or the Case of the Confusing Participle', *Catholic Biblical Quarterly,* 38 (1976).

Cross, F.L., and E. A. Livingstone (eds.), *The Oxford Dictionary of the Christian Church* (London: Oxford University Press, 1974).

Crossan, J.D., *The Historical Jesus* (Edinburgh: T&T Clark, 1991).

Culpeper, N., *Culpeper's Complete Herbal and English Physician* (Manchester: J. Gleave and Son, 1981).

Dalman, G., 'Zum Tanz der Tochter der Herodias' in *Palästina-Jahrbuch*, 14 (1918).

Daniélou, J., *The Theology of Jewish Christianity* (London: Darton, Longmann & Todd Ltd, 1964).

Davies, S.L., 'John the Baptist and Essene Kashruth', *New Testament Studies*, 29 (1983).

Davies, W.D., D.C Allison, *The Gospel According to Saint Matthew* (Edinburgh: T. & T. Clark, 1998).

Demdike, D., 'A Season in the Sun', M. Green (ed.) *Quest Witchcraft Anthology* (London: Quest, BCM-SCL Quest, 1982).

Dibelius, M.,'Jungfrauensohn und Krippenkind: Untersuchungen zur Geburtsgeschichte Jesu im Lukas-Evangelium' *Botschaft und Geschichte: Gesammelte Aufsätze von Martin Dibelius*, Bd 1: *Zur Evangelienforschung*. G. Bornkamm (Tubingen: J. C. B. Mohr [Paul Seibeck], 1953).

Dibelius, M., *From Tradition to Gospel* (Cambridge: James Clark, 1971; reprint of 1934 edition).

Dodd, C.H., *The Interpretation of the Fourth Gospel* (Cambridge: Cambridge University Press, 1953).

Dodd, C.H., *Historical Tradition in the Fourth Gospel* (Cambridge: Cambridge University Press, 1963).

Duling, D.C. and N. Perrin, *The New Testament. Proclamation and Parenesis, Myth and History*, third edition (Orlando: Harcourt Brace & Company, 1994).

Duling, D.C. and N. Perrin, 'Spirit-and-Fire Baptism', *Novum Testamentum*, 14 (1972).

Duling, D.C. and N. Perrin, *Jesus and the Spirit* (London: SCM Press, 1975).

Duling, D.C. and N. Perrin, 'John the Baptist's use of Scripture', in C. A. Evans and W. R. Stegner (eds.), *The Gospels and the Scriptures of Israel* (Journal for the Study of the New

Testament, Supplement Series 104; Studies in Scripture in Early Judaism and Christianity 3; Sheffield: JSOT Press, 1994).

Dunn, James, *Jesus and the Spirit* (London: SCM Press, 1975).

Elliott, J.K., *The Apocryphal New Testament* (Oxford: Clarendon Press, 1993).

Enslin, M.S., 'John and Jesus,' *Zeitschrift Für Die Neutestamentliche Wissenschaft*, 66 (1975).

Enslin, M.S., 'John the Baptist and his Followers' in R. J. Hoffmann (ed.), *The Origins of Christianity* (Buffalo, NY: Prometheus, 1985).

Ernst, J., *Johannes der Täufer: Interpretation — Geschichte — Wirkungsgeschichte* (Beihefte zur *Zeitschrift für die neuentestamentliche Wissenschaft* 53; Berlin and New York: de Gruyter, 1989).

Evans, C.A., *Life of Jesus Research: An Annotated Bibliography* (Leiden, New York, and Köln: Brill, 1996).

Farmer, W.R., *Maccabees, Zealots, and Josephus* (Westpoint: Greenwood Press, 1956).

Farmer, R.R., 'John the Baptist,' *Interpreter's Dictionary of the Bible*, 2 (1962).

Fetellus, '*Palestine Pilgrims' Text Society* vol. 5 (London: no publisher given, 1896).

Filson, F.V., 'John the Baptist', *International Standard Bible Encyclopedia*, 2 (1982).

Fitzmyer, J.A., *The Gospel According To Luke I-IX* (Anchor Bible [Commentary] 28; Garden City: Doubleday, 1981).

Fitzmyer, J.A., *Luke the Theologian, Aspects of His Teaching* (London: Geoffrey Chapman, 1989).

Fleddermann, H., 'John and the Coming One (Matt. 3. 11-12//Lk. 3. 16-17)', in K.H. Richards (ed.), *Society of Biblical Literature 1984 Seminar Papers* (SBLSP 23; Chico: Scholars Press, 1984).

Fortini, A., *Francis of Assisi* (New York: Crossroad, 1985).

France, R.T., 'Jesus the Baptist?' in J.B. Green and M. Turner (eds.), *Jesus of Nazareth: Lord and Christ: Essays on the*

Historical Jesus and New Testament Christology (Carlisle: Paternoster; Grand Rapids, Eerdmans, 1994).

Frazer, J. G., *The Golden Bough: A Study in Magic and Religion* (London: Macmillan Press, 1983).

Fredriksen, Paula, *Jesus of Nazareth, King of the Jews: A Jewish Life and the Emergence of Christianity* (New York: Vintage, 2000).

Goguel, M., *Au seuil de l'évangile Jean-Baptiste* (Paris: Payot, 1928).

Goulder, M.D. and M.L Sanderson, 'St Luke's Genesis' in *Journal of Theological Studies* 8 (1957).

Green, M. J., 'Mistletoe', *Dictionary of Celtic Myth and Legend* (London: Thames and Hudson, 1992).

Gregory of Nazianzus, *Homily* 42.75 (Patrologiae Graecae, 36; Turnhout: Typographi Brepols Editores Pontifici, J.P. Migne, no date).

Guyénot, L., *Jésus et Jean Baptiste: Enquête Historique sur une Rencontre Légendaire* (Chambéry: Imago Exergue, 1999).

Harrington, D.J., 'Mark', in R.E. Brown, J.A. Fitzmyer, R.E. Murphy (eds.), *The New Jerome Biblical Commentary* (London: Geoffrey Chapman, 1989).

Harrington, D. J., 'The Gospel According to Mark', R.E. Brown, J.A. Firzmyer and R.E. Murphy (eds.) *The New Jerome Biblical Commentary* (London: Geoffrey Chapman, 1991).

Harvey, A.E., *The New English Bible Companion to the New Testament* (Oxford: University Press: Cambridge: University Press, 1971).

Heard, W.J., 'Revolutionary Movements' in *Dictionary of Jesus and the Gospels*, J.B. Green, S. McKnight and I.H. Marshall (eds.) (Downes Grove, Il.: Inter Varsity Press, 1992).

Hill, D., *New Testament Prophecy* (Marshalls Theological Library; London: Marshall, Morgan & Scott, 1979).

Hoehner, H. W., *Herod Antipas* (Cambridge: Cambridge University Press, 1972).

Hollenbach, P.W., 'Social Aspects of John the Baptist's Preaching Mission in the Context of Palestinian Judaism', in W. Haase and E. Temporini (eds.), *Aufsteig und Neidergang römischen Welt I*, 19. 1 (1979).

Hollenbach, P.W., 'The Conversion of Jesus: From Jesus the Baptizer to Jesus the Healer' in W. Haase and E. Temporini (eds.), *Aufsteig und Neidergang römischen Welt II*, 25. 1 (1982).

Hollenbach, P.W., 'John the Baptist', *Anchor Bible Dictionary*, 3 (1992).

Horsley, R.A., '"Like One of the Prophets of Old": Two Types of Popular Prophets At The Time Of Jesus', *Catholic Biblical Quarterly*, 47 (1985).

Houlden, J.L., 'John the Baptist' in R.J. Coggins and J.L. Houlden (eds.), *A Dictionary of Biblical Interpretation* (London: SCM Press and Trinity Press International, 1990).

Hughes, J.H., 'John the Baptist: The Forerunner of God Himself', *Novum Testamentum*, 14 (1972).

Hutchison, C. A., *The Hermit Monks of Grandmont* (Kalamazoo: Cistercian Publications, 1989).

Jacobsen Buckley, J., 'Ginza' in M. Eliade (ed.) *The Encyclopedia of Religion* vol. 5. (New York: Macmillan publishing Company; London: Collier Macmillan Publisers, 1987).

Jeremias, J., *New Testament Theology Part One: The Proclamation of Jesus* (London: SCM Press, 1971).

Jerome, *Vita Pauli, Vita Hilarionis, Vita Malchi monaci captivi* (Patrologiae Latinae, 23; Paris: J.-P. Migne, 1883).

Jöckle, C., *Encyclopaedia of Saints* (London: Alpine Fine Arts Collection (UK) Ltd, 1995).

Jones, A., *The Wordsworth Dictionary of Saints* (Ware, Hertfordshire: Wordsworth Editions, Ltd, 1992).

Josephus, Flavius, *The Complete Works*, trans. William Whiston London, New York: The London Printing and Publishing Company Limited, 1870).

Josephus, *The Jewish War of Flavius Josephus with his autobiography* (London; Houlston and Stoneman, 1847).

Josephus, *The Jewish War*, translated by G. A. Williamson (New York: Harmondsworth, Penguin Press, 1970).

Käsemann, E. 'The Disciples of John the Baptist in Ephesus' in *Essays on New Testament Themes*, 136-48. Translated by W.J. Montague. SBT 41 (London: SCM Press, 1964).

Kazmierski, C.R., *John the Baptist: Prophet and Evangelist* (Collegeville, MN: The Liturgical Press/Michael Glazer, 1996).

Keiffer, R., 'John', J. Barton and J. Muddleman (eds.) *The Oxford Bible Commentary* (Oxford: Oxford University Press, 2001).

Kraeling, C., *John The Baptist* (New York and London: Charles Scribner's Sons, 1951).

Le Braz, A., *The Land of Pardons*, trans. F. M. Gostling (London: Methuen & Co., 1924).

Lachs, S.T., 'John the Baptist and his Audience', *Gratz College Annual of Jewish Studies*, 4 (1975)

Lampe, G.W.H., *The Seal of the Spirit* (London, New York, Toronto: Longmans, Green and Co., 1956).

Lang, F., πυρ, in G. Kittel and G. Friedrich (eds.), *Theological Dictionary of the New Testament*, VI (1964).

Laurentin, R., *Petite vie de Jean Baptiste* (Paris: Desclée de Brouwer, 1993).

Lightfoot, J.B, *The Apostolic Fathers* (Baker Book House: Grand Rapids, 1956).

Lightfoot, J.B. and Charles, R.H., *The Lost Books of the Bible* and *The Forgotten Books of Eden* (Oxford: The Clarendon Press, 1913).

Livingston, E.A., *The Concise Oxford Dictionary of the Christian Church* (Oxford: Oxford University Press, 1980).

Lohse, E., *The New Testament Environment*, translated by J. E. Steely (London: SCM Press, 1994).

Loisy, A., *Les évangiles synoptiques* (Ceffonds: privately published, 1907).

Lüdemann, G., *Jesus After 2000 Years* (London: SCM Press, 2000).

Lupieri, E., 'John the Baptist: The First Monk: A Contribution to the History of the Figure of John the Baptist in the Early Monastic World', *Monasticism: A Historical Overview* (Word and Spirit 6 Still River: St Bede's Publications, 1984).

MacCulloch, J. A., 'Relics, Primitive and Western', J. Hastings (ed.) *Encyclopaedia of Religion and Ethics* vol. 10 (Edinburgh: T & T Clark, 1918).

McCown, C.C., 'The Scene of John's Ministry', *Journal of Biblical Literature*, 59 (1940).

McGreal, W., *At the Fountain of Elijah: The Carmelite Tradition* (London: Darton, Longman and Todd Ltd, 1999).

Maier, B., *Dictionary of Celtic Religion and Culture*, trans. C. Edwards (Woodbridge: The Boydell Press, 1997).

McKenzie, J.L., *Dictionary of the Bible* (London, Dublin, Melbourne: Geoffrey Chapman, 1968).

Manson, T.W., 'John the Baptist', *Bulletin of the John Rylands Library*, 36 (1953).

Marcus, J., 'The Beelzebul Controversy and the Eschatologies of Jesus' in Chilton, B. and C.A, Evans, *Authenticating the Activities of Jesus* (Authenticating the Words of Jesus & Authenticating the Activities of Jesus, New Testament Tools and Studies, 28; Leiden: Brill, 2002).

Martin, R.P., *Acts* (London: Scripture Union, 1697).

Martyn, J.L., 'We have Found Elijah', in R. Hammerton-Kelly and R. Scroggs (eds.), *Jews, Greeks and Christians: Religious Cultures in Late Antiquity* (W. D. Davies Festschrift; Studies In Judaism In Late Antiquity, 21; Leiden: Brill, 1976).

Martyr, A., 'Of the Holy Places Visited', trans. A. Stewart. *The Library of the Palestine Pilgrims' Text Society*, vol 2 (London: Committee of the Palestine Exploration Fund, 1897).

Medici, M., *Good Magic* (London: Macmillan London Ltd, 1988).

Meier, J.P., 'John the Baptist in Matthew's Gospel', *Journal of Biblical Literature*, 99 (1980).

Metford, J. C. J., *Dictionary of Christian Lore and Legend* (London: Thames and Hudson, 1983).

Meyer, B.F., *The Aims of Jesus* (London: SCM Press, 1979).

Meyer, B.F., 'Phases in Jesus' Mission', *Gregorianum*, 73 (1992).

Mowinckel, S., *He That Cometh* (Oxford: Basil Blackwell, 1959).

Murphy, C.M., *John the Baptist. Prophet of Purity for a New Age* (Collegeville, MN.: Liturgical Press, 2003).

Murphy-O'Connor, J., 'John the Baptist and Jesus: History and Hypotheses', *New Testament Studies*, 36 (1990).

Neill, S., Wright, N. T., *The Interpretation of the New Testament: 1861-1986*, second edition (Oxford: Oxford University Press, 1988).

Palestine Pilgrims Text Society (London: no publisher, 1896).

Palladius, *The Lausiac History*, translated and annotated by R. T. Meyer (Westminster, Maryland: The Newman Press; London: Longmanns, Green and Co, 1965).

Perkins, P., 'The Gospel According to John', R.E. Brown, J.A. Firzmyer and R.E. Murphy (eds.) *The New Jerome Biblical Commentary* (London: Geoffrey Chapman, 1991).

Perrin, N., *Rediscovering the Teaching of Jesus* (London: SCM Press, 1967).

Perrin, N. *The Kingdom of God in the Teaching of Jesus*, fourth edition (London: SCM Press, 1984).

Pesch, R., *Das Markusevangelium*. HTKNT 2.1-2. 2 Vols. (Freiburg: Herder, 1976).

Prior, J. W., 'John the Baptist and Jesus: Tradition and Text in John 3. 25', *Journal for the Study of the New Testament*, 66 (1997).

Rhoads, D.M., *Israel in Revolution: 6-74 CE. A Political History Based on the Writings of Josephus* (Philadelphia: Fortress Press, 1976).

Richardson, P., *Herod, King of the Jews and Friend of the Romans* (Columbia: University of South Carolina Press, 1996).

Riley-Smith, J., *The Knights of St. John in Jerusalem and Cyprus* (London: Macmillan, 1967).

Robinson, J.A.T., 'Elijah, John and Jesus', *New Testament Studies*, 4 (1957).

Robinson, J.A.T., *Twelve New Testament Studies* (Studies in Biblical Theology, 34, London: SCM Press, 1962).

Robinson, J.A.T., *Twelve More New Testament Studies*, (London: SCM Press, 1984).

Robinson, J.M., P. Hoffmann and J. Kloppenborg (eds.) *The Critical Edition of Q* (Minneapolis, MN: Augsburg Fortress Publishers, 2000).

Rodd, C.S., 'Talking Points from Books', *Expository Times*, 99 (1987).

Rudolph, K., 'Mandaean Sources' in W. Foerster (ed.) *Gnosis. Volume II: Coptic and Mandaean Sources* (Oxford: Clarendon Press, 1974).

Sanders, E.P., *Jesus and Judaism* (London: SCM; Philadelphia: Fortress, 1985)

Sanders, E.P. and Davies, M., *Studying the Synoptic Gospels* (London: SCM Press, 1996).

Sanuto, M., 'Secrets for True Crusaders to help them to Recover the Holy Land', trans. A. Stewart, *Palestine Pilgrims' Text Society* (London: [no publisher given], 1896).

Schuster, Ildefonso and Levelis-Marke, Arthur (trans) *The Sacramentary (Liber Sacramentorum)*, (London: Burns & Oates, 1924-1930).

Scobie, C.H.H., *John the Baptist* (London: SCM, 1964).

Scobie, C.H.H., 'John the Baptist', in *The Scrolls and Christianity*, (M. Black (ed.), London: SPCK, 1969).

Sheerin, D., 'St John the Baptist in the Lower World', *Vigiliae Christianae*, 30 (1976).

Sinker, R., 'John the Baptist, fire of', 'John the Baptist, St., Festivals and Legends of' in W. Smith and S. Cheetham (eds.) *A Dictionary of Christian Antiquities* vol. 1 (London: John Murray, 1875.

Sire, H. J. A., *The Knights of Malta* (New Haven; London: Yale University Press, 1994).

Smith, L. M., *Cluny in the Eleventh and Twelfth Centuries* (London: Philip Allen & Co. Ltd, 1930).

Socrates, *Church History* (London: Bohn's Ecclesiastical Library, 1853).

Stanton, G.N., *The Gospels and Jesus*, (Oxford: Oxford University Press, 1989).

Stern, D. H., *Jewish New Testament Commentary* (Clarksville, Maryland: Jewish New Testament Publications, Inc. 1992).

Tatum, W. B., *John the Baptist and Jesus: A Report of the Jesus Seminar* (Sonoma: Polebridge, 1994).

Taylor, B., 'Midsummer Customs', *The Supernatural* 1(1987).

Taylor. G., *Saints and their Flowers* (London: A. R. Mowbury & Co, 1956).

Taylor, J., *John the Baptist within Second Temple Judaism, a historical study* (London: SPCK, 1997).

Taylor, T.M., 'The Beginnings of Jewish Proselyte Baptism', *New Testament Studies*, 2 (1955).

Taylor, V., *The Gospel According to St. Mark*, second edition (London: Macmillan and Co. Ltd, 1966).

Tenney, Merrill C., *The Expositor's Bible Commentary: John* (Grand Rapids, Mn: Zondervan Publishing House, 1995).

Telford, W.R., *Mark* (Sheffield: Sheffield Academic Press, 1985).

Telford, W.R., 'Major Trends and Interpretive Issues in the Study of Jesus', in B. Chilton and C.A. Evans (eds.) *Studying the Historical Jesus, Evaluations of the State of Current Research* (Leiden, New York, Köln: Brill, 1994).

Telford, W.R., *The Theology of the Gospel of Mark* (Cambridge: Cambridge University Press, 1999).

Theissen, G. and A. Merz *The Historical Jesus* (London: SCM Press, 1998).

Thomas of Celano, 'Second Life of Saint Francis' *St Francis of Assisi, Writings and Early Biographies: English Omnibus of the Sources for the Life of St Francis*. M. A. Habig (ed.) (London: SPCK, 1973).

Thomas of Celano, 'First Life of Saint Francis' *St Francis of Assisi, Writings and Early Biographies: English Omnibus of the*

Sources for the Life of St Francis M. A. Habig (ed.) (London: SPCK, 1973).

Throckmorton, B.H., *Gospel Parallels: A Comparison of the Synoptic Gospels*, fifth edition (Nashville: Thomas Nelson, Inc., 1992).

Thyen, H., 'ΒΑΠΤΙΣΜΑ ΜΕΤΑΝΟΙΑΣ ΕΙΣ ΑΦΕΣΙΝ ΑΜΑΡΤΙΩΝ', in J.M. Robinson (ed.), *The Future of Our Religious Past* (R. Bultmann Festschrift; London: SCM; New York: Harper & Row, 1971).

Torrance, T. F., 'Proselyte Baptism', *New Testament Studies*, 1 (1954).

Trumbower, J.A., 'The Role of Malachi in the Career of John the Baptist', in C.A. Evans and W.R. Stegner (eds.), *The Gospels and the Scriptures of Israel* (Journal for the Study of the New Testament, Supplement Series, 104; Studies in Scripture in Early Judaism and Christianity 3; Sheffield, JSOT Press, 1994).

Tuckett, C., *Reading the New Testament, Methods of Interpretation* (London: SPCK, 1987).

Tuckett, C.M., 'Synoptic Problem', in R.J. Coggins and J.L. Houlden (eds.), *A Dictionary of Biblical Interpretation* (London: SCM Press & Trinity Press International, 1990).

Tuckett, C.M., *Q and the History of Early Christianity* (Peabody, Mass.: Hendrickson Publishers, Inc., 1996)..

Van Dam, R., 'The Miracles of St Martin', *Saints and their Miracles in Late Antique Gaul* (Princeton, NJ: Princeton University Press, 1993).

Vermes, G., *The Complete Dead Sea Scrolls in English* (Middlesex: Allen Lane, The Penguin Press, 1997).

Vermes, G., *Jesus the Jew* (London: Collins, 1973).

Viviano, B.T., 'Matthew', in R. E. Brown, J.A. Fitzmyer, R.E. Murphy (eds.), *The New Jerome Biblical Commentary* (London:Geoffrey Chapman, 1989).

Voragine, J. de, *The Golden Legend: Readings on the Saints* vol 1, trans. W. G. Ryan (Princeton, New Jersey: Princeton University Press, 1993a).

Voragine, J. de, *The Golden Legend: Readings on the Saints* vol 2, trans. W. G. Ryan (Princeton, New Jersey: Princeton University Press, 1993b).

Walsh, M. (ed.), 'John the Baptist', *Butler's Lives of Patron Saints* (San Francisco: Harper & Row, 1987).

Webb, R.L., 'The Activity of John the Baptist's Expected Figure at the Threshing Floor (Matthew 3. 12 = Luke 3. 17)', *Journal for the Study of the New Testament*, 43 (1991a).

Webb, R.L., *John the Baptizer and Prophet: A Socio-Historical Study* (Journal for the Study of the New Testament, Supplement Series 62; Sheffield, JSOT Press, 1991b).

Webb, R.L., 'John the Baptist and his Relationship to Jesus', in B.D. Chilton and C.A. Evans (eds.), *Studying the Historical Jesus: Evaluations of the State of Current Research* (New Testament Tools And Studies 19; Leiden: Brill, 1994).

Wilson, S., 'The Fire Festivals', *Prediction,* 55 (1989).

Wilson, S., *Saints and Their Cults* (Cambridge: Cambridge University Press, 1983).

Wink, W., *John the Baptist in the Gospel Tradition* (Society for New Testament Studies Monograph Series, 7; Cambridge: Cambridge University Press, 1968).

Winter, D. (ed) *Matthew Henry's Commentary: The Four Gospels* (London, Sydney, Auckland and Toronto: Hodder and Stoughton, 1974).

Wright, N.T., 'Constraints and the Jesus of History', *Scottish Journal of Theology*, 39 (1986).

Yates, J.E., 'The Form of Mark 1.8b', *New Testament Studies* (1957).

Zeitlin, I. M., *Jesus and the Judaism of his Time* (Oxford: Polity Press, 1989).

INDEX

Also available from Amberley Publishing

The Young
Queen To Be

B

Anne
Boleyn

JOSEPHINE
WILKINSON

'Based on meticulous research & hard evidence... highly recommended'
THEANNEBOLEYNFILES.COM

Available from all good bookshops or to order direct
Please call **01453-847-800**
www.amberley-books.com